The Korean War and the Vietnam War

People, Politics, and Power

America at War

The Korean War and the Vietnam War

People, Politics, and Power

Edited by William L. Hosch, Associate Editor, Science and Technology

in association with

Published in 2010 by Britannica Educational Publishing
(a trademark of Encyclopædia Britannica, Inc.)
in association with Rosen Educational Services, LLC
29 East 21st Street, New York, NY 10010.

Distributed exclusively by Rosen Educational Services.
For a listing of additional Britannica Educational Publishing titles, call toll free (800) 237-9932.

First Edition

Britannica Educational Publishing
Michael I. Levy: Executive Editor
Marilyn L. Barton: Senior Coordinator, Production Control
Steven Bosco: Director, Editorial Technologies
Lisa S. Braucher: Senior Producer and Data Editor
Yvette Charboneau: Senior Copy Editor
Kathy Nakamura: Manager, Media Acquisition
William L. Hosch: Associate Editor, Science and Technology

Rosen Educational Services
Hope Lourie Killcoyne: Senior Editor and Project Manager
Maggie Murphy: Editor
Nelson Sá: Art Director
Matthew Cauli: Designer
Introduction by Holly Cefrey

Library of Congress Cataloging-in-Publication Data

Korean War and the Vietnam War: people, politics, and power / edited by William L. Hosch.—1st ed.
p. cm.—(America at war)
"In association with Britannica Educational Publishing, Rosen Educational Services."
Includes bibliographical references.
ISBN 978-1-61530-011-2 (library binding)
1. Korean War, 1950–1953—Juvenile literature. 2. Korean War, 1950–1953—United States—Juvenile literature. 3. Vietnam War, 1961–1975—Juvenile literature. 4. Vietnam War, 1961–1975—United States—Juvenile literature. I. Hosch, William L.
DS918.K5655 2010
951.904'2—dc22

2009036105

Manufactured in the United States of America

On the cover: (Left) *American soldiers of an artillery gun crew load a howitzer during the Korean War,* c. *July 1950.* U.S. Army/Hulton Archive/Getty Images; (Right) *A U.S. Army patrol being led by Captain Robert Bacon,* c. *1964, Vietnam.* Larry Burrows/Time & Life Pictures/Getty Images.
Korean War Chapter Opener Image: *One of the 19 statues of soldiers at the Korean War Veterans Memorial in Washington, D.C.* © www.istockphoto.com/Gary Blakeley.
Vietnam War Chapter Opener Image: *Taken from a 1999 United States Postal Service commemorative stamp, soldiers are seen leaping from a helicopter near Chu Lai, Vietnam, in the spring of 1967.* © www.istockphoto.com/Ray Roper

CONTENTS

46

77

99

112
120

123
U.S. AIR FORCE

215

INTRODUCTION

The Korean War and the Vietnam War were conflicts that involved far more than either the geographic inhabitants or local military personnel. Countries across the globe weighed in with pro-war and antiwar sentiments, with many nations sending aid—monetary or military—to one side or the other. Both wars involved complicated opposing issues that led to escalation rather than resolution, creating a stage for some memorable people history will never see again, nor soon forget.

The Korean War, also known as the Korean Conflict, began on June 25, 1950. At that time in the United States, Harry S. Truman was president, *The Third Man* by Anton Karas was the number-one song, 17-year-old Elizabeth Taylor was on the cover of *Movie Picture Magazine*, and frozen pizza had just been invented. Half a globe away, North Korean forces launched an invasion into South Korea.

It was with a thunderous artillery barrage that Communist North Korean forces overran American-occupied South Korea. But a fast defeat of South Korea was not to be. Instead, Republic of Korea Army (ROKA) forces formed a strong defence that held the North Korean army at bay. Still, if the South was to stave off collapse, it would need outside help.

Indeed, the conflict escalated, becoming a battleground between communism and democracy, which many leaders, political theorists, and activists felt were in complete and irreconcilable opposition to each other. The involvement of the United States as well as the Soviet Union, and later China, further complicated matters.

If there is one number associated with the Korean War, it is 38. The 38th parallel, bisecting Korea, became a border dividing that nation into two halves, North Korea and South Korea. The crossing of this line by either side was considered an act of aggression. However, the existence of the parallel as a border predates the Korean War, being a result of the end of World War II. When Japan was about to lose that war, its control over colonies such as Korea was thrust to the victors, which included the United States, Britain, France, and the Soviet Union. While the Allies had been united against the Axis powers—Germany, Italy, and Japan—political and ideological conflict over what the world should be like after World War II arose among them, particularly pitting Britain and the United States against the Soviet Union. This ideological standoff became known as the Cold War. While the two superpowers never fought each other directly,

The Vietnam Veterans Memorial in Washington D.C. honours members of the U.S. armed forces who served and died in the Vietnam War. A boy runs his fingers along names of soldiers in 1982, the year the monument was dedicated. Owen Franken/Time & Life Pictures/ Getty Images.

conflicts such as that in Korea were impacted, and some say, furthered, if not altogether caused by it.

Three days before Japan's August 15, 1945, surrender, the Soviet Union quickly advanced into Korea from the north. U.S. officials, fearing a communist takeover of the country, quickly offered a solution to keep the peace between the U.S.S.R. and the United States, proposing the 38th parallel as the military dividing line for Japanese surrender.

The Soviets agreed. In the North, the Japanese would surrender to the Soviets; in the South, to the Americans. The division was meant only as a temporary measure, with the understanding that the Korean halves would unite under a new unified government of their choosing. This, however, would not come to pass, and has remained a remnant of unfulfilled peacetime promises.

During the delay of peacetime reparations and the establishing of a new order, North Korea elected its own communist leader, receiving support from the Soviet Union. In 1948, North Korea refused to take part in an election controlled by the United Nations, the goal of the UN having been to create and all-Korean government. Following this outright refusal to unite with the South, South Korea sought its own solution through the UN. In late 1948, the UN approved the elections that had taken place, thereby validating the new South Korean government. The United States withdrew its occupying forces during 1949, but later returned to aid in the conflict against the North. The North was known as the Democratic People's Republic of Korea (DPRK); the South was known as the Republic of Korea (ROK).

Though the war lasted only three years, many North and South Koreans died, along with members of UN forces and Soviet forces. To this day, the United States has a force of over 35,000 troops stationed in South Korea. When two U.S. journalists were captured and imprisoned by the North Koreans for illegally entering the country in March of 2009, it took an unannounced visit by former U.S. president Bill Clinton and a subsequent pardon by North Korean leader Kim Jong Il to secure their release.

Dramatic, complicated, and unresolved, the schism between North and South Korea is presented for readers to consider. Among those profiled is legendary military leader General Douglas MacArthur, relieved of duty by Pres. Harry S. Truman in 1951 for fear of his bringing about a war with China over the Korean Conflict. Kim Dae Jung, who, passed away August 18, 2009, is also profiled. Though not a key figure during the Korean War itself, Kim would go on to champion democratic government, becoming South Korea's 15th president. His so-called "sunshine" policy allowed South Koreans to visit relatives in the North. In 2000, Kim became the only Korean to receive the Nobel Prize for Peace, an award granted for his efforts to

North Korean leader Kim Il-sung at a rally, August 1966. Kim Il-sung ruled the Democratic People's Republic of Korea (North Korea) from its founding in 1948 until his death in 1994. Three Lions/Hulton Archive/Getty Images

restore democracy in South Korea and improve relations with North Korea.

After the Korean War, the long shadow of the Cold War would soon be cast upon another eastern country: Vietnam. Much like Korea, the end result was a country divided geographically by a parallel—and politically and philosophically as a people. Lasting far longer than the Korean War—from 1955 to 1975—the Vietnam War was also subject to much more stateside criticism than the conflict in Korea.

Vietnam's rich cultural history spans hundreds of years across independent dynasties, beginning with the break from China in the 900s. Ancient Vietnamese society enjoyed many advances, including metalworking, plant cultivation, creation of various musical instruments, and art dating back as far as the Stone Age. This flourishing was supplanted by the French when they began efforts to colonize Vietnam in 1859. By 1885, Vietnam was fully absorbed by French Indochina. The French imposed a new way of life, including large-scale changes in labour, which was welcomed by only a few. Powerful Japanese forces eventually set up camp in French Indochina, where they had free reign over Vietnam's resources.

Tired of living without their own identity, the Vietnamese started speaking out, uniting behind Ho Chi Minh. One of the most influential communist leaders of the 20th century, Ho's impact on the Vietnamese people was profound. His new communist, nationalist liberation movement, Viet Minh, was rallying to gain freedom from France, and to fight the Japanese forces. With his power seated in the north, Ho declared his country's independence in 1946. At this time, there were those Vietnamese who supported French rule, opposing the idea of a new communist regime. The French reached an agreement with Ho, that Vietnam would be a "free state"—but within the French Union. However, it was all or nothing for Viet Minh, so the agreement soon dissolved.

This conflict led to the First Indochina War, lasting from 1946 until 1954. Viet Minh's forces received support from Russia and China starting in 1950. The United States lent backing to the French and non-communist Vietnamese in the south. The ending result was another Cold War Korea; Vietnam was divided by the 17th parallel, with communist forces on one side, non-communists on the other, and various countries involved in the future of this divided nation. National elections were to be held in 1956 to unify the country, but as with Korea, this event never came to pass because the temporary government of the south refused to take part in the election. Ngo Dinh Diem, leader of the South, said national elections couldn't possibly be "free" under the communist government of the north. The government of the South was the Government of the Republic of Vietnam (GVN). The northern government was the Democratic Republic of Vietnam (DRV).

Ngo Dinh Diem made it possible to throw anyone even suspected of being a communist into jail without proof or due process. His fear of communism led to extremes, which divided many U.S. officials as to whether they should support the GVN. The Americans did support them however, lending military aid as Diem insisted that his new country was under attack by the DRV both within his own boundaries and beyond.

In 1961, Pres. John F. Kennedy sent weaponry and support to Diem, but limited the number of troops. By 1963, Diem's people, including Buddhist monks, were crying out for a leadership change. The

A group of U.S. Marines and U.S. Navy medics carrying a wounded American soldier near Dong Ha, Vietnam, August 1967. Bruce Axelrod/Hulton Archive/GettyImages

United States supported the call to replace Diem, who was captured and assassinated on November 2, 1963. Less than three weeks later, Kennedy was assassinated as well, leaving the troubles of Vietnam to his successor, Pres. Lyndon B. Johnson. During Johnson's presidency, America's involvement in the war increased dramatically. Johnson's successor, Richard M. Nixon, though campaigning on a policy to end the war, which he termed seeking "peace with honour," instead expanded it into neighbouring Cambodia and Laos. Nixon's 1972 Christmas bombings of northern cities caused an international outrage, calling for him to change his country's involvement. In April of 1975, Saigon fell, as did the GVN, ending the war.

As the war played out on television sets across the country, Americans were divided—often passionately so—regarding their country's involvement in the war. Antiwar demonstrations, begun under LBJ's presidency, became more widespread under that of his successor. In the spring of 1970, one such antiwar/anti-Nixon demonstration turned deadly when soldiers of the Ohio National Guard fired into a crowd of approximately 2,000 people at Kent State, killing four college students.

Reporting on this event, as he did so many others, was journalist Walter Cronkite (1916–2009). "The most trusted man in America" died on July 17, 2009, at the age of 92. A CBS News anchorman for 19 years, Cronkite kept countless Americans abreast of events at home and abroad.

Earlier in July of 2009, another great player in the Korean and Vietnam wars passed. Secretary of Defense Robert S. McNamara (1916–2009) served as America's eighth Secretary of Defense. A master of statistical analysis, McNamara was hand picked by Pres. John F. Kennedy to run the Pentagon within his new administration. Called a "primary architect" of the Vietnam War, McNamara, in his memoir, *In Retrospect: The Tragedy and Lessons of Vietnam*, offered something that many proponents of U.S. involvement in the war never did—an admittance that he and his peers were "wrong, terribly wrong." McNamara acknowledged that he misunderstood the Asian way in general, and that he lacked the necessary courage to tell Pres. Lyndon B. Johnson that the war was futile. His memoir was a sensational best seller, providing insight from a historical perspective that few experienced firsthand.

The cost of these two wars was quite high. The Korean War resulted in the deaths of approximately 2,000,000 Koreans, 600,000 Chinese, 37,000 Americans, and 3,000 Turks, Britons, and other nationals in the UN forces. The death toll in the Vietnam War was even higher. More than 3,000,000 people (including 58,000 Americans) died over the course of the war, more than half of them civilians. This book aims to help the reader understand the causes, the unfolding of events, the chemistry of the various key figures, and the aftermath.

CHAPTER 1

PRECURSORS TO THE KOREAN WAR

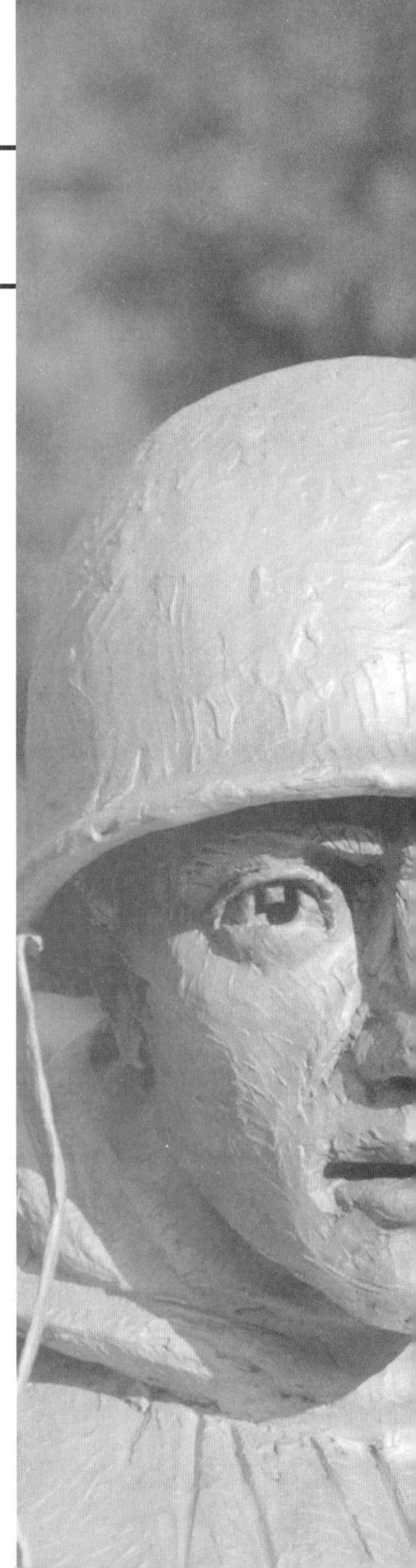

The Korean War was precipitated by the collapse of the Japanese empire at the end of World War II, in September 1945. Following the war, China, Manchuria, and the former Western colonies seized by Japan in 1941–42 had either a native government or a colonial regime waiting to return to power after hostilities ceased. Having been annexed to Japan since 1910, Korea did not have a native government waiting to return. Most claimants to Korean power were harried exiles in China, Manchuria, Japan, the U.S.S.R., and the United States who fell into two broad categories. The first was made up of committed Marxist revolutionaries who had fought the Japanese as part of the Chinese-dominated guerrilla armies in Manchuria and China. One of these exiles was a minor but successful guerrilla leader named Kim Il-sung, who had received some training in Russia and had been made a major in the Soviet army. The other category was made up of members of the Korean nationalist movement, no less revolutionary, who drew their inspiration from the best of science, education, and industrialism in Europe, Japan, and America. These "ultranationalists" were split into rival factions. Notably, one of these factions centred on the leadership of Syngman Rhee, educated in the United States and was at one time the president of a dissident Korean Provisional Government in exile.

In their hurried effort to disarm the Japanese army and repatriate the Japanese population in Korea (estimated at

700,000), the United States and the Soviet Union agreed in August 1945 to divide the country for administrative purposes at the 38th parallel (latitude 38° N). At least from the American perspective, this geographic division was a temporary expedient. However, the Soviets began a short-lived reign of terror in northern Korea that quickly politicized the division by driving thousands of refugees south. The two sides could not agree on a formula that would produce a unified Korea, and the division ultimately would lead to civil war between the new North and South within a few years.

The creation of an independent South Korea became UN policy in early 1948. Southern communists opposed this, and by autumn partisan warfare had engulfed parts of every Korean province below the 38th parallel. The fighting expanded into a limited border war between the South's newly formed Republic of Korea Army (ROKA) and the North Korean border constabulary as well as the North's Korean People's Army (KPA). The North launched 10 cross-border guerrilla incursions in order to draw ROKA units away from their guerrilla-suppression campaign in the South.

In its larger purpose the partisan uprising failed: the Republic of Korea (ROK) was formed in August 1948, with Syngman Rhee as president. Nevertheless, almost 8,000 members of the South Korean security forces and at least 30,000 other Koreans lost their lives. Many of the victims were not security forces or armed guerrillas at all, but simply people identified as "rightists" or "reds" by the belligerents. Small-scale atrocities became a way of life.

The partisan war also delayed the training of the South Korean army. In early 1950, American advisers judged that fewer than half of the ROKA's infantry battalions were even marginally ready for war. U.S. military assistance consisted largely of surplus light weapons and supplies. Indeed, Gen. Douglas MacArthur, commander of the United States' Far East Command (FECOM), argued that his Eighth Army, consisting of four weak divisions in Japan, required more support than the Koreans did. By mid-1950, ROKA forces in the South were still unprepared for the impending invasion from the North.

KOREA OCCUPIED AND DIVIDED, 1910–50

Japanese Occupation

Japan annexed Korea in 1910, before the onset of World War I. A Japanese government was established quickly in Korea, with the governor-generalship filled by generals or admirals appointed by the Japanese emperor. The Koreans were deprived of freedom of assembly, association, the press, and speech. Many private schools were closed because they did not meet certain arbitrary standards set by the Japanese government. The colonial authorities used their own school system as a tool for assimilating Korea to Japan,

Japanese gendarmes in Korea, 1910. The gendarmes served as the police force in Korea during the oppressive Japanese occupation of the country (1910–45). Topical Press Agency/ Hulton Archive/Gettty Images

placing primary emphasis on teaching the Japanese language and excluding from the educational curriculum such subjects as Korean language and Korean history. The Japanese built nationwide transportation and communications networks and established a new monetary and financial system. They also promoted Japanese commerce in Korea while barring Koreans from similar activities.

The colonial government promulgated a land-survey ordinance that forced landowners to report the size and area of their land. By failing to do this, many farmers were deprived of their land. Farmland and forests owned jointly by a village or a clan were likewise expropriated by the Japanese since no single individual could claim them. Much of the land thus expropriated was then sold cheaply to Japanese landlords. Many of the dispossessed Korean farmers took to the woods and subsisted by slash-and-burn tillage, while others emigrated to Manchuria and Japan in search of jobs. The majority of ethnically Korean residents now in those areas are the descendants of those emigrants.

IN FOCUS: KOREAN PROVISIONAL GOVERNMENT

In April 1919 Korean patriots organized a provisional government in exile in Shanghai in reaction to Japanese suppression of the March 1st Movement. This movement for Korean independence from Japanese rule was so named for a proclamation of independence issued by 33 prominent Koreans on March 1, 1919, which resulted in a number of massive demonstrations that occurred in Korea wherever the proclamation was read. Leading members of the Korean Provisional Government included such national leaders as Syngman Rhee, An Ch'ang-ho, and Kim Ku.

With the establishment of the provisional government, Korea was able to make more concerted efforts toward achieving independence from Japan, and it made immediate contacts with various independence groups both at home and abroad. By 1922 all of the Korean resistance groups in Manchuria were unified under the provisional government's leadership. To help gain their aims, the leaders published a newspaper, The Independent, *which greatly enhanced popular consciousness of political participation. They also sent delegations to the United States and Europe to draw attention to their cause.*

Nevertheless, the Korean Provisional Government soon encountered insurmountable problems. Internally, the Japanese suppressed all nationalistic dissension in Korea, even going so far as to prohibit use of the Korean language in the later 1930s. Externally, the coalition of exiled Koreans that had formed the provisional government began to grow apart. Although Syngman Rhee was elected the nominal president, he remained in the United States, attempting to solicit Western moral support. The premier, Yi Tong-hwi, began to seek Soviet military aid for revolutionary operations in Manchuria. Kim Ku drew close to the right-wing Chinese Nationalists of Chiang Kai-shek.

With the liberation of Korea from Japanese occupation at the end of World War II, the Korean Provisional Government came to an end. Its members returned to Korea, where they put together their own political organizations in what came to be South Korea and competed for power.

DIVISION OF KOREA

The Cairo Declaration, issued on Dec. 1, 1943, by the United States, Great Britain, and China, pledged independence for Korea "in due course." This vague phrase aroused the leaders of the Korean provisional government in Chongqing to request interpretation from the United States. Their request, however, received no answer. At the Yalta Conference held in February 1945, U.S. Pres. Franklin D. Roosevelt proposed to Soviet Premier Joseph Stalin a four-power trusteeship for Korea consisting of the United States, Great Britain, the U.S.S.R., and the Republic of China. While Stalin agreed to Roosevelt's suggestion in principle, they did not reach any formal agreement on the future status of Korea, and after the Yalta meeting there was a growing uneasiness between the Anglo-American allies and the U.S.S.R.

Throughout the Potsdam Conference in July 1945, U.S. military leaders insisted on encouraging Soviet entry into the war against Japan. The Soviet military leaders asked their U.S. counterparts about invading Korea, and the Americans replied that such an expedition would not be practicable until after a successful landing had taken place on the Japanese mainland. The ensuing Potsdam Declaration included the statement that "the terms of the Cairo Declaration," which promised Korea its independence, "shall be carried out." In the terms of its entry into the war against Japan on August 8, the U.S.S.R. also pledged to support the independence of Korea. On the following day Soviet troops went into action in Manchuria and northern Korea.

The General Order No. 1, drafted on August 11 by the United States for Japanese surrender terms in Korea, provided for Japanese forces north of latitude 38° N (the 38th parallel) to surrender to the Soviets and those south of that line to the Americans. Stalin did not object to the contents of the order, and on September 8 American troops landed in southern Korea, almost a month after the first Soviet entry. On the following day the United States received the Japanese surrender in Seoul. There were now two zones of occupied Korean territory—northern and southern—for the Soviets had already begun to seal off the 38th parallel.

The historic decision to divide the peninsula into two has aroused speculation on several counts. Some historians attribute the division of Korea to military expediency in receiving the Japanese surrender, while others believe that the decision was a measure to prevent the

In Focus: 38th Parallel

Latitude 38° N, or the 38th parallel, in East Asia roughly demarcates North Korea and South Korea. The line was chosen by U.S. military planners at the Potsdam Conference (July 1945) near the end of World War II as an army boundary. North of the 38th parallel the U.S.S.R. was to accept the surrender of the Japanese forces in Korea, and south of it the Americans were to accept the Japanese surrender. The line was intended as a temporary division of the country, but the onset of the Cold War led to the establishment of a separate U.S.-oriented regime in South Korea under Syngman Rhee and a communist regime in North Korea under Kim Il-sung.

After the outbreak of the Korean War between North and South Korea in June 1950, United Nations (UN) forces, which under U.S. Gen. Douglas MacArthur had come to the aid of the South, moved north of the 38th parallel in an attempt to occupy North Korea. With the intervention of Chinese troops in support of the North, the war came to a stalemate roughly along that parallel. The cease-fire line, fixed at the time of the armistice agreement, gave South Korea possession of an eastern mountainous area north of the parallel, which was the major battlefront when the demarcation line was fixed. Likewise, North Korea was given a roughly triangular portion of territory south of the 38th parallel and west of longitude 127° E that includes the city of Kaesŏng.

A demilitarized zone (DMZ) was created by pulling back the respective forces 1.2 miles (2 km) along each side of the boundary. It runs for about 150 miles (241 km) across the peninsula, from the mouth of the Han River on the west coast to a little south of the North Korean town of Kosŏng on the east coast. Located within the DMZ is the "truce village" of P'anmunjŏm, about 5 miles (8 km) east of Kaesŏng. It was the site of peace discussions during the Korean War and has since been the location of various conferences over issues related to North and South Korea, their allies, and the UN.

The areas north and south of the DMZ are heavily fortified, and both sides maintain large contingents of troops there. Over the years there have been occasional incidents and minor skirmishes but no significant conflicts. Since the end of the Korean War the DMZ, which was once farmland, has lain almost untouched and, to a large extent, has reverted to nature. In mid-2007 limited cargo-train service was resumed across the zone.

A sign in English identifying the 38th parallel, 1950. The 38th parallel roughly marks the border between North and South Korea and is at the center of the demilitarized zone (DMZ). Time & Life Pictures/Getty Images

Soviet forces from occupying the whole of Korea. Since U.S. policy toward Korea during World War II had aimed to prevent any single power's domination of Korea, it may be reasonably concluded that the principal reason for the division was to stop the Soviet advance south of the 38th parallel.

The Southern Zone

The end of Japanese rule caused political confusion among Koreans in both zones. In the south various political parties sprang up. Although they were roughly divided into rightists, leftists, and middle-of-the-roaders, they had a common goal: the immediate attainment of self-government. As early as Aug. 16, 1945, some Koreans organized a Committee for the Preparation of Korean Independence, headed by Woon-hyung Lyuh (Yŏ Un-hyŏng), who was closely associated with the leftists. On September 6 the delegates attending a "national assembly" called by the committee proclaimed the People's Republic of Korea. But the U.S. military government in South Korea, under Lieut. Gen. John R. Hodge, the commanding general of the U.S. armed forces in Korea, refused to recognize the republic, asserting that the military government was the "only government" in Korea, as stipulated in General Order No. 1. The exiled Korean provisional government, on returning, also was compelled by the military government to declare itself a political party, not a rival government. U.S. policy in Korea was to establish a trusteeship that would supersede both the American and the Soviet occupation forces in Korea.

In late December the Council of Foreign Ministers (representing the United States, the Soviet Union, and Great Britain) met in Moscow and decided to create a four-power trusteeship of up to five years. Upon receiving the news, Koreans reacted violently. In February 1946, to soothe the discontent, the military government created the Representative Democratic Council as an advisory body to the military government. This body was composed of Koreans and had as its chairman Syngman Rhee, former president of the Korean government-in-exile.

In October the military government created an Interim Legislative Assembly, half of whose members were elected by the people and half appointed by the military government. The assembly was empowered to enact ordinances on domestic affairs but was subject to the veto of the military government. The feeling against trusteeship came to a climax several months later when the assembly formally condemned trusteeship in Korea.

The Northern Zone

Unlike the U.S. forces in the south, the Soviet army marched into the north in 1945 accompanied by a band of expatriate Korean communists. By placing the latter in key positions of power, the

Soviet Union easily set up a communist-controlled government in the north. On August 25 the People's Executive Committee of South Hamgyŏng province was created by the South Hamgyŏng province Communist Council and other nationalists. The Soviet authorities recognized the committee's administrative power in the province, thus setting a precedent for the committee's role throughout the provinces of the northern zone. In this way the Soviet Union placed the north under its control without actually establishing a military government. In October Korean leaders in the north organized the Bureau of Five Provinces Administration, a central governing body, and this was replaced in February 1946 by the Provisional People's Committee for North Korea. This new agency, a de facto central government, adopted the political structure of the Soviet Union.

Communist leader Kim Il-sung arrived in P'yŏngyang in the uniform of a major of the Red Army and was introduced to the people as a national hero on Oct. 14, 1945. Shortly after his public appearance, Kim was elected first secretary of the North Korean Central Bureau of the Communist Party. After the Provisional People's Committee was organized, with Kim as its chairman, it assumed the helm of existing central administrative bureaus. A year later, in February 1947, a legislative body was established under the name of the Supreme People's Assembly, and, with the strong support of the Soviet occupation authorities, Kim commenced consolidating his political power.

Establishment of the Two Republics

The Moscow Conference of December 1945 created a Joint U.S.-U.S.S.R. Commission of the rival U.S. and Soviet military commands in Korea to settle the question of establishing a unified Korea. When the commission convened in Seoul from March to May 1946, the Soviet delegates demanded that those Korean political groups that had opposed trusteeship be excluded from consultation. The United States refused, and on this rock foundered all attempts by the commission to prepare for the unification of Korea. The commission met again from May to August 1947, but it achieved nothing toward the creation of a unified Korea.

The United States presented the question of Korean unification to the United Nations (UN) in September 1947. In November the UN General Assembly in New York City adopted a resolution, proposed by the United States, that called for general elections in Korea under the observation of a UN Temporary Commission on Korea. Those elected were to make up a National Assembly, establish a government, and arrange with the occupying powers for the withdrawal of their troops from Korea. The U.S.S.R., however, barred the Temporary

Commission from entering the northern zone. The South, however, held elections under the supervision of the Temporary Commission on May 10, 1948. The National Assembly convened on May 31 and elected Syngman Rhee as its speaker. Shortly afterward a constitution was adopted, and Rhee was elected president of the new government on July 20. Finally, on August 15, the Republic of Korea was inaugurated, with Seoul as the capital, and the military government in South Korea came to an end. In December the UN General Assembly declared that the republic was the only lawful government in Korea, despite the presence of the communist-controlled government under Kim Il-sung in the North.

Meanwhile, on Nov. 18, 1947, the Supreme People's Assembly of North Korea set up a committee to draft a constitution. The committee adopted the new constitution in April 1948, and on August 25 elections for members of the Supreme People's Assembly were held with a single list of candidates. On September 3 the constitution was ratified by the Supreme People's Assembly, which was holding its first meeting in P'yŏngyang. Kim Il-sung was appointed premier, and on September 9 the Democratic People's Republic of Korea was proclaimed, with the capital at P'yŏngyang. On October 12 the U.S.S.R. recognized this state as the only lawful government in Korea.

CHAPTER 2

KOREA AT WAR, 1950–53

PREPARATIONS FOR WAR

In December 1948 the Republic of Korea's Department of National Defense was established. By June 1950, when the war between the North and South broke out, South Korea had a 98,000-man force equipped only with small arms, which was barely enough to deal with internal revolt and border attacks. The U.S. occupation forces completely withdrew from Korea by June 1949, leaving behind them a force of about 500 men as a U.S. Military Advisory Group to train the South Korean armed forces. In October 1949 the United States granted South Korea $10,200,000 for military aid and $110,000,000 for economic aid for the fiscal year 1950, the first year of a contemplated three-year program. In addition the U.S. Congress approved $10,970,000 for military aid in March 1950. The military equipment committed under the U.S. military assistance program was still en route, however, when North Korean troops invaded the South in June. South Korea was thus unprepared to resist the total invasion from the North.

Military preparations for the conflict with the South had been much more extensive in North Korea. Early in 1946 the Soviet authorities had organized a 20,000-man constabulary and army units, and in August the North Korean army was established (its title changing to the Korean People's Army in February 1948). The Soviet occupation forces left North Korea in December 1948, leaving behind for training purposes 150 advisers for each army division. In March 1949 the U.S.S.R. concluded a reciprocal-aid agreement with North Korea, in which it agreed to furnish heavy military equipment, and by June 1950 North Korean forces numbered 135,000, including a tank brigade. As early as 1946 the Soviets were sending thousands of Koreans to the U.S.S.R. for specialized training, and during 1949–50 China transferred about 12,000 Korean troops from its army to the North Korean forces. The North Korean forces were thus far superior to those of South Korea in training and equipment when, on June 25, 1950, North Korean troops launched a full-scale invasion of the south.

INVASION AND COUNTERINVASION, 1950–51

South to Pusan

In early 1949 Kim Il-sung pressed his case with Stalin that the time had come for a conventional invasion of the South. Stalin refused, concerned about the relative unpreparedness of the North Korean armed forces and about possible U.S. involvement in the South's defense. However, over the course of the next year, the communist leadership built the KPA into a formidable offensive force modeled after a Soviet mechanized army. The Chinese released Korean veterans from the People's Liberation Army so that they could join the KPA efforts, while the Soviets provided armaments. By 1950 the North Koreans enjoyed substantial advantages over the South in every category of equipment. After another Kim visit to Moscow in March–April 1950, Stalin finally approved an invasion.

Soldiers in a tank regiment of the North Korean People's Army (KPA) line up in this undated photograph taken during the Korean War. AFP/Getty Images

In the predawn hours of June 25, the North Koreans struck across the 38th parallel behind a thunderous artillery barrage. The principal offensive, conducted by the KPA I Corps (53,000 men), drove across the Imjin River toward Seoul. The II Corps (54,000 soldiers) attacked along two widely separated axes, one through the cities of Ch'unch'ŏn and Inje to Hongch'ŏn and the other down the east coast road toward Kangnŭng. The KPA entered Seoul in the afternoon of June 28, but the North Koreans did not accomplish their goal of a quick surrender by the Rhee government and the disintegration of the South Korean army. Instead, remnants of the Seoul-area ROKA forces formed a defensive line south of the Han River, and on the east coast road ROKA units gave ground in good order. Still, if the South was to stave off collapse, it would need help. Their only possible allies at this time were the U.S. armed forces.

Truman's initial response to North Korea's invasion of the South was to order MacArthur to transfer munitions to the ROKA and to use air cover to protect the evacuation of U.S. citizens. Instead of pressing for a congressional declaration of war against North Korea, which he regarded as too alarmist and time-consuming when time was of the essence, Truman went to the United Nations for sanction. Under U.S. guidance, the UN called for the invasion to halt (June 25), then for the UN member states to provide military assistance to the ROK (June 27). By charter the Security Council considered and passed the resolutions, which could have been vetoed by a permanent member such as the Soviet Union. The Soviets, however, were boycotting the Council over the issue of admitting communist China to the UN. Congressional and public opinion in the United States, meanwhile, supported military intervention without significant dissent.

Having demonstrated its political will, the Truman administration faced the unhappy truth that it did not have much effective military power to meet the invasion. MacArthur secured the commitment of three divisions from Japan, but U.S. ground forces only expanded the scope of defeat. For almost eight weeks, near Osan, along the Kum River, through Taejŏn, and south to Taegu, U.S. soldiers fought the KPA and died—and some fled. Weakened by inadequate weapons, limited numbers, and uncertain leadership, U.S. troops were frequently beset by streams of refugees fleeing south, which increased the threat of guerrilla infiltration. These conditions produced unfortunate attacks on Korean civilians, such as the firing on hundreds of refugees at a railroad viaduct near the hamlet of Nogun-ri, west of the Naktong River, during the last week in July.

It was not until the first weeks of August that the United Nations Command, or UNC, as MacArthur's theatre forces had been redesignated, started to slow the North Koreans. The Eighth Army,

Primary Document: Harry S. Truman's "United Nations Police Action in Korea" Statement

Two days after the June 25 invasion of South Korea by the KPA, President Truman released a statement, excerpted below, on the American government's attitude toward the Korean crisis.

Bulletin, July 3, 1950, p. 5.

In Korea, the government forces, which were armed to prevent border raids and to preserve internal security, were attacked by invading forces from North Korea. The Security Council of the United Nations called upon the invading troops to cease hostilities and to withdraw to the 38th parallel. This they have not done, but, on the contrary, have pressed the attack. The Security Council called upon all members of the United Nations to render every assistance to the United Nations in the execution of this resolution. In these circumstances, I have ordered United States air and sea forces to give the Korean government troops cover and support . . .

I have similarly directed acceleration in the furnishing of military assistance to the forces of France and the Associated States in Indochina and the dispatch of a military mission to provide close working relations with those forces.

I know that all members of the United Nations will consider carefully the consequences of this latest aggression in Korea in defiance of the Charter of the United Nations. A return to the rule of force in international affairs would have far-reaching effects. The United States will continue to uphold the rule of law.

commanded by Lieut. Gen. Walton H. Walker, one of the best corps commanders in Europe in 1944–45, and the ROKA, led by Maj. Gen. Chung Il Kwon, rallied and fought back with more success. Supplies came through the port at Pusan, where the Eighth Army's logistics system depended on Korean and Japanese technicians and on thousands of Korean labourers. To stop the North Koreans' tanks and supporting artillery and infantry, Walker brought in Sherman and Pershing medium tanks, rocket launchers, artillery pieces, anti-aircraft guns, and, most important of all, close-air-support aircraft. The Fifth Air Force attacked forward units of the KPA with World War II–era P-51 Mustangs, new jet-powered F-80s and F-84s, and even B-26 and B-29 bombers. U.S. Marine Corps squadrons, embarked on navy light carriers, were capable of flying anywhere along the front in quick response to requests from ground forces, and on the east coast the U.S. Navy's cruisers and destroyers became a seagoing heavy artillery for the ROK I Corps. Meanwhile, fresh U.S. Army and Marine Corps units began to arrive, supplemented by a British Commonwealth brigade. In the same period, the ROKA, which had shrunk to half its prewar strength through deaths, surrenders, a few defections, and substantial desertions, began to bring its ranks back up with reservists, student volunteers, and men impressed from cities' streets as the South Koreans fell back.

Concerned that the shift of combat power toward the UNC would continue into September, the field commander of the KPA, Gen. Kim Chaek, ordered an advance against the Naktong River–Taegu–Yŏngdŏk line, soon to become famous as the "Pusan Perimeter." The major effort was a double envelopment of Taegu, supplemented by drives toward Masan and P'ohang, the southwestern and northeastern coastal anchors of the perimeter. None reached significant objectives. At the Battle of Tabu-dong (August 18–26), the ROK 1st Division and the U.S. 27th Regimental Combat Team defeated the North Koreans' main armoured thrust toward Taegu. By September 12 the KPA, its two corps reduced to 60,000 men and its tank forces destroyed, had been driven back in most places west of the Naktong and well away from Taegu and P'ohang. At that moment the entire strategic balance of the war was shifted by the sudden appearance of the U.S.-led X Corps at Inch'ŏn.

North to the Yalu

MacArthur did not believe that he could win the war without an amphibious landing deep behind enemy lines, and he had started to think about a landing as early as July. For the core of his landing force, he and the Joint Chiefs of Staff assembled the X Corps, to be commanded by Maj. Gen Edward M. Almond, MacArthur's chief of staff. The corps included both U.S. and South Korean marine and infantry divisions, as well as an assortment of U.S. support troops.

For the landing site, MacArthur himself fixed on Inch'ŏn, the port outlet of Seoul on Korea's west coast. After a naval gun and aerial bombardment on September 14, marines assaulted a key harbour defense site, Wŏlmi Island, the next day and then in the late afternoon took Inch'ŏn itself. The North Korean resistance was spread too thinly over the area, and the 1st Marine Division, accompanied by ROK and U.S. army units, entered Seoul on September 25. The bulk of the 7th Division advanced to Suwŏn, where it contacted the Eighth Army on the 26th. MacArthur and Syngman Rhee marched into the damaged capitol building and declared South Korea liberated.

As an organized field force, the KPA disintegrated, having lost 13,000 as prisoners and 50,000 as casualties in August and September. Nevertheless, about 25,000 of its best troops took to the mountains and marched home as cohesive units, while another 10,000 remained in South Korea as partisans. As the communists headed north, they took thousands of South Koreans with them as hostages and slave labourers. They also left additional thousands of South Koreans executed in their wake—most infamously at Taejŏn, where 5,000 civilians were massacred.

The ROK army and national police, for their part, showed little sympathy to any southern communists they found or even suspected, and U.S. aircraft attacked people and places with little restraint. As a result, the last two weeks of September saw gruesome atrocities rivaling those seen in Europe during the fratricidal Thirty Years' War of the 17th century.

Even before the Inch'ŏn landing, MacArthur had thought ahead to a campaign into North Korea, though his plans never went beyond establishing a line across the so-called waist of Korea, from P'yŏngyang in the west to Wŏnsan in the east. On September 27 the Joint Chiefs gave him final authority to conduct operations north of the 38th parallel although he was instructed to limit operations in the event of Russian or Chinese intervention. For the UNC the war aim was expanded. As announced by the UN General Assembly on October 7, their goal was to include the occupation of all of North Korea and the elimination of the KPA as a threat to the political reconstruction of Korea as one nation. To that end, ROKA units crossed the parallel on October 1, and U.S. Army units crossed on October 7. The ROK I Corps marched rapidly up the east coast highway, winning the race for Wŏnsan and P'yŏngyang fell to the U.S. I Corps on October 19. The Kim Il-sung government, with the remnants of nine KPA divisions, fell back to the mountain town of Kanggye. Two other divisions, accompanied by Soviet advisers and air defense forces, struggled northwest toward the Yalu River and the Chinese border at Sinŭiju. The UNC assumed that the KPA had lost its will to fight. In reality, it was awaiting rescue.

In Focus: Inch'ŏn Landing

On Sept. 15-26, 1950, an amphibious landing was made by U.S. and South Korean forces at the port of Inch'ŏn, near the South Korean capital, Seoul. A daring operation planned and executed under extremely difficult conditions by MacArthur, the amphibious landing reversed the tide of the war, forcing the invading North Korean army to retreat in disorder up the Korean peninsula.

MacArthur had started to think about a landing somewhere behind enemy lines in early July 1950. On August 12 he ordered his staff to prepare for an amphibious landing at Inch'ŏn, despite the coastline there presenting every possible disadvantage for such an operation. The tidal variation was approximately 30 feet, permitting use of the beaches for only 6 hours out of each 24. The only approach to the port was through a narrow, tortuous channel, blocked by a key harbour defense site, Wolmi Island, and the port facilities of Inch'ŏn were inadequate to support a major operation. However, MacArthur knew that practically the entire KPA had been committed to the assaults on Pusan. The Inch'ŏn–Seoul area was weakly held, and nowhere else were the North Koreans' lines of communication so vulnerable or accessible. Furthermore, Seoul, as South Korea's capital, was psychologically important to the restoration of South Korea's independence, and MacArthur was determined to reverse the war and restore the United States' damaged prestige as soon as possible.

For the core of his landing force, MacArthur and the joint chiefs selected the 1st Marine Division and the 7th Infantry Division. As the force developed, it also included two South Korean marine battalions, an elite ROKA infantry regiment, and an assortment of support troops from the U.S. Army and Marine Corps. The entire force was designated the X Corps and was placed under Almond's command. The landing force became part of Joint Task Force 7, directed by Vice Adm. Arthur D. Struble, the U.S. Navy's 7th Fleet commander.

After a naval gun and aerial bombardment on September 14, U.S. marines assaulted Wolmi Island the next day. Later that day additional marine units landed along Inch'ŏn's waterfront. The North Koreans' resistance was not stubborn, and their armoured counterattacks over the next two days did little to slow the marines' advance on Seoul. With Kimpo airfield secured on September 18, the 1st Marine Division put all three of its infantry regiments across the Han River on September 20–25. Then they captured Seoul with some last-minute and largely unnecessary help from a South Korean and a U.S. infantry regiment. Meanwhile, the 7th Infantry Division came ashore on September 18 and fanned out quickly to the south. On September 26, the day Seoul fell to the marines, an armoured spearhead of the Eighth Army dashing north from the Pusan Perimeter met the 7th Infantry Division at Suwon, south of Seoul. The KPA, completely shattered, had ceased to exist as a cohesive force in the South. Many of its survivors were able to escape northward through the wild, rugged country in the central and eastern portion of the peninsula, but more than 125,000 prisoners fell into UNC hands.

The amazement created by the sudden appearance of the X Corps at Inch'ŏn added more lustre to MacArthur's already brilliant career, and the landing is still considered to be one of the greatest operations in military history.

Back to the 38th Parallel

As UNC troops crossed the 38th parallel, Chinese Communist Party Chairman Mao Zedong received a plea for direct military aid from Kim Il-sung. The chairman was willing to intervene on behalf of North Korea, but he needed assurances of Soviet air power. Stalin promised to extend China's air defenses (manned by Soviets) to a corridor above the Yalu, thus protecting air bases in Manchuria and hydroelectric plants on the river. He also promised new Soviet weapons and armaments factories. After much debate, Mao ordered the Renmin Zhiyuanjun, or Chinese People's Volunteers Force (CPVF), to cross into Korea. It was commanded by Gen. Peng Dehuai, a veteran of 20 years of war against the Chinese Nationalists and the Japanese.

The Chinese First Offensive (Oct. 25–Nov. 6, 1950) had the limited objective of testing U.S.-ROK fighting qualities and slowing their advance. In the battle of Onjŏng-Unsan along the Ch'ŏngch'ŏn

River, the Chinese ruined seven Korean and U.S. regiments—including the only Korean regiment to reach the Yalu, cut off in the vastness of the cold northern hills near Ch'osan. The Chinese suffered 10,000 casualties, but they were convinced that they had found a formula for fighting UNC forces: attack at night, cut off routes of supply and withdrawal, ambush counterattacking forces, and exploit all forms of concealment and cover. Stunned by the suddenness of the Chinese onslaught and almost 8,000 casualties (6,000 of them Koreans), the Eighth Army fell back to the south bank of the Ch'ŏngch'ŏn and tightened its overextended lines. With a harsh winter beginning and supplies in shortage, this pause in action was wise.

Another matter of concern to the UNC was the appearance of MiG-15 jet fighters above North Korea. Flown by Soviet pilots masquerading as Chinese and Koreans, the MiGs stopped most of the daytime raids on North Korea in one week's action (November 1–7). The U.S. Air Force immediately dispatched a crack wing of F-86 Sabre jet interceptors to Japan. Over the course of the war, the F-86s succeeded in allowing the Far East Air Forces (FEAF) to conduct offensive air operations anywhere in North Korea, and they also protected the Eighth Army from communist air attack. However, they were never able to provide perfect protection for B-29s flying daylight raids into "MiG Alley," a corridor in northwestern Korea where MiGs based near An-tung, Manchuria (now Dandong, China), fiercely defended bridges and dams on the Yalu River.

The FEAF also turned its fury on all standing structures that might shield the Chinese from the cold; cities and towns all over North Korea went up in flames. But the air assault did not halt the buildup for the Chinese Second Offensive. This time Peng's instructions to his army commanders stressed the necessity to lure the Americans and "puppet troops" out of their defensive positions between the Ch'ŏngch'ŏn and P'yŏngyang, giving the impression of weakness and confusion, while Peng would surround their forward elements with his much-enlarged force of 420,000 Chinese and North Korean regulars. MacArthur, in what may have been his only real military mistake of the war, ordered the Eighth Army and X Corps northward into the trap on November 24, and from November 25 to December 14 the Chinese battered them back to South Korea. Falling upon the U.S. IX Corps and the ROK II Corps from the east, Peng's Thirteenth Army Group opened up a gap to the west and almost cut off the I Corps north of the Ch'ŏngch'ŏn. The I Corps managed to fight its way through Chinese ambushes back to P'yŏngyang. In the eastern sector the Chinese Ninth Army Group sent two armies against the 1st Marine Division near the Changjin Reservoir (known to the Americans by its Japanese name, Chosin). Under the worst possible weather conditions, the marines turned and fought their way south, destroying seven Chinese divisions

In Focus: Battle of the Chosin Reservoir

Chosin was the name given on old Japanese military maps to the Changjin Reservoir, a dammed lake in the Taebaek Mountains of North Korea. There, in November–December 1950, isolated and surrounded units of the 1st U.S. Marine Division and a regimental combat team of the 7th U.S. Infantry Division fought their way through 12 Chinese divisions until they reached waiting transport ships at the coast.

Following the successful Inch'ŏn landing of September 1950, MacArthur ordered a general advance into North Korea. On the eastern side of the Korean peninsula's rocky spine, the 1st Marine Division, Maj. Gen. Oliver Smith, commander, began to disembark at Wonsan on October 26. On October 29 the 7th Infantry Division landed farther north at Iwon. In mid-November the marines and the 31st Regimental Combat Team (hastily assembled from units of the 7th Division) were ordered up to Chosin. The marines were to take Yudam-ni on the west side of the reservoir as the prelude of a stroke farther north against Kanggye, and the 31st RCT was to relieve a marine battalion on the east side of the reservoir and prepare to push toward the Yalu River, at the border with China. Smith was extremely skeptical of these plans, and so he ordered the marines to move cautiously northward, detaching forces to maintain their vital supply route to the ports in the Hungnam-Hamhung area, some 50 miles away.

Unknown to the UNC, the Chinese Ninth Army Group (comprising 12 divisions in four armies) was deployed along the eastern ridges of the Taebaek range. On the night of November 27–28 the Chinese struck. They sent one army against the 31st RCT, two armies against the marines at Yudam-ni and at Hagaru-ri (at the base of the reservoir, where Smith had his headquarters), and a fourth army against the road to Hungnam deep in the rear. The 31st RCT was destroyed. Fewer than half of its original 2,500 troops managed to struggle on foot and in small, disorganized groups around the frozen reservoir or directly across the ice to Hagaru-ri. There Smith consolidated his forces and had the dead and wounded flown out on transport planes that operated from a rudimentary airfield. On December 6, spurning the idea of withdrawal or retreat and refusing to have his able-bodied troops airlifted out without their equipment, he faced his division southward toward Hungnam to begin "attacking in another direction." Under weather conditions as cold as -20 °F (-29 °C), the 1st Marine Division, along with the remnants of the 31st RTC, a commando of Royal Marines, and attached South Korean troops, fought its way out against constant Chinese attack.Smith's forces retraced their route from the coast down a single narrow, vulnerable road through several mountain passes and bridged chasms. The Chinese, suffering as much as the Americans from the cold and subjected during daylight hours to attack by U.S. Air Force and Marine Corps planes, were unable to halt the marines' steady advance. On December 11 the 1st Marine Division reached Hungnam, whence it was evacuated by sea. Of the almost 12,000 marines who began the breakout from Hagaru-ri, 178 were killed, 749 were wounded, and 23 were missing in action; in addition, there were some 1,500 nonbattle casualties, a large number of them from frostbite. The Battle of the Chosin Reservoir quickly became one of the most storied exploits in Marine Corps history. However, for the American participants the brilliance of the breakout could not completely dispel the gloom of defeat.

before reaching sanctuary at the port of Hŭngnam on December 11.

At the height of the crisis, MacArthur conferred with Walker and Almond, and they agreed that their forces would try to establish enclaves in North Korea, thus preserving the option of holding the P'yŏngyang-Wŏnsan line. In reality, Walker had finally reached the limits of his disgust with MacArthur's meddling and posturing, and he started his men south. By December 6 the Eighth Army had destroyed everything it could not carry and had taken the road for Seoul. Walker's initiative may have saved his army, but it also meant that much of the rest of the war would be fought as a UNC effort to recapture ground surrendered with little effort in December 1950. Walker himself died in a traffic accident just north of Seoul on December 23 and was succeeded by Lieut. Gen. Matthew B. Ridgway.

Heartened by the ease with which the CPVF had driven the UNC out of North Korea, Mao Zedong expanded his war aims to demand that the Chinese army unify all of Korea and drive the Americans and puppets off the peninsula. His enthusiasm increased when the Chinese Third Offensive (Dec. 31, 1950–Jan. 5, 1951) retook Seoul. The Chinese attacks centred on ROKA divisions, which were showing signs of defeatism and ineptness. Ridgway,

Lt. Gen. Walton H. Walker (front left) *consults with Gen. Douglas MacArthur* (front right), *November 1950.* Carl Mydans/Time & Life Pictures/Getty Images

therefore, had to rely in the short term upon his U.S. divisions, many of which had now gained units from other UN participants. In addition to two British Commonwealth brigades, there were units from Turkey, France, Belgium, the Netherlands, Greece, Colombia, Thailand, Ethiopia, and the Philippines. Pulling his multinational force together, Ridgway pushed back to the Han River valley in January 1951.

The Chinese, now reinforced by a reborn North Korean army, launched their Fourth Offensive on Feb. 11, 1951. Again the initial attacks struck ill-prepared South Korean divisions, and again the UNC gave ground. Again the Eighth Army fought back methodically, crossing the 38th parallel after two months. At that point Peng began the Fifth Offensive (First Phase) with 11 Chinese armies and two North Korean corps. The attacks came at an awkward moment for the Eighth Army. On April 11 Truman, having reached the opinion that MacArthur's independence amounted to insubordination, had relieved the general of all his commands and recalled him to the United States. The change elevated Ridgway to commander in chief of both FECOM and the UNC, and brought Lieut. Gen. James A. Van Fleet to command the Eighth Army. Like Ridgway, Van Fleet had earned wide respect as a division and corps commander during World War II against the Germans in 1944–45.

Before Van Fleet could re-form the ROK Army and redeploy his own divisions, the Chinese struck. At a low point in Korean military history, the battered ROKA II Corps gave way. The U.S. divisions then peeled back to protect their flanks and rear until Van Fleet could commit five more U.S. and Korean divisions and a British brigade to halt the Chinese armies on April 28. Mao refused to accept Peng's report that the CPVF could no longer hold the initiative, and he ordered the Second Phase of the offensive, which began on May 16 and lasted another bloody week. Once again allied air power and heavy artillery stiffened the resistance, and once again the UNC crossed the 38th parallel in pursuit of a battered (but not beaten) Chinese expeditionary force.

Primary Document: Harry S. Truman's "Korea and the Policy of Containment" Speech

The differences between MacArthur and the Truman administration over Korean War policy intensified during the spring of 1951, when the UNC, made up mostly of Americans, faced upwards of 400,000 Red Chinese "volunteers" in addition to the well-trained and Soviet-equipped divisions of North Korea. While MacArthur wanted an all-out war, including permission to bomb bases in China, the administration was determined to confine the war to Korea and to end it if possible with a negotiated settlement. After removing MacArthur from his command, Truman broadcast a message to the nation, excerpted below, on April 11, defining the government's aims in Korea and explaining MacArthur's recall.

Bulletin, *April 16, 1951, pp. 603–605.*

I want to talk plainly to you tonight about what we are doing in Korea and about our policy in the Far East. In the simplest terms, what we are doing in Korea is this: We are trying to prevent a third world war . . .

The aggression against Korea is the boldest and most dangerous move the Communists have yet made. The attack on Korea was part of a greater plan for conquering all of Asia . . .

The question we have had to face is whether the Communist plan of conquest can be stopped without general war. Our government and other countries associated with us in the United Nations believe that the best chance of stopping it without general war is to meet the attack in Korea and defeat it there.

That is what we have been doing. It is a difficult and bitter task. But so far it has been successful. So far, we have prevented World War III. So far, by fighting a limited war in Korea, we have prevented aggression from succeeding and bringing on a general war. And the ability of the whole free world to resist Communist aggression has been greatly improved . . .

I have thought long and hard about this question of extending the war in Asia. I have discussed it many times with the ablest military advisers in the country. I believe with all my heart that the course we are following is the best course. I believe that we must try to limit the war to Korea for these vital reasons: to make sure that the precious lives of our fighting men are not wasted; to see that the security of our country and the free world is not needlessly jeopardized; and to prevent a third world war . . .

A number of events have made it evident that General MacArthur did not agree with that policy. I have therefore considered it essential to relieve General MacArthur so that there would be no doubt or confusion as to the real purpose and aim of our policy. It was with the deepest personal regret that I found myself compelled to take this action. General MacArthur is one of our greatest military commanders. But the cause of world peace is more important than any individual . . .

We are ready, at any time, to negotiate for a restoration of peace in the area. But we will not engage in appeasement. We are only interested in real peace. Real peace can be achieved through a settlement based on the following factors:

The fighting must stop.

Concrete steps must be taken to insure that the fighting will not break out again.

There must be an end to the aggression.

A settlement founded upon these elements would open the way for the unification of Korea and the withdrawal of all foreign forces.

We do not want to widen the conflict. We will use every effort to prevent that disaster. And in so doing we know that we are following the great principles of peace, freedom, and justice.

To the Negotiating Table

By June 1951 the Korean War had reached another critical point. The Chinese–North Korean armies, despite having suffered some 500,000 casualties since November, had grown to 1,200,000 soldiers. The UNC had taken its share of casualties—more than 100,000 since the Chinese intervention—but by May 1951 U.S. ground troops numbered 256,000, the ROKA 500,000, and other allied contingents 28,000. The U.S. FEAF had grown from fewer than 700 aircraft in July 1950 to more than 1,400 in February 1951.

These developments obliged the leaders of both coalitions to consider that peace could not be imposed by either side through military victory—at least at acceptable cost. Truman and the UN, in particular, had lost their ardour for anything more than a return to status quo antebellum and were sympathetic to the idea of a negotiated settlement. On May 17, 1951, the U.S. National Security Council adopted a new policy that committed the United States to support a unified, democratic Korea, but not necessarily one unified by military action and the overthrow of Kim Il-sung.

The communist road to a negotiated peace started in Beijing, where Mao, who had no desire to end the war, approved an approach suggested by Peng and others: hold the ground in Korea and conduct a campaign of attrition, attempting to win limited victories against small allied units through violent night attacks and infantry infiltration. Protection from UNC aircraft and artillery would be provided by caves and bunkers dug into the Korean mountains. Meanwhile, negotiations would be managed by the Chinese, an unparalleled chance to appear an equal of the United States in Asia and a slap at the hated Japanese. The Koreans were not a factor for either side.

After secret meetings between U.S. and Soviet diplomats, the Soviet Union announced that it would not block a negotiated settlement to the Korean War. The Truman administration had already alerted Ridgway to the prospect of truce talks, and on June 30 he issued a public statement that he had been authorized to participate in "a meeting to discuss an armistice providing for the cessation of hostilities." On July 2 the Chinese and North Koreans issued a joint statement that they would discuss arrangements for a meeting, but only at their place of choice: the city of Kaesŏng, an ancient Korean capital, once part of the ROK but now occupied by the communists at the very edge of the front lines. The Chinese had just fired the first salvo of a new war, one in which talking and fighting for advantage might someday end the conflict.

TALKING AND FIGHTING, 1951–53

Battling for Position

From the time the liaison officers of both coalitions met on July 8, 1951, until the armistice agreement was signed on July 27, 1953, the Korean War continued as

In Focus: Kaesŏng

Kaesŏng lies just south of latitude 38° N (the 38th parallel), approximately 45 miles (72 km) northwest of Seoul, S.Kor. One of the oldest cities of Korea, Kaesŏng was the capital of the Koryŏ dynasty (935–1392). It was formerly called Songdo ("City of Pine"), so named because it is surrounded by pine-covered mountains, including Mounts Songak (2,506 feet, or 764 metres) and Osŏng (3,483 feet, or 1,062 metres). Kaesŏng is a castle city enclosed by a stone wall with four gates. It was overrun by communist forces during the war, and in 1951 it was chosen as the site of the first truce talks. After the war, Kaesŏng was included in North Korea.

The area is home to the Kaesŏng Industrial Complex, an industrial park and duty-free trade facility established as a joint venture between the North and South Korean governments to allow South Korean companies to manufacture goods in the North. Financed and managed for the most part by South Korea, it was planned during a period of warming North-South relations in the late 1990s, and construction began in 2003. Within a few years, several dozen South Korean companies had facilities there, among them textile, chemical, machinery, and electronics factories. The businesses employed both North and South Koreans. Tourist groups were permitted to visit the complex from South Korea by means of a road built from the latter.

Although some of the city's Koryŏ-era monuments were destroyed during the war, many temples, tombs, and palaces remain, including some that have been restored. The medicinal herb ginseng is a famous product of the area that has been exported to China and Southeast Asian countries since ancient times. Kaesŏng is also a notable cultural and educational centre.

a "stalemate." This characterization is appropriate in only two ways: (1) both sides had given up trying to unify Korea by force; and (2) the movement of armies on the ground never again matched the fluidity of the war's first year. Otherwise, the word *stalemate* has no meaning, for the political-geographic stakes in Korea remained high.

As the negotiations at Kaesŏng developed, neither Ridgway nor Van Fleet believed that the talks would produce anything without more UNC offensives beyond the 38th parallel. Ridgway was particularly convinced that UNC forces should take the "Iron Triangle," a key area between the headwaters of the Imjin River and the highest eastern mountain ranges that was anchored on the cities of Ch'ŏrwŏn (west), P'yŏnggang (north), and Kimhwa (east). Communist planners were equally convinced that control of this terrain offered advantages for defending North Korea or for continuing the war with offensives to the south and east.

Ground actions never actually ceased in 1951, but none matched the ferocity and frustration of the Eighth Army's Autumn Offensive (August 31–November 12). Van Fleet's general concept envisioned operations by the I Corps (five divisions) in the west and the X Corps (five divisions) in the central-eastern sector. In the I Corps sector, the ROK 1st Division and the British Commonwealth Division made notable advances beyond the Imjin valley, while other U.S. and ROK divisions advanced past Ch'ŏrwŏn and then stalled in heavy fighting. The X Corps, fighting a crack Chinese army and two North Korean corps, pushed northward through the mountains and succeeded only in making "Bloody Ridge," "Heartbreak Ridge," "The Punchbowl," and Kanmubong Ridge bad memories for thousands of army and marine veterans. The KPA I, III, and VI Corps, holding the eastern mountains, proved especially difficult to dislodge, for Kim Il-sung had issued a "stand or die" order to his much-enlarged and improved armed forces. The most surprising advance occurred in the X Corps sector, where two U.S. and two ROK divisions pushed the Chinese back almost 10 miles (16 km) from Kimhwa to Kŭmsong, pushing the front line out in a salient that exposed their flanks but also establishing a strong position to advance west to P'yŏnggang. The cost of the campaign troubled Van Fleet and Ridgway, with 60,000 casualties and 22,000 of them American soldiers.

The campaign did not discourage the Chinese leadership, since in their eyes the strategy of "active defense" had worked. The UNC gave up major offensive operations in November, and the Chinese actually struck back in places with some success. Communist losses of some 100,000–150,000 were significant but not crippling—certainly not enough to drive the Chinese to end the war, only to talk some more about it.

In late October 1951 the communists agreed to move the truce negotiations to a more secure area, a village named P'anmunjŏm. Within two months they accepted the current line of contact between the armies as the military demarcation line; they also accepted related measures for the creation of a demilitarized zone. The UNC accepted that there would be no verification activities outside of the DMZ, and both sides agreed to work on a regime for enforcement of the armistice after the shooting stopped. Much work on these items remained to be done, but the outline of an agreement was becoming apparent as the year ended. However, there was one major exception to the accordance reached between the North and South: how each side would handle their prisoners of war.

Battling over POWs

As another bitterly cold Korean winter congealed operations on the ground, repatriation of prisoners of war (POWs) became the most intractable issue at P'anmunjŏm. The initial assumption of the negotiators was that they would follow the revised Geneva Convention of 1949, which required any "detaining authority" that held POWs to return all of them to their homelands as rapidly as possible when a war ended. This "all for

In Focus: P'anmunjŏm

P'anmunjŏm is a village in the demilitarized zone of central Korea, established after the Korean War, 5 miles (8 km) east of Kaesŏng and 3 miles (5 km) south of the 38th parallel, on the Kyŏngŭi high road (from Seoul to Sinŭiju). It was the location of the truce conference that was held for two years (1951–53) between representatives of the United Nations forces and the opposing North Korean and Chinese armies during the war. After the armistice, signed there July 27, 1953, both the liaison officers and the guards of the four countries forming the Neutral Nations Supervisory Commission (Sweden, Switzerland, Poland, and Czechoslovakia) were located there. In 1968 the U.S. intelligence ship Pueblo *was seized off the North Korean coast by North Korean patrol boats, and its officers and crew were incarcerated and charged with espionage. P'anmunjŏm was then used as the negotiation site between the United States and North Korea, and the crew were released through the village. Subsequently, it has served as a meeting place for conferences between North and South Korea, including Red Cross conferences to establish means of communication and contact between people on either side of the truce line.*

all" policy of a complete—even forced—exchange of prisoners was certainly favoured by the U.S. military, which was alarmed by early reports from Korea of atrocities against allied POWs. The South Korean government, on the other hand, was adamantly opposed to complete and involuntary repatriation, since it knew that thousands of detainees in the South were actually South Korean citizens who had been forced to fight with the KPA. Indeed, the North Koreans knew that they had much to answer for regarding their impressment, murder, and kidnapping of South Koreans. The Chinese army leaders, meanwhile, knew that some of their soldiers, impressed from the ranks of the Nationalist army, would refuse repatriation if it was not made mandatory.

Both sides agreed to exchange the names of POWs and the numbers held in various categories. The results of the tally shocked all the participants. The U.S. armed forces were carrying 11,500 men as missing in action (MIA), but the communists reported only 3,198 Americans in their custody (as well as 1,219 other UNC POWs, mostly Britons and Turks). The accounting for the South Koreans was even worse: of an estimated 88,000 MIAs, only 7,142 names were listed. The numbers fed the fears of the allies that the murder rate of POWs had been even worse than they suspected. In truth, most of the MIAs had died in battle, but perhaps 15,000 (all but 2,000 of them South Koreans) had died in communist hands from torture, execution, starvation, and medical mistreatment.

The communists, too, found little comfort in the numbers. Early unofficial estimates of POWs in UNC custody had been either too low, around 90,000, or too high, around 170,000. Now the official list produced 95,531 North Koreans, 20,700 Chinese, and 16,243 South Koreans, for a total of 132,474. The UNC reported that the 40,000 "missing" men were South Koreans who had already passed loyalty investigations and would not be counted as potential repatriates. Against this background, Truman ruled in January 1952 that no POW in UNC custody would be forced to return to North Korea or China against his will. Koreans choosing to go north would be exchanged on a "one for one" formula until all 12,000 allied POWs had been returned. Such a process, however, would require extensive screening of individuals about their preferences, a condition that soon created open warfare in the camps.

The communists had taken steps in 1951 to infiltrate political officers into the UNC POW camps, and now orders came from P'yŏngyang to obstruct the screening process without regard for loss of life. The goal was to make the POWs so obnoxious that the UNC would use force if necessary to send every one of them back to communist control. And so, beginning in December 1951, a series of revolts broke out "inside the wire," culminating in pitched battles between armed prisoners and entire guard battalions in which hundreds of POWs and a small number of UNC troops lost their lives. Finally, in May 1952, Gen. Mark W. Clark, who had just replaced Ridgway as UNC commander, ordered the execution of Operation BREAKUP, which over the following months crushed the revolt with tanks, gas, and bullets. By the end of the year, all the Chinese had been sent to Cheju Island, repatriate and nonrepatriate POWs segregated, refugees resettled, some of the communist intelligence network disrupted, and camp administration improved. Vigilantism and gang warfare never ceased entirely, however.

Guerrilla Warfare

The POW revolt was only one aspect of the "other war" raging behind UNC lines. Another was waged by communist partisans and stay-behind units of the KPA, who, based in South Korea's mountainous southern provinces, plagued the UNC lines of communication, rear-area camps, and Korean towns. In the autumn of 1951 Van Fleet ordered Maj. Gen. Paik Sun-yup, one of the ROKA's most effective officers, to break the back of guerrilla activity. From December 1951 to March 1952, ROK security forces killed 11,090 partisans and sympathizers and captured 9,916 more—a ratio suggesting something close to a "scorched earth, no-quarter" policy. Previous ROKA counterguerrilla operations had resulted in the war's worst atrocity by a UNC unit, the execution of 800 to 1,000 villagers at Kŏch'ang in February 1951.

Air Warfare

Air power gave the UNC its greatest hope to offset Chinese manpower and increasing firepower. The FEAF clearly won the battle for air superiority, pitting fewer than 100 F-86s against far more numerous Soviet, Chinese, and North Korean MiG-15s. Pilots from all the U.S. armed forces downed at least 500 MiGs at a loss of 78 F-86s. The Soviets rotated squadrons of their air defense force to Korea, losing more than 200 pilots.

Strategic bombing by the UNC was at first limited by policy to attacks on North Korean cities and military installations—a campaign pursued until P'yŏngyang resembled Hiroshima or Tokyo in 1945.

In Focus: MiG-15 and F-86 Sabres

In December 1950, U.S. pilots flying F-86 Sabres and Soviet pilots flying MiG-15s over North Korea began history's first large-scale jet fighter combat. The appearance of Soviet pilots marked a major turning point in the war. One of China's conditions for entering the war in October 1950 was Soviet air support, and to that end Soviet fighter units were sent to bases in Manchuria, close to the border with North Korea. The aircraft bore Chinese markings, and the pilots were ordered to speak only Chinese or Korean, but to the crews of U.S. B-29 bombers and their escort fighters, there was no doubt as to the pilots' nationality—a nationality that was eventually confirmed when the Soviet pilots, in the pressure of combat, abandoned the ruse and communicated by radio in Russian.

The MiG-15 was the first "all-new" Soviet jet aircraft, one whose design did not simply add a jet engine onto an older piston-engine airframe. Employing swept-back wings, tailfin, and horizontal stabilizers to reduce drag as the plane approached the speed of sound, it clearly exploited aerodynamic principles learned from German engineering at the close of World War II. It was powered by a centrifugal-flow engine that had been licensed from the British Rolls-Royce company and then upgraded by the Soviet manufacturer Klimov. The plane was first flown in 1947, and deliveries to front-line fighter units began in 1949. Designed as a bomber interceptor, the MiG-15 carried a formidable armament of two 23-mm guns and one 37-mm gun firing exploding shells.

Shocked by the speed, climbing ability, and high operating ceiling of the Soviet fighter, the United States hurried delivery to Korea of the new F-86 Sabre, a single-seat, single-engine jet fighter built by North American Aviation, Inc. Like the MiG-15, the F-86 was built with swept-back wings, was first flown in 1947, and became operational in 1949. Unlike its Soviet counterpart, it was designed for air-superiority combat with other jet fighters; it was powered by a General Electric turbojet engine, and its armament consisted of six .50-inch machine guns (though later versions also carried 20-mm cannons). Though inferior to the MiG-15 in weight of armament, turn radius, and maximum speed at combat altitude, the F-86 quickly re-established U.S. air supremacy over Korea, in part because of its superior handling characteristics, a radar-ranging gunsight, and a superior pilot-training system instituted by the U.S. Air Force. Nevertheless, the MiG-15 virtually ended daylight bombing runs by the huge, slow B-29s, and Soviet pilots continued to engage in combat with U.S. and allied planes even as they trained Chinese and North Koreans to fly in the new jet age.

In 1952 the bombing of power plants and dams along the Yalu also was authorized, and the following year approval was given to attack dams and supporting irrigation systems in North Korea. The bombing caused great suffering for the North Koreans, but they had to follow the Chinese and Russians in the war's strategic direction, and the Chinese and Russians were hurt very little.

Throughout the war U.S. political and military leaders studied the possible use of nuclear weapons, and upon four separate occasions they gave this study serious attention. The answer was always the same: existing atomic bombs, carried by modified B-29s, would have little effect except for leveling cities. The one time that Truman suggested (in December 1950) that he was considering the nuclear option, the British led the allied charge to stop such talk.

Without question the UNC air campaign hurt the communists, and in retaliation the Chinese and North Koreans (with Soviet collusion) treated captured pilots with special brutality. Air crewmen made up the largest single group of U.S. POWs who truly disappeared without a trace, presumably dying under interrogation in Manchuria, elsewhere in China, and possibly in Russia. The communists also claimed that FEAF bombers were spreading epidemic diseases among the

U.S. Air Force mechanics prepare F-86 Sabres for combat at the Suwon Air Base in South Korea. F-86s were used by the Far East Air Forces (FEAF) throughout the Korean War. U.S. Air Force photo

civilian population, and they tortured captured American pilots until they extracted incriminating statements of terror bombing and germ warfare.

Strengthening the ROK

U.S. air power might have held the communists at bay in the near term, but the long-term security of the ROK depended on (1) the enlargement and improvement of its own armed forces and (2) the stability of its government. The first requirement was accomplished by the United States' Korean Military Advisory Group, which modernized the ROKA and also organized an effective training program. In the political arena, however, the UNC had to deal with the aging Rhee, who was convinced that he had an unfinished divine mission to save Korea.

In 1952 Rhee forced the National Assembly to make the election of the president a matter of popular vote, immediately calling an election and winning a second term with five million of the six million votes cast. Rhee's political coup had a ripple effect that spread to the armistice negotiations, as his dogmatic opposition to a cease-fire increased in scope and vigour. Essentially, Rhee could not believe that a likely new Republican administration in Washington, led by two other venerable Cold Warriors, Dwight D. Eisenhower and John Foster Dulles, would be satisfied to have U.S. soldiers "die for a tie." Neither could the Russians, Chinese, and North Koreans.

The Final Push

From September to November 1952, the Chinese expeditionary force staged its sixth major offensive of the war, this time to force the allies back to the 38th parallel and to inflict unacceptable casualties on them. Raging from the valley of the Imjin through the Iron Triangle to the eastern mountains, the ground war followed the same dismal pattern. The Chinese infiltrated allied outposts at night, then attacked under the support of short, intense artillery barrages. Submachine guns and hand grenades ruled the trenches, and flamethrowers and demolitions became standard weapons for assault units. Obscure hills acquired memorable names: White Horse Mountain, Bunker Hill, Old Baldy, Sniper Ridge, Capitol Hill, Triangle Hill, Pike's Peak, Jackson Heights, and Jane Russell Hill. By the time fighting faded in mid-November, the Eighth Army had lost 10,000 men, the Chinese 15,000. Chinese commanders hoped that they had persuaded president-elect Eisenhower to abandon any ambitious plans for a major offensive in 1953.

The Chinese need not have worried, for both Eisenhower and secretary of state-designate Dulles viewed continuation of the Korean War as incompatible with U.S. national security interests. In their view the People's Republic of China was indeed the enemy in Asia, but Korea was only one theatre in the struggle. They also knew that the voting public's support

Pres. Dwight D. Eisenhower (right) *meets with his Secretary of State, John Foster Dulles* (left), *September 1954.* Carl Iwasaki/Time & Life Pictures/Getty Images

for the war had thinned throughout 1952 as the talking and fighting continued abroad and the talking and taxing continued at home. As for the negotiations, Dulles conceded the communists' point that voluntary repatriation should involve screening by an international agency, not just U.S.-ROK teams. When the UN and the International Committee of the Red Cross called for an exchange of sick and disabled POWs as a goodwill gesture, Eisenhower approved.

The plan proved a good test of communist intentions—by sheer chance. On March 5, 1953, Joseph Stalin died, and within weeks the Politburo of the Soviet Communist Party voted that the war in Korea should be ended. Mao Zedong received the news with dismay, but he knew that his army could not continue the war without Soviet assistance. With a speed that amazed the negotiating teams on both sides, the Chinese accepted voluntary repatriation. POWs who wanted to return to their homelands would be released immediately, and those who chose to stay would go into the custody of a neutral international agency for noncoercive screening. The Chinese and North Koreans also agreed to the exchange of sick and disabled POWs, which took place between April 20 and May 3.

Peace was not yet at hand, however. Rhee had never publicly surrendered his "march north and unify" position, and in private he hinted that he might "accept" an armistice only in return for serious commitments by the United States, including an unambiguous mutual security alliance and $1 billion in economic aid. The Chinese, meanwhile, saw but one way to win concessions and territory in a peace agreement: on the battlefield. Their seventh and final offensive opened in the Imjin River sector in May against U.S. and Commonwealth divisions, then

Primary Document: Dwight D. Eisenhower's "I Shall Go to Korea" speech

Eisenhower would probably have won in any event, but his election was assured when, in a campaign speech at Detroit on Oct. 24, 1952, he pledged to go to Korea immediately after election day if he were chosen as America's next president. He did win, and he did go to Korea, on December 2. The Detroit speech is excerpted below.

New York Times, *Oct. 25, 1952.*

In this anxious autumn for America, one fact looms above all others in our people's mind. One tragedy challenges all men dedicated to the work of peace. One word shouts denial to those who foolishly pretend that ours is not a nation at war.

This fact, this tragedy, this word is: Korea.

A small country, Korea has been, for more than two years, the battleground for the costliest foreign war our nation has fought, excepting the two world wars. It has been the burial ground for 20,000 American dead. It has been another historic field of honor for the valor and skill and tenacity of American soldiers.

All these things it has been—and yet one thing more. It has been a symbol—a telling symbol—of the foreign policy of our nation. It has been a sign—a warning sign—of the way the administration has conducted our world affairs. It has been a measure—a damning measure—of the quality of leadership we have been given . . .

The biggest fact about the Korean War is this: It was never inevitable; it was never inescapable; no fantastic fiat of history decreed that little South Korea—in the summer of 1950—would fatally tempt Communist aggressors as their easiest victim. No demonic destiny decreed that America had to be bled this way in order to keep South Korea free and to keep freedom itself self-respecting . . .

The record of failure dates back—with red-letter folly—at least to September of 1947. It was then that Gen. Albert Wedemeyer—returned from a presidential mission to the Far East—submitted to the President this warning: "The withdrawal of American military forces from Korea would result in the occupation of South Korea by either Soviet troops or, as seems more likely, by the Korean military units trained under Soviet auspices in North Korea." That warning and his entire report were disregarded and suppressed by the administration . . .

When the enemy struck on that June day of 1950, what did America do? It did what it always has done in all its times of peril—it appealed to the heroism of its youth. This appeal was utterly right and utterly inescapable. It was inescapable not only because this was the only way to defend the idea of collective freedom against savage aggression. That appeal was inescapable because there was now in the plight into which we had stumbled no other way to save honor and self-respect.

The answer to that appeal has been what any American knew it would be. It has been sheer valor—valor on all the Korean mountainsides that each day bear fresh scars of new graves.

Now—in this anxious autumn—from these heroic men there comes back an answering appeal. It is no whine, no whimpering plea. It is a question that addresses itself to simple reason. It asks: Where do we go from here? When comes the end? Is there an end?

My answer—candid and complete—is this: The first task of a new administration will be to review and reexamine every course of action open to us with one goal in view—to bring the Korean War to an early and honorable end. That is my pledge to the American people.

For this task a wholly new administration is necessary. The reason for this is simple. The old administration cannot be expected to repair what it failed to prevent.

Where will a new administration begin? It will begin with its President taking a simple, firm resolution. That resolution will be: To forgo the diversions of politics and to concentrate on the job of ending the Korean War—until that job is honorably done.

That job requires a personal trip to Korea. I shall make that trip. Only in that way could I learn how best to serve the American people in the cause of peace.

shifted to the South Koreans, who were driven back about 19 miles from the Kŭmsong salient.

Armistice

The battle of the Kŭmsong salient ended the shooting war. On May 25 the P'anmunjŏm negotiators had worked out the details of the POW exchange, making provisions for "neutral nation" management of the repatriation process. They began to plan for an armistice signing. Then, on June 18–19, Rhee arranged for his military police to allow 27,000 Korean internees in their custody to "escape." Enraged, the Chinese ordered further attacks on the ROKA. The Americans shared their fury but, in the interest of compromise, convinced Rhee that the United States would meet all his preconditions for an armistice. On July 9 Rhee agreed to accept the armistice, though no representative of the ROK ever signed it. On July 27 Mark W. Clark for the UNC, Peng Dehuai for the Chinese, and Kim Il-sung for the North Koreans signed the agreement. That same day the shooting stopped (more or less), and the armies began the awkward process of disengagement across what became a 2.5-mile-wide DMZ.

Supervision of the armistice actions fell to a Military Armistice Commission

North Korean prisoners of war leaving a prison camp on Koja Island, South Korea, en route to Inch'ŏn as a condition of North-South armistice, August 1953. Central Press/Hulton Archive/Getty Images

(10 officers representing the belligerents), a Neutral Nations Supervisory Commission (Sweden, Switzerland, Poland, and Czechoslovakia), and a Neutral Nations Repatriation Commission (the same four states, plus India as the custodian of the POWs). From August 5 to September 6, a total of 75,823 communist soldiers and civilians (all but 5,640 of them Koreans) returned to their most-favoured regime, and 7,862 ROK soldiers, 3,597 U.S. servicemen, and 1,377 persons of other nationalities (including some civilians) returned to UNC control. The swap became a media event of potent possibilities: the communist POWs stripped off their hated capitalist prison uniforms and marched off singing party-approved songs.

The handling of those who refused repatriation turned into a nightmare, as agents among the communist POWs and interrogators made life miserable for the Indians. By the time the Neutral Nations Repatriation Commission gave up the screening process in February 1954, only 628 Chinese and Koreans had changed their minds and gone north, and 21,839 had returned to UNC control. Most of the nonrepatriates were eventually settled in South Korea and Taiwan.

In Focus: Demilitarized Zone (DMZ)

The demilitarized zone (DMZ) on the Korean peninsula demarcates North Korea from South Korea. It roughly follows latitude 38° N (the 38th parallel), the original demarcation line between North Korea and South Korea at the end of World War II.

The DMZ incorporates territory on both sides of the cease-fire line as it existed at the end of the Korean War (1950–53) and was created by pulling back the respective forces 1.2 miles (2 km) along each side of the line. It runs for about 150 miles (241 km) across the peninsula, from the mouth of the Han River on the west coast to a little south of the North Korean town of Kosŏng on the east coast. Located within the DMZ is the "truce village" of P'anmunjŏm, about 5 miles (8 km) east of Kaesŏng, N. Kor. It was the site of peace discussions during the Korean War and has since been the location of various conferences over issues related to North and South Korea, their allies, and the United Nations.

The areas north and south of the DMZ are heavily fortified, and both sides maintain large contingents of troops there. Over the years there have been occasional incidents and minor skirmishes but no significant conflicts. Once farmland and subsequently a devastated battleground, the DMZ has lain almost untouched since the end of hostilities and has reverted to nature to a large extent, making it one of the most pristine undeveloped areas in Asia. The zone contains many ecosystems including forests, estuaries, and wetlands frequented by migratory birds. It serves as a sanctuary for hundreds of bird species, among them the endangered white-naped and red-crowned cranes, and is home to dozens of fish species and Asiatic black bears, lynxes, and other mammals. In mid-2007 limited freight-train service was resumed across the zone.

As provided for in the armistice agreement, the United States organized an international conference in Geneva for all the belligerents to discuss the political future of Korea. The actual meetings produced no agreement. The Korean peninsula would continue to be caught in the coils of Cold War rivalry, but the survival of the Republic of Korea kept alive the hope of civil liberties, democracy, economic development, and eventual unification—even if their fulfillment might require another 50 years or more.

The war had lasted for three years and one month and resulted in roughly 4,000,000 casualties, including civilians. South Korean casualties were some 1,313,000 (1,000,000 civilians); communist casualties were estimated at 2,500,000 (including 1,000,000 civilians). The United States lost about 37,000 in action (the official figure, which had been recorded as some 54,000, was revised in 2000 after it was discovered that a clerk had incorrectly included military noncombatant deaths worldwide), South Korea some 47,000, and the UN forces 3,194; but the estimated losses of China in action were 900,000 men and of North Korea 520,000. During the war, two-fifths of Korea's industrial facilities were destroyed and one-third of its homes devastated.

The U.S. Army had provided South Korea with $181,200,000 during the occupation period of 1946–48. This money, which was provided under the assistance programs for occupied areas, was spent mainly on preventing hunger and disease. For the period 1949–52 the U.S. provided $485,600,000 for economic aid and $12,500,000 for military aid. Following the war, the UN Korean Reconstruction Agency (UNKRA) was established to carry out economic aid to South Korea, with most of the contributions being provided by the United States. The UNKRA came to an end in 1958, but UN Emergency Relief and aid from other international voluntary agencies continued.

CHAPTER 3

Political Leaders of the Korean War

The following brief biographies of major political leaders from North Korea, South Korea, the United States, the Soviet Union, and China concentrate on their actions during the Korean War.

NORTH KOREA

Kim Il-sung

(b. April 15, 1912, Man'gyŏndae, near P'yŏngyang, Korea [now in North Korea]—d. July 8, 1994, P'yŏngyang)

Kim Il-sung was the communist leader of North Korea from 1948 until his death in 1994. He was the nation's premier from 1948 to 1972, chairman of its dominant Korean Workers (Communist) Party from 1949, and president and head of state from 1972.

Kim was the son of parents who fled to Manchuria in 1925 to escape the Japanese rule of Korea. He joined the Korean guerrilla resistance against the Japanese occupation in the 1930s and adopted the name of an earlier legendary Korean guerrilla fighter against the Japanese. Kim was noticed by the Soviet military authorities, who sent him to the Soviet Union for military and political training. There he joined the local Communist Party.

During World War II, Kim led a Korean contingent as a major in the Soviet army. After the Japanese surrender in 1945, Kim returned with other Soviet-trained Koreans to establish a communist provisional government under Soviet auspices in what would become North Korea. He became the first premier of the newly formed Democratic People's Republic of Korea in 1948, and in 1949 he became chairman of the Korean Workers' Party. Hoping to reunify Korea by force, Kim launched an invasion of South Korea in 1950, thereby igniting the Korean War. His attempt to extend his rule to the South was repelled by U.S. troops and other UN forces, however, and it was only through massive Chinese support that he was able to repel a subsequent invasion of North Korea by UN forces.

The Korean War ended in a stalemate in 1953. As head of state, Kim crushed the remaining domestic opposition and eliminated his last rivals for power within the Korean Workers' Party. He became his country's absolute ruler and set about transforming North Korea into an austere, militaristic, and highly regimented society devoted to the twin goals of industrialization and the reunification of the Korean Peninsula under North Korean rule. Kim introduced a philosophy of *juche*, or "self-reliance," under which North Korea tried to develop its economy with little or no help from foreign countries. North Korea's state-run economy grew rapidly in the 1950s and '60s but eventually stagnated, with shortages of food occurring by the early '90s. The omnipresent personality cult sponsored by Kim was part of a highly effective propaganda system that enabled him to rule unchallenged for 46 years over one of the world's most isolated and repressive societies. In his foreign policy he cultivated close ties with both the Soviet Union and China and remained consistently hostile to South Korea and the United States.

While retaining control of the Korean Workers' Party, Kim relinquished the office of premier and was elected president of North Korea in December 1972. In 1980 he raised his eldest son, Kim Jong Il, to high posts in the party and the military, in effect designating the younger Kim as his heir. However, Kim remained in power for more than a decade more, until his death in 1994.

Kim Jong Il

(b. Feb. 16, 1941, Siberia, Russia, U.S.S.R.)

Kim Jong Il, son of the former North Korean premier and (communist) Korean Workers' Party (KWP) chairman Kim Il-sung, was the successor to his father as ruler of North Korea.

The official North Korean version of Kim Jong Il's life, different from the biography documented elsewhere, says that he was born at a guerrilla base camp on Mount Paektu, the highest point on the Korean peninsula; it attributes many precocious abilities to him; and it claims his birth was accompanied by such auspicious signs as the appearance of a double rainbow in the sky. During the Korean

War (1950–53) he was placed in safety in northeastern China (Manchuria) by his father, although the official biography does not mention the episode. After attending a pilot's training college in East Germany for two years, he graduated in 1963 from Kim Il-sung University. He served in numerous routine posts in the KWP before becoming his father's secretary. He worked closely with his father in the 1967 party purge and then was assigned several important jobs. Kim was appointed in September 1973 to the powerful position of party secretary in charge of organization, propaganda, and agitation.

Kim was officially designated his father's successor in October 1980, was given command of the armed forces in 1990–91, and held high-ranking posts on the Central Committee, in the Politburo, and in the Party Secretariat. When Kim Il-sung died of a heart attack in 1994, Kim Jong Il became North Korea's de facto leader. He was named chairman of the KWP in October 1997, and in September 1998 he formally assumed the country's highest post. Since the position of president had been eliminated by the Supreme People's Assembly, which reserved for Kim Il-sung the posthumous title of "eternal president," the younger Kim was reelected chairman of the National Defense Commission, an office whose powers were expanded.

During his leadership of the country, Kim built on the mystique already surrounding his father and himself. Conflicting information circulated regarding his personal life, most of it unreliable and—perhaps deliberately—serving to add to the mystery. It was known that Kim took an interest in the arts and encouraged greater creativity in literature and film, although the products remained primarily propaganda tools. A well-known film buff, Kim headed a movie studio before ascending to the country's leadership. It produced works celebrating socialist values, Kim Il-sung and his national policy of self-reliance (*juche*), and, later, Kim Jong Il himself and his "military first" (*sŏngun chŏngch'i*) policy. As part of his desire to create better films, in the late 1970s the younger Kim had a South Korean film director, Shin Sang-ok, and his wife, actress Choi Eun-hee, abducted to the north, where they were pressed into service until their 1986 escape.

After becoming North Korea's leader, and with his country facing a struggling economy and a famine, Kim made moves toward amending North Korea's long-standing policy of isolationism. Throughout the late 1990s and the early 21st century, Kim sought to improve ties with a number of countries. However, these relations with the international community have been strained over the issue of nuclear weapons. The first decade of the 21st century was characterized by negotiations and sanctions over North Korea's nuclear program, particularly with the United States. Furthermore, despite reaching an agreement with South

Korea to take steps toward reunification in 2000, inter-Korean relations have deteriorated. Kim's regime announced that it planned to close the land border and all nonmilitary telephone links with South Korea in 2008.

A positive note was sounded in August 2009, when Kim agreed to the release of two American journalists. The two women, Euna Lee and Laura Ling, had been imprisoned in March 2009 by North Korea for having illegally entered the country. On August 4, 2009, former U.S. president Bill Clinton flew to P'yŏngyang for a private meeting with the North Korean leader, after which Kim issued a special pardon. The two women flew back to the United States with Clinton the following day.

SOUTH KOREA

Syngman Rhee

(b. March 26, 1875, P'yŏngsan, Hwanghae province, Korea [now in North Korea]—d. July 19, 1965, Honolulu, Hawaii, U.S.)

Syngman Rhee was the first president of the Republic of Korea (South Korea).

Rhee completed a traditional classical Confucian education and then entered a Methodist school, where he learned English. He became an ardent nationalist and, ultimately, a Christian. In 1896 he joined with other young Korean leaders to form the Independence Club, a group dedicated to asserting Korean independence from Japan. When right-wing elements destroyed the club in 1898, Rhee was arrested and imprisoned until 1904. On his release he went to the United States, where in 1910 he received a Ph.D. from Princeton University, becoming the first Korean to earn a doctorate from an American university. He returned home in 1910, the year in which Korea was annexed by Japan.

Rhee found it impossible to hide his hostility toward Japanese rule, and, after working briefly in a YMCA and as a high-school principal, he emigrated to Hawaii, which was then a U.S. territory. He spent the next 30 years as a spokesman for Korean independence, trying in vain to win international support for his cause. In 1919 he was elected (in absentia) president of the newly established Korean Provisional Government, in Shanghai. Rhee relocated to Shanghai the following year but returned to Hawaii in 1925. He remained president of the Provisional Government for 20 years, eventually being pushed out of the leadership by younger Korean nationalists centred in China. (Rhee had refused to recognize an earlier impeachment, for misuse of his authority, by the Provisional Government in the 1920s.) Rhee moved to Washington, D.C., and spent the World War II years trying to secure Allied promises of Korean independence.

After the war, since Rhee was the only Korean leader well known to Americans, he was returned to Korea ahead of the other members of the Provisional

Government. He campaigned for a policy of immediate independence and unification of the country. He soon built up a mass political organization supported by strong-arm squads and a following among the police. With the assassination of the major moderate leaders, including Song Jin Woo and Chang Duk Soo, Rhee remained the most influential leader, and his new party won the elections in South Korea. In 1948 he became president of the Republic of Korea, a post to which he was reelected in 1952, 1956, and 1960.

As president, Rhee assumed dictatorial powers, tolerating little domestic opposition to his program. Rhee purged the National Assembly of members who opposed him and outlawed the opposition Progressive Party, whose leader, Cho Bong Am, was executed for treason. He controlled the appointment of mayors, village headmen, and chiefs of police. He even defied the United Nations (UN) during the Korean War (1950–53). Hoping that UN forces would continue to fight and eventually unite North and South Korea under one government, Rhee hindered the truce talks by ordering the release in June 1953 of some 25,000 anti-communist North Korean prisoners. (Under the agreed-upon truce settlement, these men were to have been repatriated to North Korea.) Stunned, the communists broke off the negotiations and renewed their attack, largely ignoring the UN forces and concentrating their fire on Rhee's South Korean troops. Having made their point, the communists then resumed negotiations, and a truce settlement was speedily signed.

In spite of his authoritarian policies, Rhee failed to prevent the election of an opposition vice president, Chang Myŏn, in 1956. Government claims that the March 1960 elections gave Rhee more than 90 percent of the popular vote (55 percent in 1956) provoked student-led demonstrations against election fraud, resulting in heavy casualties and demands for Rhee's resignation. These demands were supported by the unanimous vote of the National Assembly and by the U.S. government. Rhee resigned on April 27, 1960, and went into exile in Hawaii.

Yun Po Sŏn

(b. 1897, Asan, Korea [now in South Korea]—d. July 18, 1990, Seoul, S.Kor.)

Yun Po Sŏn served (1960–62) as a liberal president of South Korea during the Second Republic.

Yun received an M.A. (1930) from the University of Edinburgh and managed his family's business affairs. When Japanese rule of Korea ended in 1945, Yun entered politics; his mentor, President Rhee, appointed him mayor of Seoul in 1948 and minister of commerce and industry in 1949. In time, however, he came to disagree with Rhee's authoritarian rule. He was elected to the National Assembly in 1954, and the next year he was among the founders of the opposition Democratic Party.

After the student-led pro-democracy uprising of 1960 forced Rhee to resign, Yun was elected president. Internal rivalries within the Democratic Party rendered his leadership ineffectual, however. In less than a year a coup brought the army's Maj. Gen. Park Chung Hee to power. Though Yun was initially persuaded to stay in office, he resigned in 1962.

He then became a vehement critic of Park's repressive regime and opposed Park in the 1963 and 1967 presidential elections. He was twice convicted of instigating the overthrow of the government and received suspended prison sentences. After Park's assassination in 1979, Yun was tried for organizing a mass pro-reform rally, and again he received a suspended sentence. He retired from politics in 1980.

Park Chung Hee

(b. Sept. 30 or Nov. 14, 1917, Kumi, North Kyŏngsang province, Korea [now in South Korea]—d. Oct. 26, 1979, Seoul, S.Kor.)

Park Chung Hee was president of the Republic of Korea (South Korea) from 1963 to his death. His 18-year rule brought about enormous economic expansion, though at the cost of civil liberties and political freedom.

Born into an impoverished rural family, Park graduated (1937) with top honours from Taegu (Daegu) Normal School, after which he taught primary school. After attending a Japanese military academy, Park served as a second lieutenant in the Japanese army during World War II and became an officer in the Korean army when Korea was freed

South Korean President Park Chung Hee (at podium) *with U.S. President Lyndon B. Johnson* (right), *1965*. Francis Miller/Time & Life Pictures/ Getty Images

from Japanese rule after the war. He was made a brigadier general (1953) during the Korean War (1950–53) and was promoted to general in 1958. On May 16, 1961, he led a military coup that overthrew the Second Republic. He remained the leader of the junta until two years later, when he won the first of his three terms as president of the Third Republic.

At home Park maintained a policy of guided democracy, with restrictions on personal freedoms, suppression of the press and of opposition parties, and control over the judicial system and the universities. He organized and expanded the Korean Central Intelligence Agency (KCIA; now the National Intelligence Service), which became a much-feared agent of political repression. Park claimed that all his measures were necessary to fight communism. In foreign affairs, he continued the close relations his predecessors Rhee and Yun had maintained with the United States. Park was responsible in large part for South Korea's "economic miracle"; the programs he initiated gave his country one of the fastest-growing economies in the world.

On Oct. 17, 1972, Park declared martial law, and one month later he installed a repressive authoritarian regime, the Yushin ("Revitalization Reform") order, with a new constitution that gave him sweeping powers. He grew increasingly harsh toward political dissidents. After Park's dismissal (1979) of popular opposition leader Kim Young Sam from the National Assembly, Korea erupted with severe riots and demonstrations. Park was assassinated by his lifelong friend Kim Jae Kyu, the head of the KCIA.

Chun Doo Hwan

(b. Jan. 18, 1931, Hapch'ŏn, South Kyŏngsang, Korea [now in South Korea])

Chun Doo Hwan was president of South Korea from 1980 to 1988.

Born into a peasant family, Chun entered the Korean Military Academy in 1951. Following his graduation in 1955, he became an infantry officer and in 1958 married Lee Soon Ja, daughter of Brig. Gen. Lee Kyu Dong. Chun commanded a South Korean division in South Vietnam during the Vietnam War and rose rapidly through the ranks. After Park seized power in 1961, Chun served as civil service secretary for the junta (1961–62) and, in 1963, with the nominal restoration of civilian government, as chief of personnel of the KCIA. He served in various other official posts and was made a brigadier general in 1978.

After Park's assassination in 1979, Chun, as the chief of army security command, took charge of the investigation of his death. He arrested several suspects, including his rival, the army chief of staff, Gen. Chung Sŭng Hwa (December 1979), and he purged many of Chung's supporters in a virtual coup by one military faction against another. Although the official president was Choi Kyu Hah, Chun emerged as the real holder of power, and in April 1980 he became head of the KCIA. In May the military under Chun's leadership dropped all pretense of civilian rule, declared martial law, and brutally suppressed democratic civilian opposition in the city of Kwangju.

After President Choi resigned on August 16, Chun resigned from the army and on August 27 became president. With the country still under martial law, Chun pushed through a new constitution in late 1980 that allowed him to govern with a firm hand. Chun's tenure was punctuated by several crises, notably a financial scandal in 1982 that forced him to replace half his cabinet and an assassination attempt in Burma (Myanmar) by North Korean agents in 1983 that resulted in the deaths of several top aides and ministers. As president, Chun devoted his efforts to maintaining economic growth and political stability. South Korea continued its export-led economic growth under Chun, and the nation industrialized rapidly.

Chun was prohibited by the terms of the 1980 constitution from serving more than one seven-year term, and in 1987 he picked Roh Tae Woo to be the candidate of the ruling Democratic Justice Party (now part of the Grand National Party). He retired from politics after being succeeded by Roh in 1988. Despite public gestures of atonement for abuses of power during his presidency, Chun could not distance himself from the lingering public memory of his actions. In December 1995 both he and Roh were indicted on charges of having accepted bribes during their terms as president. In addition, the outcry over the extent of the fraud (hundreds of millions of dollars) prompted prosecutors to pursue charges (which had been brought by the prosecutor's office in 1994) related to their involvement in the 1979 coup and their actions during the 1980 uprising in Kwangju. Both were found guilty of all charges in August 1996. Chun was sentenced to death and Roh to 2,212 years in prison. Chun's sentence was later reduced to life imprisonment and Roh's to 17 years; both received presidential pardons in December 1997.

Roh Tae Woo

(b. Dec. 4, 1932, near Taegu, Korea [now in South Korea])

Roh Tae Woo was president of South Korea (1988–93) and is remembered for instituting democratic reforms.

While a high-school student in Taegu (Daegu), Roh became friends with a fellow student, Chun Doo Hwan. Following the outbreak of the Korean War (1950–53), Roh joined the South Korean army and with Chun attended the Korean Military Academy, where they both graduated in 1955. Roh rose steadily through the ranks thereafter, becoming a general by 1979.

In October 1979 Pres. Park Chung Hee was assassinated, and in December Chun and some fellow officers launched a coup against the civilian government; Roh, who was then an army division commander, gave them crucial support. Roh was a member of the Chun-led junta that ordered the brutal suppression of demonstrators in Kwangju (Gwangju) in May 1980. Chun became president in August of that year. Roh resigned from the military in 1981 and held a series of ministerial posts in Chun's government, including minister of political affairs (1981), sports (1982), and home affairs (1982). As head of the Seoul Olympic Organizing Committee from 1983 to 1986, he oversaw South Korea's preparations for the 1988 Summer Olympic Games held in Seoul.

In 1985 Chun chose Roh to become the new chairman of Chun's ruling political party, the Democratic Justice Party (DJP), and in June 1987 Chun chose Roh to be the candidate of the DJP in the upcoming presidential elections. Under the country's existing constitution, Roh was thus practically guaranteed to win the presidency, and this prospect ignited widespread popular unrest. In response, on June 29, 1987, Roh made a historic speech in which he proposed a broad program of democratic reforms, which led to the drafting of a new constitution (approved in October 1987). Chief among its provisions was the direct election of the president by popular vote.

In the December 1987 election, both major opposition candidates, Kim Young Sam and Kim Dae Jung, ran against Roh, splitting the opposition vote and thus enabling Roh's victory. He began his five-year term as president on Feb. 25, 1988.

As president, the moderate and conciliatory Roh committed himself to the democratization of South Korean politics. Partly as a result of Roh's reforms, the DJP failed to gain a majority of seats in the National Assembly in elections in April 1988, but in 1990 the party, under Roh's leadership, merged with two moderate opposition parties to form a new majority party called the Democratic Liberal Party. In foreign affairs, Roh's government cultivated new ties with the Soviet Union (and later Russia) and China, obtained South Korea's admission (1991) to the United Nations, and signed an agreement (1991) with North Korea calling for nonaggression between the two Koreas. In February 1993 he was succeeded by Kim Young Sam, whose subsequent anticorruption reforms targeted Roh and Chun.

In October 1995 Roh publicly apologized for having illegally amassed hundreds of millions of dollars in secret political donations during his term as president. He subsequently was indicted and tried for corruption as well as for mutiny and sedition for his involvement in the 1979 coup (charges that had been leveled in 1994 but not pursued at that time). In August 1996 he was convicted on all counts; he was sentenced to 2,212 years in prison, which was later reduced to 17 years, and was fined about $300 million, a sum equivalent to the amount he was convicted of having taken illegally.

Former South Korean President Roh Tae Woo prepares to stand trial on corruption charges in the Seoul District Criminal Court Building, December 1995. Choo Youn-Kong/AFP/ Getty Images

Roh received a pardon in December 1997 from outgoing president Kim Young Sam and President-elect Kim Dae Jung.

KIM YOUNG SAM

(b. Dec. 20, 1927, Kŏje Island, South Kyŏngsang province, Korea [now in South Korea])

Kim Young Sam was president of South Korea from 1993 to 1998.

Kim graduated from Seoul National University in 1952 and was first elected to the National Assembly in 1954. A centrist liberal, he was successively reelected until 1979, when he was expelled (on October 9) from the assembly for his opposition to Park's presidency. His expulsion touched off riots and demonstrations. To protest Kim's dismissal, all 66 opposition members of the assembly resigned. After Park's assassination on October 26, it was assumed that Kim would be a contender in the presidential election, but Chun's military takeover of the government in May 1980 precluded this possibility. Soon after taking power, Chun put Kim under house arrest; in November 1980, Kim was banned from political activity for eight years, and his party was also banned.

The Chun government lifted his house arrest in June 1983, after Kim staged a 23-day hunger strike, and he resumed his political activity in 1985. That year he reasserted his leadership of the moderate opposition to President Chun. Kim ran unsuccessfully for the South Korean presidency in 1987, splitting the antigovernment vote with the rival opposition leader and presidential candidate Kim Dae Jung. In 1990 Kim Young Sam merged his Reunification Democratic Party with the ruling Democratic Justice Party, led by President Roh, thus forming a centre-right party, called the Democratic Liberal Party (DLP), that dominated Korean politics. As the candidate of the DLP, Kim won election to the presidency in December 1992, defeating Kim Dae Jung and another opposition candidate, Chung Joo Youn, chairman of the Hyundai *chaebŏl* (conglomerate).

Once in power, Kim established firm civilian control over the military and tried to make the government more responsive to the electorate. He launched reforms designed to eliminate political corruption and abuses of power, and he even allowed two of his presidential predecessors, Roh Tae Woo and Chun Doo Hwan, to be prosecuted for various crimes they had committed while in power. The South Korean economy continued to grow at a rapid rate during Kim's presidency, and, with wages rising rapidly, the standard of living reached that of other industrialized countries.

Kim was constitutionally barred from seeking a second term as president. His popularity declined rapidly in the last year of his five-year term because of corruption scandals in his administration and the increasingly precarious state of the South Korean economy, which was caught in a financial crisis that swept through Southeast and East Asia in late 1997. He was succeeded as president by Kim Dae Jung.

Kim Dae Jung

(b. Dec. 3, 1925, Mokp'o, Haeui Island, Korea [now in South Chŏlla province, South Korea]—d. Aug. 18, 2009, Seoul, South Korea)

Kim Dae Jung was a South Korean politician who became a prominent opposition leader during the tenure of Park Chung Hee. He became the first opposition leader to win election to his country's presidency (1998–2003). Kim received the Nobel Prize for Peace in 2000 for his efforts to restore democracy in South Korea and to improve relations with North Korea.

Kim was the son of a middle-class farmer, and he graduated from the Mokp'o Commercial High School at the top of his class in 1943. He began working as a clerk in a Japanese-owned shipping company and in 1945 took over the company, eventually becoming a wealthy businessman. During the Korean War he was captured by the communists and sentenced to be shot, but he managed to escape.

In the 1950s Kim became an ardent pro-democracy activist and in 1954 voiced opposition to Rhee's policies. After five attempts at elective office, Kim finally won a seat on the National Assembly in 1961, but the election was nullified following a military coup d'état led by Park Chung Hee. By the age of 40 he had earned a reputation as one of South Korea's most gifted orators and charismatic politicians. He became increasingly critical of Park's policies, and in 1971, a year after becoming president of the National Democratic Party, Kim ran against Park in a national presidential election. Kim lost, despite winning more than 40 percent of the vote. He was by then an outspoken critic of the repressive policies of the Park government.

In 1973 Kim was kidnapped from his hotel in Tokyo by agents of the Korean Central Intelligence Agency and was returned forcibly to South Korea; this act severely strained relations between Japan and South Korea. In 1976 Kim was again arrested, having agitated for the restoration of democracy. He was released from house arrest in 1979 just two months after Park's assassination on October 26 of that year. Kim was arrested in May 1980 on charges of sedition and conspiracy and sentenced to death, but Park's successor, Chun, commuted the sentence to life imprisonment and later to 20 years. In December 1982 Kim was allowed to leave South Korea for medical treatment in the United States, but the trip became an exile. Able to return to South Korea in 1985, he resumed his role as one of the principal leaders of the political opposition. In 1987 he ran for the presidency and lost after splitting the antigovernment vote with rival opposition candidate Kim Young Sam. He ran again for the presidency in 1992 but was defeated by Kim Young Sam, who had merged his own Reunification Democratic Party with the ruling Democratic Justice Party to form the DLP.

Kim formed a new political party, the National Congress for New Politics, in 1995 and made his fourth bid for the presidency in 1997. By this time the ruling Democratic Liberal Party had lost popularity because of corruption scandals in Kim Young Sam's administration and the electorate's outrage over the increasing instability of the South Korean economy, which was caught in the financial crisis sweeping through Southeast and East Asia. Kim formed an electoral coalition with the conservative United Liberal Democrats led by Kim Jong Pil, and in the presidential election of Dec. 18, 1997, Kim Dae Jung won a narrow victory over the ruling party's candidate, Lee Hoi Chang.

Once in office Kim immersed himself in overcoming the financial crisis and restructuring banking, business, and labour practices. Under his leadership, South Korea emerged from International Monetary Fund bailout programs in a shorter time than expected. He then set about improving relations with North Korea. His "sunshine" policy allowed South Koreans to visit relatives in the North and eased rules governing South Korean investment in the country. In 1998 direct talks between the two countries resumed after a four-year hiatus, and from June 13 to 15, 2000, Kim met with North Korean ruler Kim Jong Il. During the historic summit, which marked the first meeting between leaders of North and South Korea, both sides agreed to work toward eventual reunification. Barred by electoral rules from running for a second term, Kim left office in 2003; he was succeeded by Roh Moo Hyun. Kim died on August 18, 2009, in a Seoul hospital. He was 85.

Roh Moo Hyun

(b. Aug. 6, 1946, Gimhae, near Pusan, Korea [now in South Korea]—d. May 23, 2009, Pusan, S.Kor.)

Roh Moo Hyun was president of South Korea from 2003 to 2008.

Born into a poor family, Roh worked as a night watchman in high school and later served in the military (1968–71). Although he did not attend college, he was able to pass the bar exam in 1975. He was appointed a judge in 1977 and later became a highly respected human rights lawyer, defending student protestors accused of being pro-communist.

In the late 1980s, Roh entered politics at the invitation of then-opposition leader Kim Young Sam. Roh won a seat in the National Assembly in 1988 and gained notice for criticizing Chun's military regime. In 1990 he split with his party when Kim made an alliance with general-turned-president Roh Tae Woo. That alliance led to Kim's election as president, and Roh Moo Hyun's political fortunes seemed to crumble. He lost his seat in the National Assembly in 1992 and failed to regain it in 1996. He also lost a bid to become mayor of Pusan in 1995. Nevertheless, Roh continued to favour democratic reforms and refused to compromise with the pro-military party. He eventually led a small opposition party into an alliance with Kim Dae Jung, and when Kim came to power in 1998, Roh served in his cabinet.

In 2002 Roh, supported by outgoing president Kim, made a bid for the presidency. Roh favoured negotiating with North Korea rather than isolating it. He preferred using diplomacy in persuading North Korea to abandon its nuclear weapons policy, and he was openly critical of U.S. policy toward the Korean peninsula, a stance that appealed to the growing anti-American sentiment in the country. In December 2002 Roh defeated Lee Hoi Chang in a tightly contested presidential race, receiving 48.9 percent of the vote to Lee's 46.6 percent.

After taking office in February 2003, Roh faced a faltering economy and labour unrest. He also found himself in the midst of a financial scandal after several of his aides were accused of accepting illegal campaign donations. In October 2003

Roh called for a national vote of confidence, but parliament opposed the referendum, which was not provided for in South Korea's constitution. Allegations of election law violations and economic mismanagement soon followed, and in March 2004 Roh was impeached by parliament, a move that was highly unpopular with the public. Forced to temporarily step down, he was reinstated as president in May after the Constitutional Court overturned the impeachment. Under the shadow of scandal for most of his term, Roh was unable to take advantage of the parliamentary majority that his party achieved in late 2004. Continuing economic malaise in South Korea caused his poll numbers to drop to the single digits, and a North Korean nuclear test in 2006 was seen as a sign of failure for the soft diplomacy championed by Roh and his predecessor. While Roh was unable to run for a second term because of South Korean election law, in December 2007 his chosen successor, Chung Dong-young, was soundly defeated by Grand National Party candidate Lee Myung-bak. Roh was later investigated over allegations of bribery, and in May 2009 he committed suicide by jumping off a cliff.

Lee Myung-bak
(b. Dec. 19, 1941, Osaka, Japan)

Lee Myung-bak was elected president of South Korea in 2008.

Lee was born in wartime Japan and was the fifth of seven children. In 1946 his family returned to Korea, but their boat capsized during the journey, and they landed ashore with little more than the clothes they were wearing. They settled in his father's hometown of P'ohang, and, to help support his family, Lee sold rice snacks during the day and attended school at night. He enrolled at Korea University, Seoul, in 1961, paying his tuition by working as a garbage collector. He was imprisoned in 1964 for participating in protests against the normalization of relations between South Korea and Japan.

Lee was blacklisted by the government for his student activism, which limited his job prospects with some of the larger established firms. He joined the fledgling Hyundai Construction company in 1965. At the time, it had fewer than 100 employees, and Lee advanced quickly through the executive ranks. When he resigned as CEO in 1992, the Hyundai Group had some 160,000 employees, and its products ranged from automobiles to heavy machinery to consumer electronics.

Lee entered politics in 1992, winning election to the National Assembly as a member of the conservative New Korea Party. He was reelected in 1996, only to resign two years later after he was found guilty of violating campaign spending limits. He withdrew from politics and spent a year of self-imposed exile in the United States. He returned to South Korea and was elected mayor of Seoul in 2002. His administration focused on improving the livability of the central business district, most notably through an ambitious urban beautification project. This included the restoration of the Cheonggye stream, a downtown waterway paved over by Hyundai some four decades earlier. While business owners initially balked at the project's $900 million price tag, it proved to be a success with both Seoul natives and tourists when it opened in September 2005.

Upon completion of his term as mayor, Lee successfully campaigned for the presidency of South Korea, winning election by a landslide on Dec. 19, 2007. A 2001 business scandal surfaced in the days leading up to the election, however, and the matter was directed to an independent counsel.

UNITED STATES

Harry S. Truman

(b. May 8, 1884, Lamar, Mo., U.S.—d. Dec. 26, 1972, Kansas City, Mo.)

Harry S. Truman was the 33rd president of the United States (1945–53). He led his nation through the final stages of World War II and through the early years of the Cold War, vigorously opposing Soviet expansionism in Europe and sending U.S. forces to turn back a communist invasion of South Korea.

In June 1950 military forces of communist North Korea suddenly plunged southward across the 38th parallel boundary in an attempt to seize noncommunist South Korea. Outraged, Truman reportedly responded, "By God, I'm going to let them [North Korea] have it!" Truman did not ask Congress for a declaration of war, and he was later criticized for this decision. Instead, he sent to South Korea, with UN sanction, U.S. forces under Gen. Douglas MacArthur to repel the invasion. Ill-prepared for combat, the Americans were pushed back to the southern tip of the Korean peninsula before MacArthur's brilliant Inch' ŏn offensive drove the communists north of the 38th parallel. South Korea was liberated, but MacArthur wanted a victory over the communists, not merely restoration of the status quo. U.S. forces drove northward, nearly to the Yalu River boundary with Manchuria. Hundreds of thousands of Chinese troops then poured into North Korea, pushing the fighting once again down to the 38th parallel.

When MacArthur insisted on extending the war to China and using nuclear weapons to defeat the communists, Truman removed him from command—a courageous assertion of civilian control over the military. The administration was devoted to its policy of containment. The war, however, dragged on inconclusively past the end of Truman's presidency, eventually claiming the lives of more than 33,000 Americans and leaving a residual bitterness at home.

The inability of the United States to achieve a clear-cut victory in Korea following Soviet conquests in eastern Europe and the triumph of communism in China led many Americans to conclude that the United States was losing the Cold War. Accusations began to fly that the president and some of his top advisers were "soft on communism," thereby explaining why the United States—without question the world's greatest power in 1945—had been unable to halt the communist advance. As the nation's second "Red Scare" (the fear that communists had infiltrated key positions in government and society) took hold in the late 1940s and early '50s, Truman's popularity began to plummet. In March 1952 he announced he was not going to run for reelection. By the time he left the White House in January 1953, his approval rating was just 31 percent; it had peaked at 87 percent in July 1945.

U.S. Secretary of State Dean Acheson (centre) *calls to order a meeting of the North Atlantic Treaty Organization (NATO) on September 15, 1950.* Encyclopædia Britannica, Inc.

Dean Acheson

(b. April 11, 1893, Middletown, Conn., U.S.—d. Oct. 12, 1971, Sandy Spring, Md.)

Dean Acheson was a U.S. secretary of state (1949–53) and adviser to four presidents. He was the principal creator of U.S. foreign policy in the Cold War period following World War II, and he helped to create the Western alliance in opposition to the Soviet Union and other communist nations.

Appointed secretary of state by Truman in January 1949, Acheson promoted the formation of the North Atlantic Treaty Organization (NATO), the first peacetime defensive alliance entered into by the United States.

Despite his strong stance in what he conceived to be a global confrontation with communism, Acheson was the target of attack by foreign-policy critics within both political parties. His enemies were particularly inflamed when, during the congressional hearings of Senator Joseph R. McCarthy on subversive activities (1949–50), Acheson refused to fire any of his State Department subordinates. His most widely publicized remark was, "I will not turn my back on Alger Hiss"—a former State Department officer later convicted of perjury in denying that he had engaged in espionage in the 1930s.

U.S. Secretary of State Dean Acheson signs the North Atlantic Treaty on April 4, 1949, as U.S. President Harry S. Truman (second from left) *and Vice President Alben W. Barkley* (left) *look on.* Encyclopædia Britannica, Inc.

Demands for Acheson's resignation increased after the entry of communist China into the Korean War (1950–53). The storm of public controversy erupted more violently after the president removed MacArthur as commander of forces in Korea. Acheson subsequently established the policies of nonrecognition of China and aid to the Nationalist regime of Gen. Chiang Kai-shek on Taiwan; later he also supported U.S. aid to the French colonial regime in Indochina.

Dwight D. Eisenhower

(b. Oct. 14, 1890, Denison, Texas, U.S.—d. March 28, 1969, Washington, D.C.)

Dwight D. Eisenhower was the supreme commander of the Allied forces in western Europe during World War II and the 34th president of the United States (1953–61).

As early as 1943 Eisenhower was mentioned as a possible presidential candidate. His personal qualities and military

Dwight D. Eisenhower (centre), *the Republican Party nominee for U.S. president, with running mate Richard Nixon* (left, holding child) *at campaign headquarters in Washington, D.C., September 10, 1952.* Encyclopædia Britannica, Inc.

reputation prompted both parties to woo him. As the campaign of 1952 neared, Eisenhower let it be known that he was a Republican, and the eastern wing of the party, headed by Governor Thomas E. Dewey of New York, made an intensive effort to persuade him to seek the Republican presidential nomination. His name was entered in several state primaries against the more conservative Senator Robert A. Taft of Ohio. Although the results were mixed, Eisenhower decided to run. In June 1952 he retired from the army after 37 years of service, returned to the United States, and began to campaign actively. At the party convention in July, after a bitter fight with Taft supporters, Eisenhower won the nomination on the first ballot. His running mate was Senator Richard M. Nixon of California. The Democrats nominated Governor Adlai E. Stevenson of Illinois for president and Senator John Sparkman of Alabama for vice president.

Eisenhower urged economy and honesty in government and promised to visit Korea to explore the possibilities for ending the Korean War, which had broken out in 1950 between communist North Korea and pro-Western South Korea and soon involved United Nations (mainly U.S.) troops and communist Chinese forces. Many Republicans, including his running mate Sen. Richard M. Nixon of California, spoke of pro-communist disloyalty within the Truman administration and called for stringent antisubversive measures. The Eisenhower-Nixon ticket won handily, carrying 39 states, winning the electoral vote 442 to 89, and collecting more than 33 million popular votes.

Eisenhower kept his campaign promise and visited Korea shortly after his inauguration. Partly, perhaps, because of Joseph Stalin's death in March 1953 and partly because Eisenhower hinted at his willingness to use nuclear weapons, the president was able to negotiate a truce for the Korean War in July 1953.

Dwight D. Eisenhower delivering his "Atoms for Peace" speech to the United Nations General Assembly in New York City, December 1953. © United Nations/IAEA

John Foster Dulles

(b. Feb. 25, 1888, Washington, D.C.—d. May 24, 1959, Washington, D.C.)

John Foster Dulles was the U.S. secretary of state (1953–59) under Eisenhower. He was the architect of many major elements of U.S. foreign policy in the Cold War with the Soviet Union after World War II.

Dulles viewed his appointment as secretary of state by Eisenhower, in January 1953, as a mandate to originate foreign policy. "The State Department," Dulles once told an aide, "can only keep control of foreign policy as long as we have ideas." A man bent on realizing his ideas, he was an assiduous planner, and, once he enjoyed Eisenhower's complete confidence, policy planning flourished during his administration.

Dulles, fully aware that NATO would be effective only for the defense of western Europe, leaving the Middle East, the Far East, and the Pacific islands unprotected, was eager to fill those gaps. He initiated the Manila conference in 1954, which resulted in the Southeast Asia Treaty Organization (SEATO) pact that united eight nations either located in Southeast Asia or with interests there in a neutral defense pact. This treaty was followed in 1955 by the Baghdad Pact, later renamed the Central Treaty Organization (CENTO), uniting the so-called northern tier countries of the Middle East—Turkey, Iraq, Iran, and Pakistan—in a defense organization.

Three factors determined Dulles' foreign policy: his profound detestation of Communism, which was in part based on his deep religious faith; his powerful personality, which often insisted on leading rather than following public opinion; and his strong belief, as an international lawyer, in the value of treaties. Of the three, passionate hostility to Communism was the leitmotiv of his policy. Wherever he went, he carried with him Joseph Stalin's *Problems of Leninism* and impressed upon his aides the need to study it as a blueprint for conquest similar to Adolf Hitler's *Mein Kampf*. He seemed to derive personal satisfaction from pushing the Soviet Union to the brink. In fact, in 1956 he wrote in a magazine article that "if you are scared to go to the brink, you are lost."

SOVIET UNION AND CHINA

JOSEPH STALIN

(b. Dec. 21 [Dec. 9, Old Style], 1879, Gori, Georgia, Russian Empire—d. March 5, 1953, Moscow, Russia, U.S.S.R.)

Joseph Stalin was secretary-general of the Communist Party of the Soviet Union (1922–53) and premier of the Soviet state (1941–53). For a quarter of a century, Stalin dictatorially ruled the Soviet Union and transformed it into a major world power.

During the quarter of a century preceding his death, Stalin probably exercised greater political power than any other figure in history. Stalin industrialized the Union of Soviet Socialist Republics, forcibly collectivized its agriculture, consolidated his position by intensive police terror, helped to defeat Germany in 1941–45, and extended Soviet controls to include a belt of eastern European states. Chief architect of Soviet totalitarianism and a skilled but phenomenally ruthless organizer, he destroyed the remnants of individual freedom and failed to promote individual prosperity, yet he created a mighty military-industrial complex and led the Soviet Union into the nuclear age.

Far from continuing his World War II alliance with the United States and

Joseph Stalin, 1950. Sovfoto

Great Britain, Stalin now regarded these countries—and especially the United States—as the arch-enemies that he needed after Hitler's death. At home, the primacy of Marxist ideology was harshly reasserted. Stalin's chief ideological hatchet man, Andrey Zhdanov, a secretary of the Central Committee, began a reign of terror in the Soviet artistic and intellectual world; foreign achievements were derided, and the primacy of Russians as inventors and pioneers in practically every field was asserted. Hopes for domestic relaxation, widely aroused in the Soviet Union during World War II, were thus sadly disappointed.

Mao Zedong

(b. Dec. 26, 1893, Shaoshan, Hunan province, China—d. Sept. 9, 1976, Beijing)

Mao Zedong was the principal Chinese Marxist theorist, soldier, and statesman who led his nation's communist revolution. Leader of the Chinese Communist Party from 1935, he was chairman (chief of state) of the People's Republic of China from 1949 to 1959 and chairman of the party until his death.

When China emerged from a half century of revolution as the world's most populous nation and launched itself on a path of economic development and social change, Mao Zedong occupied a critical place in the story of the country's resurgence. To be sure, he did not play a dominant role throughout the whole struggle. In the early years of the Chinese Communist Party, he was a secondary figure, though by no means a negligible one, and even after the 1940s (except perhaps during the Cultural Revolution) the crucial decisions were not his alone. Nevertheless, looking at the whole period from the foundation of the Chinese Communist Party in 1921 to Mao's death in 1976, one can fairly regard Mao Zedong as the principal architect of the new China.

Mao Zedong. Encyclopædia Britannica, Inc.

In December 1949 Mao, now chairman of the People's Republic of China, traveled to Moscow, where, after two months of arduous negotiations, he succeeded in persuading Stalin to sign a treaty of mutual assistance accompanied by limited economic aid. Before the Chinese had time to profit from the resources made available for economic development, however, they found themselves dragged into the Korean War in support of the Moscow-oriented regime in P'yŏngyang. Only after this baptism of fire did Stalin, according to Mao, begin to have confidence in him and believe he was not first and foremost a Chinese nationalist as opposed to a real communist.

Despite these tensions with Moscow, the policies of the People's Republic of China in its early years were in very many respects based, as Mao later said, on "copying from the Soviets." While Mao and his comrades had experience in guerrilla warfare, mobilization of the peasants in the countryside, and political administration at the grassroots level, they had no firsthand knowledge of running a state or of large-scale economic development. In such circumstances the Soviet Union provided the only available model of a Communist government to emulate. A five-year plan was therefore drawn up under Soviet guidance; it was put into effect in 1953 and included Soviet technical assistance and a number of complete industrial plants. Yet, within two years, Mao had taken steps that were to lead to the breakdown of the political and ideological alliance with Moscow.

CHAPTER 4

Military Commanders of the Korean War

The following brief biographies of major military commanders concentrate on their actions during the Korean War.

CHUNG IL KWON

(b. Nov. 21, 1917, North Hamgyong province, Korea [now in North Korea]—d. Jan. 17, 1994, Hawaii, U.S.)

Chung Il Kwon was the commander of South Korean troops during some of the most intense fighting against North Korean and Chinese forces during the Korean War (1950–53).

Chung was a 1940 graduate of Tokyo's Military Academy and served in Japan's Imperial Army in Manchuria during World War II. He then joined the Chinese Nationalist army before entering the Republic of Korea Army. After North Korean troops invaded South Korea in June 1950, Chung was made commander of all ROKA forces. He led ROKA units during the difficult retreat in July–August to Pusan, in coordination with the U.S. Eighth Army, and also during the surprise landing in September at Inch'ŏn, which crippled the North Korean offensive. Hailed as a national hero, Chung was made chairman of the South Korean joint chiefs of staff in 1956, and he retired from the military in 1957 as a four-star general. During his retirement he was ambassador to the United States, France, and several Latin American countries. He also served as Park Chung Hee's prime minister (1964–70). Chung then held a number of other government posts before Chun Doo Hwan assumed the presidency in 1980.

PENG DEHUAI

(b. Oct. 24, 1898, Xiangtan, Hunan province, China—d. Nov. 29, 1974, Beijing)

Peng Dehuai was one of the greatest military leaders in Chinese communist history. He was minister of national defense of China from 1954 until 1959, when he was removed for criticizing the military and economic policies of the party.

Peng was a military commander under a local warlord and later under Chiang Kai-shek but broke with him in 1927 when Chiang attempted to rid the Nationalist Party of leftist elements. In 1928 Peng became a communist and soon afterward became involved in guerrilla activity, leading a series of peasant uprisings. He then became a senior military commander under Mao Zedong and participated in the Long March (1934–35).

Peng was the second-ranking man in the communists' military hierarchy from the outbreak of the Sino-Japanese War in 1937 to 1954 and was a member of the Political Bureau (Politburo) of the Chinese Communist Party from 1936. He led Chinese forces in the Korean War and signed the armistice at P'anmunjŏm on July 27, 1953. In 1954 he became minister of national defense. In 1959, however, he criticized as impractical the policies of the Great Leap Forward, which emphasized ideological purity over professional expertise in both the military forces and the economy. Peng was deprived of office for a while and in 1965 was sent to the CCP's Southwest Bureau in Sichuan province. Peng was posthumously "rehabilitated" in December 1978 under the post-Mao regime.

DOUGLAS MACARTHUR

(b. Jan. 26, 1880, Little Rock, Ark., U.S.—d. April 5, 1964, Washington, D.C.)

Douglas MacArthur was the U.S. general who commanded the Southwest Pacific Theatre in World War II. He administered postwar Japan during the Allied occupation that followed and led United Nations forces during the first nine months of the Korean War.

When the Korean War began in 1950, MacArthur was soon selected to command United Nations forces there. After stemming the North Korean advance near Pusan, he carried out a daring landing at Inch'ŏn in September and advanced into North Korea in October as the North Korean Army rapidly disintegrated. In November, however, massive Chinese forces attacked MacArthur's divided army above the 38th parallel and forced it to retreat to below Seoul. Two months later MacArthur's troops returned to the offensive, driving into North Korea again. On April 11, 1951, Truman relieved MacArthur of his commands because of the general's insubordination and unwillingness to conduct a limited war. Returning to the United States for the first time since before World War II, MacArthur at first received widespread popular support; the excitement waned after a publicized Senate investigation of his dismissal.

In 1944, 1948, and 1952, conservative Republican groups tried in vain to obtain MacArthur's nomination for the presidency. MacArthur accepted the board chairmanship of the Remington Rand Corporation in 1952; thereafter, except for these duties and rare public appearances, he lived in seclusion in New York City. He died in Washington, D.C., in 1964 and was buried at Norfolk, Virginia.

WALTON H. WALKER

(b. Dec. 3, 1899, Belton, Texas, U.S.—d. Dec. 23, 1950, near Seoul, S.Kor.)

Walton H. Walker was commander of the U.S. Eighth Army during the difficult opening months of the Korean War.

In September 1948 Walker was transferred to Japan to command the Eighth Army, which constituted the ground arm of MacArthur's Far East Command. Following the North Korean invasion of South Korea on June 25, 1950, Eighth Army headquarters transferred to Taegu, S.Kor. Walker also received command of the Republic of Korea Army and of other United Nations forces as they arrived. With most of his U.S. units understrength, his ROKA forces demoralized, and tactical air support insufficient, Walker was forced to fight a stubborn withdrawal into the southeast corner of the Korean peninsula. On July 29 he issued a "stand or die order," declaring "there will be no Dunkirk, there will be no Bataan." Nevertheless, his defensive line continued to contract until the arrival of reinforcements, heavy armaments, and increased air support enabled him to establish a 140-mile (225 km) "Pusan Perimeter," centred on the port of Pusan. His skill in shifting reserves to blunt North Korean attacks on the perimeter held the line and gained time for the organization of the X Corps under Edward M. Almond and its landing at Inch'ŏn on September 15. The pressure thus relieved, Walker was able to go on the offensive. Although the ROKA and X Corps pushed into North Korean territory and briefly held the North's capitol, P'yŏngyang, by December they again had been forced back to the 38th parallel by a Chinese offensive. The Eighth Army made contact with the X Corps on September 26, and, with some reluctance on Walker's part but on the orders of MacArthur, they pushed together into North Korean territory. The ROKA I Corps took Wonsan, the U.S. I Corps took the North's capital, P'yŏngyang. Then on November 25 a massive offensive by Chinese forces on UN lines at the Ch'ŏngch'ŏn River quickly turned the tide. Falling back under extreme pressure, Walker abandoned P'yŏngyang on December 5 and 10 days later established a new line roughly on the 38th parallel, the original dividing line between North and South Korea. He was killed in a jeep accident on the road between Seoul and the new front established at the 38th parallel. Walker was succeeded as commander of the Eighth Army by Matthew B. Ridgway.

EDWARD M. ALMOND

(b. Dec. 12, 1892, Luray, Va., U.S.—d. June 11, 1979, Anniston, Ala.)

Edward M. Almond held important command positions with the U.S. Army during the Korean War.

In June 1946 Almond was transferred to MacArthur's FECOM headquarters in Tokyo, eventually becoming chief of staff (with a permanent rank of major general). With the outbreak of the Korean War in

Maj. Gen. Edward M. Almond (third from right) *with some of his staff officers, October 1950.* Popperfoto/Getty Image

June 1950, he assisted MacArthur in planning for an amphibious assault midway up the west coast of the Korean peninsula. In recognition of Almond's services, MacArthur appointed him commander of the newly created X Corps. After landing at Inch'ŏn on September 15, Almond's corps quickly took Seoul, the South Korean capital, and linked up with Walker's Eighth Army, trapping some 120,000 North Korean troops between them. In October the X Corps moved by sea around the peninsula and landed unopposed at Wonsan, on the east coast of North Korea. Following MacArthur's plan, Almond pushed north and reached the Chinese border at the Yalu River by November 21, but massive Chinese counterattacks forced UN forces to withdraw. By December 11 the X Corps had concentrated in the port of Hungnam, whence it embarked for Pusan. Incorporated into the Eighth Army, the X Corps reentered the line in east-central Korea and participated in the gradual advance back across the 38th parallel.

Almond remained in command of the X Corps until July 1951. He was then given command of the Army War College, a post he held until his retirement from the military in January 1953.

JAMES ALWARD VAN FLEET

(b. March 19, 1892, Coytesville, N.J., U.S.—d. Sept. 23, 1992, Polk City, Fla.)

James Alward Van Fleet was a division and corps commander in the U.S. Army during crucial World War II battles, notably the Normandy Invasion and the Battle of the Bulge, and was commander of U.S. ground forces during much of the Korean War.

In April 1951 Van Fleet was named to succeed Matthew B. Ridgway as commander of the Eighth Army in Korea, which included all U.S. ground forces as well as South Korean and other units. His command lasted through months of bitter fighting for small tactical advantages while armistice negotiations dragged on. He was promoted to general in July 1951, but he grew impatient with what he viewed as restrictions placed on his army's ability to fight and was replaced by Maxwell Taylor in February 1953. At that point he retired from the military. He was the recipient of the Purple Heart, the Distinguished Service Cross, the Silver Star, the Bronze Star, and, his most-prized commendation, the Combat Infantryman's Badge.

MATTHEW B. RIDGWAY

(b. March 3, 1895, Fort Monroe [Hampton], Va., U.S.—d. July 26, 1993, Fox Chapel, near Pittsburgh, Pa.)

Matthew B. Ridgway was the U.S. Army officer who planned and executed the first major airborne assault in U.S. military history with the attack on Sicily (July 1943).

Assuming command of the U.S. Eighth Army in the Korean War during the Chinese communist offensive in late

Dwight D. Eisenhower hands over his position of Supreme Allied Commander Europe (SACEUR) to Matthew B. Ridgway on May 30, 1952. Encyclopædia Britannica, Inc.

1950, Ridgway rallied the United Nations forces and initiated a counteroffensive that drove the Chinese out of South Korea. Promoted in 1951 to the rank of general, he succeeded MacArthur as Allied commander in the Far East and continued the successful defense of South Korea. He subsequently oversaw the end of the U.S. occupation of Japan in 1952.

In 1952 Ridgway succeeded Gen. Dwight D. Eisenhower as supreme commander of Allied forces in Europe, and the following year he was appointed chief of staff of the U.S. Army. He retired in 1955 as a general. Ridgway was awarded the Presidential Medal of Freedom in 1986 and the Congressional Gold Medal in 1991.

MARK CLARK

(b. May 1, 1896, Madison Barracks, N.Y., U.S.—d. April 17, 1984, Charleston, S.C.)

Mark Clark was a U.S. Army officer during World War II. He commanded Allied forces (1943–44) during the successful Italian campaign against the Axis powers.

In May 1952, during the Korean War, he was given command of all United Nations troops in Korea, holding that post until after an armistice was signed (July 1953); he retired from the army the same year. Clark served as president of the Citadel, a military college in Charleston, S.C., from 1954 to 1966.

CHAPTER 5

Korea Still Divided, 1953–

SOUTH KOREA MODERNIZED

In the 1950s South Korea had an underdeveloped, agrarian economy that depended heavily on foreign aid. The military leadership that emerged in the early 1960s and led the country for a quarter century may have been autocratic and, at times, repressive, but its pragmatic and flexible commitment to economic development resulted in what became known as the "miracle on the Han River." During the next three decades, the South Korean economy grew at an average annual rate of nearly 9 percent, and per capita income increased more than a hundredfold. South Korea was transformed into an industrial powerhouse with a highly skilled labour force. In the late 20th century, however, economic growth slowed, and in 1997 South Korea was forced to accept a $57 billion bailout from the International Monetary Fund (IMF)—then the largest such rescue in IMF history. The country also wrestled with reforming the *chaebŏl* and liberalizing its economy. Nevertheless, its economy enjoyed a recovery in subsequent years, and the country entered the 21st century on a relatively firm economic footing.

South Korean society underwent an equally rapid transformation after the Korean War. The population more than doubled between the end of the war and the turn of the 21st century. Simultaneously, modern education developed rapidly, again with considerable government involvement but also because of the resurgence of the Korean people's traditional zeal for education after decades of repression during the Japanese occupation period. The growth of educational institutions and of commercial and industrial enterprises in and around South Korea's major cities attracted an increasing number of rural people to urban areas. Seoul, in particular, grew some 10-fold to about 10 million people between the end of World War II and the early 21st century. There was a corresponding growth in communications media, especially newspaper and magazine publishing. An ambitious program was also undertaken to expand and modernize the country's transportation infrastructure.

The most conspicuous social change in South Korea, however, was the emergence of a middle class. Land reform carried out in the early 1950s, together with the spread of modern education and the expansion of the economy, caused the disappearance of the once-privileged *yangban* (landholding) class, and a new elite emerged from the ranks of the former commoners. Another significant social change was the decline of the extended-family system: rural-to-urban migration broke traditional family living arrangements, as urban dwellers tended to live in apartments as nuclear families and, through family planning, have fewer children. In addition, women strenuously campaigned for complete legal equality and won enhanced property ownership rights. Women also won the right to register as a head of family in a new family register system (*hojŏk*) that took effect in 2008. Under the old system only men could register as family heads; thus, children were legally part of the father's family register, not the mother's. The new system increased women's legal standing in, among other things, divorce and child-custody cases. This system also granted adopted and stepchildren rights that were equal to those of biological children—for example, in matters of inheritance.

Rapid urbanization, the nuclear family system, the increase in women's active participation in the economy, and lengthening life expectancies meant that by the early 21st century South Korea had decreasing birth rates and an aging population. The overall population was expected to decrease over the next decades as well. The government was concerned that fewer children and an aging society would slow economic growth and destabilize the social security system in the future.

NORTH KOREA ISOLATED

Domestic Developments

In the aftermath of the Korean War, Kim Il-sung purged the so-called "domestic faction"—an indigenous communist group that had remained in Korea during the colonial period—amid much scapegoating for the disastrous war. After 1956, as the Sino-Soviet conflict intensified, Kim shifted his positions vis-à-vis Moscow and Beijing no fewer than three times: from pro-Soviet to neutral, to pro-Chinese, and finally to independent. During 1956–58, he carried out a purge against the pro-Chinese group known as the Yenan faction and eliminated a pro-Soviet faction from the KWP Central Committee.

In 1966, after a visit to P'yŏngyang by Soviet Premier Aleksey N. Kosygin, Kim announced what became known as the independent party line in North Korea, which stressed the principles of "complete equality, sovereignty, mutual respect, and noninterference among the communist and workers' parties." From this party line, KWP theoreticians developed four self-reliance (*juche*) principles: "autonomy in ideology, independence in politics, self-sufficiency in economy, and self-reliance in defense."

In the late 1960s the regime implemented a program for strengthening the armed forces. As part of the effort to fortify the entire country, more military airfields were constructed and large underground aircraft hangars were built. In addition, a large standing army and a strong militia were maintained.

North Korean leader Pres. Kim Il-sung (front left) *with his son, Kim Jong Il* (front right), *inspecting a soccer field in P'yŏngyang, 1992.* AFP/Getty Images

North Korea's emphasis on strengthening its military forces proceeded hand in hand with its continued focus on the development of a self-reliant economy. With aid from the Soviet Union, China, and the countries of eastern Europe, North Korea implemented a series of economic development plans and made significant gains. But as external aid declined sharply—first from the Soviet Union beginning in the late 1950s and then from China at the start of the Cultural Revolution in the mid-1960s—the seven-year plan of 1961–67 was seriously affected, as indicated by the extension of the plan for another three years.

Two subsequent plans, a six-year plan (1971–76, extended to 1977) and a seven-year plan (1978–84), also failed to achieve their stated goals. While the country's economic growth was hampered by the decline in foreign aid and its heavy expenditures on defense, the continued priority assigned to heavy industry created a severe shortage of daily commodities and lowered living standards. Food shortages were aggravated, in part because of an almost threefold increase in population from 1953 to 1993.

When the 1972 constitution was adopted, the premiership was changed to a presidency, which Kim Il-sung assumed; Kim also retained his post as the chairman (renamed the secretary-general) of the KWP. In 1980 the KWP held its first party congress in a decade. During the proceedings, Kim revealed his dynastic ambition by appointing his son, Kim Jong Il, to three powerful party posts, thus making the younger Kim his heir apparent.

Relations with South Korea

During the late 1960s North Korea had significantly escalated its subversion and infiltration activities against South Korea—from about 50 incidents in 1966 to more than 500 in 1967. One of its most brazen acts occurred on Jan. 21,1968, when a group of 21 North Korean commandos managed to reach within a few hundred yards of the South Korean presidential palace in Seoul in an attempt to kill Pres. Park Chung Hee. Two days later the North Korean navy forcibly seized a U.S. intelligence ship, the USS *Pueblo*, as well as its crew, off North Korea's east coast. The crew of the *Pueblo* were held hostage for nearly a year. In April 1969 North Korea shot down a U.S. reconnaissance plane in the international airspace over the east coast of the peninsula. North Korea's armed provocations continued into the early 1970s, marking the period of highest military tension on the peninsula since the end of the Korean War.

The two Koreas subsequently decided to engage in a dialogue amid the new U.S policy of détente, or relaxation of tensions, toward the Soviet Union and China, North Korea's two major allies. The North called off its armed provocations, and talks between the North and South began at P'anmunjŏm in the demilitarized zone in

In Focus: Pueblo Incident

On Jan. 23, 1968, the USS Pueblo, *a Navy intelligence ship, and its 83 crewmen were captured by North Korean patrol boats off the coast of North Korea. The United States, maintaining that the* Pueblo *had been in international waters, began a military buildup in the area following the seizure of the ship and its crew. The United States also initiated negotiations that resulted in an agreement that secured the release of the 82 surviving crewmen (one died from wounds suffered during the capture) on Dec. 23, 1968. The agreement allowed the United States to publicly disavow the confession the crew had signed, admitting the ship's intrusion, apologizing, pledging to cease all future action, and acknowledging the truth of confessions obtained during captivity. However, a naval inquiry into these confessions and the actions of Comdr. Lloyd M. Bucher produced no apparent disciplinary action.*

September 1971. High-level discussions began in early 1972, culminating in a historic joint communiqué in July, in which both sides agreed on three principles of eventual reunification: that it be (1) peaceful, (2) without foreign influences, and (3) based on national unity. High-level discussions continued until August 1973, when they were unilaterally suspended by the North.

As the Vietnam War wound down and U.S. policies and public opinion became more focused on domestic issues, North Korea probed in vain for a chance to, in its view, "liberate" the South by means of a quick military strike. Meanwhile, South Korea tried to forestall a possible withdrawal of U.S. troops from Korea for fear of a North Korean invasion. In addition, human rights in South Korea became a thorny issue in the United States. These trends together served to worsen U.S.–South Korean relations as well as inter-Korean relations until the early 1980s. South Korea's President Park was assassinated on Oct. 26, 1979, and in 1980 Gen. Chun Doo Hwan seized power. Meanwhile, the strongly anticommunist Ronald Reagan was elected president in the United States, ushering in closer U.S.–South Korean ties and cooler U.S.–North Korean relations.

In the early 1980s North Korea's policy toward the South alternated, often bewilderingly, between peace overtures and provocation. In October 1980 Kim Il-sung unveiled a proposal for the creation of a confederate republic, the Koryŏ Confederation, through a loose merger of the two Koreas, based on equal representation. Later in the decade, however, the North engineered two major terrorist incidents against the South. The first was a bombing assassination attempt against President Chun in Rangoon, Burma (now Yangon, Myanmar), on Oct. 9, 1983, that killed 17 members of the presidential delegation. The second was the destruction by time bomb of a South Korean airliner over the Indian Ocean on Nov. 29, 1987, killing all 115 people on board. Subsequently, the U.S government placed North Korea on its list of state sponsors of terrorism. North Korea was not removed from the list until October 2008.

Because of North Korea's provocations, there was no official contact between the two Koreas in the 1980s, although there were some unofficial talks and contacts between their Red Cross societies. North-South relations reached a milestone in 1991 with the simultaneous admission of the two countries to the UN in September and a series of prime-ministerial talks that produced two agreements in December: one that pledged nonaggression, reconciliation, exchanges, and cooperation and a joint declaration on the denuclearization of the Korean peninsula. The agreements went into effect in February 1992. However, little came of them, especially after North Korea became embroiled in the controversy over its nuclear program and as it suspended all contacts with South Korea in early 1993.

International Relations

North Korea remained one of the most isolated and inaccessible countries in the international community, with severe restrictions on travel into or out of the country, a totally controlled press, and an ideology of self-reliance. In the 1970s and 1980s, the North Korean government maintained its balanced diplomatic position between the country's only two significant allies, China and the Soviet Union, while sustaining a hostile attitude toward the United States. However, the collapse of the Communist Party of the Soviet Union and the subsequent dissolution of the U.S.S.R. in the early 1990s left China as North Korea's sole major ally. Eventually, even China could no longer be relied upon fully, as it cultivated friendly relations with South Korea that culminated when the two established full diplomatic ties in August 1992.

When it became clear that North Korea could not count on its traditional allies to block South Korean membership in the United Nations, it retreated from its long-standing position of insisting on a single, joint Korean seat in the UN General Assembly. Both North Korea and South Korea were admitted to the UN on Sept. 17, 1991, as "separate and equal" members. Diplomatic breakthroughs between North and South created more cordial feelings between the two countries, but these quickly dissipated when suspicion grew throughout the international community that North Korea planned to build nuclear weapons.

North Korea Under Kim Jong Il

Domestic Priorities and International Cooperation

Kim Il-sung died on July 8, 1994, and his son Kim Jong Il succeeded him. However, he did not assume the posts of secretary-general of the KWP or president of North

Korea. Instead, he consolidated his power over several years. In 1997 he officially became head of the KWP, and in 1998 the post of president was written out of North Korea's constitution—Kim Il-sung was given the posthumous title "eternal president"—and Kim Jong Il was reelected chairman of the National Defense Commission, which became the country's highest office. His regime adopted the basic guideline of "military first politics" (*sŏngun chŏngch'i*). This policy was intended to safeguard Kim's regime from any unforeseen adverse impact resulting from such events as the collapse of the Soviet Union and eastern European communist regimes in the late 1980s and early 1990s and the persistent economic hardships at home.

The death of Kim Il-sung had come at a critical time for North Korea. The country had been locked in a dispute over nuclear issues with the United States and the International Atomic Energy Agency (IAEA). The IAEA had been denied access by the North Koreans to an experimental facility at Yŏngbyŏn, where it was suspected that North Korea was diverting plutonium to build nuclear weapons. In the summer of 1994 the North had been preoccupied with the transfer of power to Kim Jong Il; however, by October the United States and North Korea had signed a nuclear accord (the "Agreed Framework"). Under the terms of this agreement, the North renounced efforts to develop nuclear weapons and pledged to abide by the Treaty on the Non-proliferation of Nuclear Weapons (Non-proliferation Treaty; NPT), in exchange for which the United States arranged for the financing and construction of two light-water reactors (LWRs) capable of producing electric power. The agreement restored hope for North-South reconciliation and a peaceful reunification of the divided peninsula.

The United States, South Korea, and Japan formed an international consortium known as the Korean Peninsula Energy Development Organization (KEDO) for the construction of the LWRs in North Korea; South Korea was the main contractor. More than two dozen countries eventually signed onto the project, supplying material and financial help, and construction work progressed slowly but steadily for a time.

Nuclear Ambitions

In late August 1998 North Korea fired a multistage, long-range missile eastward over Japanese airspace. This new missile capability caused shock worldwide and precipitated a major global controversy. In addition, suspected underground nuclear facilities were discovered near the sites whose activities were to have been frozen under the terms of the Agreed Framework in 1994.

Furthermore, it was reported in 2002 that North Korea was pursuing work toward producing highly enriched uranium, which could then be used to make nuclear weapons. In December of that year North Korea expelled IAEA inspectors

A group of images released by North Korea's Korean Central News Agency on April 9, 2009, shows a Unha-2 rocket being launched in the North Hamgyong province on April 5. AFP/ Getty Images

from the facility at Yŏngbyŏn. In January 2003 North Korea withdrew from the Non-proliferation Treaty, and nuclear research operations openly resumed at Yŏngbyŏn. Multiparty talks were initiated to resolve the various nuclear issues and ultimately came to involve the United States, North and South Korea, Russia, China, and Japan. These Six-Party Talks, as they were termed, ended in 2004 without reaching a resolution. In 2005 North Korea claimed to have nuclear weapons capability, although it was unknown whether the claim was true. After having suspended the LWR project for several years, KEDO withdrew its workers from North Korea in January 2006, and in May the organization decided to terminate the project. In October a seismic event was detected at Kilju, North Hamgyŏng province, and North Korea announced that it had carried out an underground test of a nuclear weapon. The country conducted another, more powerful underground nuclear test in May 2009, again near Kilju.

Internal Challenges and International Relations

Throughout the 1990s North Korea suffered severe food shortages that caused widespread starvation. In efforts to help North Korea cope with this crisis, South Korea, Japan, the United States, and international relief agencies (including the UN World Food Programme), provided emergency food and medical assistance. The North Korean government's response inside the country included officially promoting what it called the "arduous march" (also termed the "meal-skipping campaign"). Despite these measures, hundreds of thousands of North Koreans died of starvation in the latter half of the 1990s, and a UN study found that life expectancy had decreased substantially and infant mortality had increased dramatically. The country's economic situation began improving in the early 21st century, in part because of North Korea's own efforts to accommodate certain aspects of market economics, including more open trading policies.

After Kim Jong Il's consolidation of power under the 1998 constitution, his regime began to pursue formal diplomatic relations with many countries, including those of western Europe. By early 2001 North Korea had established relations with most of the West, amid a friendlier climate created by the improving inter-Korean relations. The United States, South Korea, and Japan also had reasons for keeping diplomatic channels open with North Korea, such as maintaining peace and seeking improvements in the country's human rights situation. Despite its successes with other countries, however, North Korea did not make any substantive progress in its diplomatic talks with Japan and the United States, even after years of direct contact.

Relations with the United States in particular reached a low point in January 2002, when U.S. Pres. George W. Bush named North Korea, with Iran and Iraq, as part of an "axis of evil" of countries that were pursuing the development of weapons of mass destruction. Tensions remained high for several years. Multiparty talks in 2008 resulted in the U.S. government's removal of North Korea from its list of state sponsors of terrorism in October, as North Korea took certain previously agreed-upon steps in connection with the pending nuclear issues.

In contrast to the hopeful beginning of the 21st century, however, the ensuing years saw the erosion of the gains that had been made in international cooperation. The joint ventures established under the "sunshine policy" after 2000 were suspended by the North within a few years. North Korea's launch of several rockets in 2009—which the international community generally suspected were tests of ballistic missiles—were considered by many observers to be diplomatically provocative acts. Coinciding with the launches and the nuclear test, the name of Kim Jong Il's youngest son, Kim Jong-un (Kim Jong Woon), began to be mentioned as his possible successor. The reported ill health of the aging Kim Jong Il made uncertain the direction the country would take in the future.

Relations with the South

After the death of Kim Il-sung and through the early years of the Kim Jong Il regime, the situation between North and South remained fairly static, although the countries participated in multiparty negotiations on nuclear issues and South Korea supplied aid to the North. Hopes were high at the turn of the 21st century that the issues dividing the two Koreas

North (left) *and South Korean* (right) *flag bearers carrying a special flag with an image of the Korean peninsula at the opening ceremony of the 2000 Summer Olympics in Sydney, Australia.* Jeff Haynes/AFP/Getty Images

might soon be resolved. As part of his policy of reconciliation with the North, which he termed the "sunshine policy," South Korean president Kim Dae Jung visited North Korea in June 2000—the first time any Korean head of state had traveled to the other side—and the two leaders worked out a five-point joint declaration that specified steps to be taken toward the ultimate goal of national unification. A select number of North and South Koreans were permitted to attend cross-border family reunions. Later that year, at the Summer Olympic Games in Sydney, North and South Korean athletes marched together (though they competed as separate teams) under a single flag showing a silhouette of the Korean peninsula. (The countries also made a joint appearance—with separate teams—at the 2004 Summer Olympic Games in Athens but failed to reach an agreement to do likewise at Beijing in 2008.) Kim Jong Il's government reestablished diplomatic relations with several Western countries and pledged to continue its moratorium on missile testing.

Efforts to restore a North-South dialogue continue. In May 2007 trains from both the North and the South crossed the demilitarized zone to the other side, the first such travel since the Korean War. Later, in October, the two Koreas held a second summit, in which Roh Moo Hyun, the South Korean president, traveled to P'yŏngyang to meet with Kim Jong Il. The December 2007 election of Lee Myung-bak as South Korean president began another period of tension in inter-Korean relations as Lee took a more hard-line position toward P'yŏngyang.

In 2008 North Korea announced that it planned to close the land border and all telephone links with South Korea in an apparent gesture of frustration over South Korea's hard-line posture. Tensions escalated further when the North Korean government announced in January 2009 that it was nullifying all military and political agreements with South Korea. In May of the same year, North Korea also announced that it was canceling all business contracts with South Korea that pertained to the joint-venture Kaesŏng Industrial Complex. Furthermore, in the same month, North Korea announced that it was unilaterally withdrawing from the armistice agreement that ended the Korean War, and that it could attack South Korea or U.S. ships off the coast of the Korean peninsula at any time. Whether a full-scale war between the countries will be reignited has yet to be seen, but with rumours of North Korea's nuclear arms testing, the next Korean war could be very different than the last.

CHAPTER 6

Korea and the Cold War

While war raged in Korea, the French were battling the nationalist and Communist Viet Minh in Indochina. When a French army became surrounded at Dien Bien Phu in 1954, Paris appealed to the United States for air support. American leaders viewed the insurgency as part of the worldwide Communist campaign and at first propounded the theory that if Indochina went Communist, other Southeast Asian countries would also fall "like dominoes." Eisenhower, however, was reluctant to send U.S. troops to Asian jungles, to arrogate war-making powers to the executive branch, or to sully the anti-imperialist reputation of the United States, which he considered an asset in the Cold War. In any case both he and the American people wanted "no more Koreas." Hence the United States supported partition of Indochina as the best means of containing the Viet Minh, and after French Premier Pierre Mendès-France came to power promising peace, partition was effected at the Geneva Conference of 1954. Laos and Cambodia won independence, while two Vietnams emerged on either side of the 17th parallel: a tough Communist regime under Ho Chi Minh in the north and an unstable republic in the south. National elections intended to reunite Vietnam under a single government were scheduled for 1956 but never took place, and, when the

Primary Document: Dean Acheson's "The Strategy of Freedom" Speech

U.S. Secretary of State Dean Acheson's address of Nov. 29, 1950, three days after Chinese Communist troops had swept across the border into Korea and attacked the UN forces at the Yalu River, is reprinted here in part.

Bulletin, Dec. 18, 1950.

What course of action will enable us to maintain our freedom and bring about a peaceful resolution of this world crisis; or, if despite our best efforts aggression does take place, will provide a basis for defeating it? . . .

There are six main elements in the Strategy of Freedom.

First is the development of an international order for the preservation of peace and freedom under the United Nations. The Charter of the United Nations expresses the universal aspirations of mankind, and the organization itself is a symbol of these aspirations. But the United Nations is also more than a symbol. It is a means through which we can take practical, day-by-day steps toward the building of a stable international community. As an organization in which most nations participate, the United Nations can also help to bring about the accommodations of interest and the adjustments of differences which are essential to peace in a world of change . . .

The second element in the Strategy of Freedom is the development of regional groupings, within the framework of the United Nations. To insure their collective security, free nations are engaged in cooperative defense measures, not possible on a universal basis at the present time. The keystone of the defense system of the free world is being built in the North Atlantic community, and among the states of the Western Hemisphere . . .

The third element in our Strategy of Freedom is the rapid building up of military strength at home and among our allies. I stress the word "rapid" because the period of greatest danger is directly before us. Our defense must not only be strong enough, it must come soon enough . . .

The fourth element is economic cooperation. This has a dual character. It contributes powerfully to the building of our defenses against external attack. It also is an instrument for helping to build healthy societies in which the vitality and the promise of freedom find practical expression—in comparison with which the decadence and despair of Communist tyranny is starkly exposed . . .

The fifth element in the Strategy of Freedom is a readiness at all times to negotiate just settlements of international disputes and to find just accommodations of conflicting interests. Our experience has demonstrated that the Soviet rulers cannot be expected to accept fair and equal negotiation so long as they feel capable of imposing their own terms or exacting their own price. Their concept of negotiation is that it should record the facts of power rather than the requirements of justice. We shall not seek to use our power in this way, but as the free world develops strength, the Soviet rulers may find it advantageous to adjust differences equitably rather than to seek to impose their demands. The free nations must always be prepared to enter into genuine negotiations, and even to take the initiative in efforts to bring about honest negotiation.

The sixth element in the Strategy of Freedom is a firm adherence in all our actions, at home and abroad, to the moral values which give meaning to our lives.

These are the elements of our national foreign policy of the Strategy of Freedom. This is the course by which we seek to avoid war and to secure peace. No one can guarantee that war will not come. The present crisis is extremely serious. Whether reason will prevail is only partly for us to decide. We must hope and strive for the best while we prepare for the worst.

United States assumed France's former role as South Vietnam's sponsor, another potential "Korea" was indeed created as the beginnings of the Vietnam War unfolded.

The Korean War and the new administration brought significant changes in U.S. strategy. Eisenhower believed that the Cold War would be a protracted struggle and that the greatest danger for the United States would be the temptation to spend itself to death. If the United States were obliged to respond to endless Communist-instigated "brushfire wars," it would soon lose the capacity and will to defend the free world. Hence Eisenhower and Secretary of State John Foster Dulles determined to solve "the great equation," balancing a healthy economy with only what was essential by way of military force. Their answer was a defense policy whereby the United States would deter future aggression with its airborne nuclear threat. As Dulles put it, the United States reserved the right to reply to aggression with "massive retaliatory power" at places of its own choosing. In implementing this policy, Eisenhower cut overall defense spending by 30 percent over four years but beefed up the Strategic Air Command. The diplomatic side of this new policy was a series of regional pacts that linked the United States to the countries that outlined the entire Soviet bloc. Truman had already founded the NATO alliance, the ANZUS pact with Australia and New Zealand (1951), the Pact of Rio with Latin-American nations (1947), and the defense treaty with Japan (1951). Now Dulles completed an alliance system linking the 1954 Southeast Asia Treaty Organization (SEATO), stretching from Australia to Pakistan, to the 1955 Baghdad Pact Organization (later the Central Treaty Organization [CENTO]), stretching from Pakistan to Turkey, to NATO, stretching from Turkey (after 1952) to Iceland.

Dulles viewed the postwar world in the same bipolar terms as had Truman and, for that matter, Stalin. Asian independence, however, not only expanded the

Primary Document: John Foster Dulles's "Containment or Liberation?" Testimony

It was no secret that Eisenhower would name John Foster Dulles as his secretary of state, and as the new president, he wasted no time in confirming everyone's expectations. Dulles was asked to testify on the policies that he would follow in response to the Communist challenge and concerning which he had given many hints in the past year, to the Senate Foreign Relations Committee on Jan. 15, 1953, five days before the new administration took office. Portions of Dulles' testimony are reprinted here.

Nomination of John Foster Dulles, Secretary of State-Designate, Hearing Before the Committee on Foreign Relations, U.S. Senate, 83 Congress, 1 Session, Washington, 1953.

There are a number of policy matters which I would prefer to discuss with the committee in executive session, but I have no objection to saying in open session what I have said before: namely, that we shall never have a secure peace or a happy world so long as Soviet Communism dominates one-third of all of the peoples that there are, and is in the process of trying at least to extend its rule to many others.

These people who are enslaved are people who deserve to be free, and who, from our own selfish standpoint, ought to be free; because if they are the servile instruments of aggressive despotism, they will eventually be welded into a force which will be highly dangerous to ourselves and to all of the free world. Therefore, we must always have in mind the liberation of these captive peoples.

Now, liberation does not mean a war of liberation. Liberation can be accomplished by processes short of war.

It must be and can be a peaceful process, but those who do not believe that results can be accomplished by moral pressures, by the weight of propaganda, just do not know what they are talking about.

I ask you to recall the fact that Soviet Communism, itself, has spread from controlling 200 million people some seven years ago to controlling 800 million people today, and it has done that by methods of political warfare, psychological warfare and propaganda, and it has not actually used the Red Army as an open aggressive force in accomplishing that.

Surely what they can accomplish, we can accomplish. Surely if they can use moral and psychological force, we can use it; and to take a negative defeatist attitude is not an approach which is conducive to our own welfare or in conformity with our own historical ideas . . .

The threat of Soviet Communism, in my opinion, is not only the gravest threat that ever faced the United States but the gravest threat that has ever faced what we call Western civilization, or, indeed, any civilization which was dominated by a spiritual faith.

Soviet Communism is atheistic in its philosophy and materialistic. It believes that human beings are nothing more than somewhat superior animals, that they have no soul, no spirit, no right to personal dignity, and that the best kind of a world is that world which is organized as a well-managed farm is organized, where certain animals are taken out to pasture, and they are fed and brought back and milked, and they are given a barn as shelter over their heads, and that is a form of society which is most conducive to the material welfare of mankind—that is their opinion. That can be made into a persuasive doctrine if one does not believe in the spiritual nature of man.

If you do believe in the spiritual nature of man, it is a doctrine which is utterly unacceptable and wholly irreconcilable.

I do not see how, as long as Soviet Communism holds those views, and holds also the belief that its destiny is to spread those views throughout the world, and to organize the whole world on that basis, there can be any permanent reconciliation.

arena of the Cold War but also spawned the third path of nonalignment. In April 1955 delegates from 29 nations attended the Bandung (Indonesia) Afro-Asian Conference, which was dominated by Jawaharlal Nehru of India, Gamal Abdel Nasser of Egypt, and Sukarno of Indonesia. In theory the delegates met to celebrate Cold War neutrality and an end to "the old age of the white man," but in fact they castigated the imperialist West and praised, or tolerated, the U.S.S.R. Although most of the Bandung leaders were sloganeering despots in their own countries, the movement captivated the imagination of many guilt-ridden Western intellectuals.

CHAPTER 7

Precursors to the Vietnam War

At the heart of the conflict was the desire of North Vietnam, which had defeated the French colonial administration of Vietnam in 1954, to unify the entire country under a single communist regime modeled after those of the Soviet Union and China. The South Vietnamese government, on the other hand, fought to preserve a Vietnam more closely aligned with the West. U.S. military advisers, present in small numbers throughout the 1950s, were introduced on a large scale beginning in 1961, and active combat units were introduced in 1965. By 1969 more than 500,000 U.S. military personnel were stationed in Vietnam. Meanwhile, the Soviet Union and China poured weapons, supplies, and advisers into the North, which in turn provided support, political direction, and regular combat troops for the campaign in the South. However, the costs and casualties of the growing war proved too much for the United States to bear, and U.S. combat units were withdrawn by 1973. In 1975 South Vietnam, left vulnerable, fell to a full-scale invasion by the North.

VIETNAM COLONIZED AND DIVIDED, 1897–1955

The Anticolonial Movement

The anticolonial movement in Vietnam can be said to have stawrted with the establishment of French rule. France's

19th-century imperial expansion reached southeast Asia following the Sino-French War with China, when it established French Indochina in 1887. This colonial regime gathered three Vietnamese regions under French rule—Tonkin in the North, Annam in Central Vietnam, and Cochinchina in the South—as well as Cambodia. In 1893, France also incorporated Laos into its southeast Asian colony. Except in Cochinchina, the original Vietnamese, Cambodian, and Laotian royal houses continued under a federal-type central government that had exclusive authority in foreign affairs, finance, defense, customs, and public works and was headed by a French governor-general responsible to the French minister for trade. In Cochinchina the administration was under a prefect and a French bureaucracy. However, many local officials of Cochinchina refused to collaborate with the French. Some led guerrilla groups, composed of the remnants of the defeated Vietnamese armies, in attacks on French outposts. A much broader resistance movement developed in Annam in 1885, led by the great scholar Phan Dinh Phung, whose rebellion collapsed only after his death in 1895.

The main characteristic of the national movement during this first phase of resistance, however, was its political orientation toward the past. Filled with ideas of precolonial Vietnam, its leaders wanted to be rid of the French in order to reestablish the old imperial order. Because this aspiration had little meaning for the generation that came to maturity after 1900, this first stage of anticolonial resistance did not survive the death of its leader.

Modern Nationalism

A new national movement arose in the early 20th century. Its most prominent spokesman was Phan Boi Chau, with whose rise the old traditionalist opposition gave way to a modern nationalist leadership that rejected French rule but not Western ideas, science, or technology. In 1905 Chau went to Japan. His plan, mildly encouraged by some Japanese statesmen, was to free Vietnam from the French with Japanese help. Chau smuggled hundreds of young Vietnamese into Japan, where they studied the sciences and underwent training for clandestine organization, political propaganda, and terrorist action. Inspired by Chau's writings, nationalist intellectuals in Hanoi opened the Free School of Tonkin in 1907, which soon became a centre of anti-French agitation and consequently was suppressed after a few months. Also, under the inspiration and guidance of Chau's followers, mass demonstrations demanding a reduction of high taxes took place in many cities in 1908. Hundreds of demonstrators and suspected organizers were arrested. Some were condemned to death, while others were sent to Con Son (Poulo Condore) Island in the South China Sea, which the French turned into a penal camp for Vietnamese nationalists.

Phan Boi Chau went to China in 1910, where a revolution had broken out against the Qing (Manchu) dynasty. There he set up a republican government-in-exile to attract the support of nationalist groups. After the French arranged his arrest and imprisonment in China (1914–17), however, his movement began to decline. In 1925 Chau was seized by French agents in Shanghai and brought back to Vietnam for trial; he died under house arrest in 1940.

After World War I the movement for national liberation intensified. A number of prominent intellectuals sought to achieve reforms by obtaining political concessions from the colonial regime through collaboration with the French. The failure of such reformist efforts led to a revival of clandestine and revolutionary groups, especially in Annam and Tonkin; among these was the Vietnamese Nationalist Party (Viet Nam Quoc Dan Dang, founded in 1927 and usually referred to as the VNQDD). However, following an attempted military uprising against the French in 1930, the VNQDD was virtually destroyed, and for the next 15 years it existed mainly as a group of exiles in China supported by the Chinese Nationalist Party (Kuomintang).

Vietnamese Communism

The year 1930 was important in the history of Vietnam for yet another reason. Five years earlier, a new figure, destined to become the most prominent leader in

In Focus: Viet Nam Quoc Dan Dang

The Viet Nam Quoc Dan Dang, or Vietnamese Nationalist Party, was the first large-scale revolutionary nationalist organization in Vietnam. Founded officially in 1927, the VNQDD was modeled after the revolutionary Nationalist Party (Kuomintang) of China. Its aim, like that of the Nationalist Party, was the establishment of a republican democratic government free from foreign interference. Gaining the allegiance of many military officers, as well as of the young intelligentsia, the VNQDD turned to terrorist activities in the late 1920s after the French repeatedly denied it a chance to participate in the electoral process.

Its most ambitious action—an event known as the Yen Bai uprising—occurred on the night of Feb. 9, 1930, when the military garrison at Yen Bai, a small town along the Chinese border, revolted against and killed their French officers. Before the remainder of the country could follow suit, however, the French, who had been alerted, overwhelmed those involved in the uprising a day later. The mutinous troops were summarily executed. In fact, the French crushed the revolt with such severity that the VNQDD was destroyed. A wave of repression followed that took hundreds of lives and sent thousands to prison camps. Many former members joined the newly formed Indochinese Communist Party.

the national movement, had appeared on the scene as an expatriate revolutionary in South China. He was Nguyen Ai Quoc, better known by his later pseudonym of Ho Chi Minh. In June 1925 Ho Chi Minh had founded the revolutionary Youth League of Vietnam, the predecessor of the Indochinese Communist Party.

As a young seaman, Ho Chi Minh had left Vietnam in 1911 and traveled widely before settling in Paris in 1917. He joined the Communist Party of France in 1920 and later spent several years in Moscow and China in the service of the international communist movement. After making his Revolutionary Youth League the most influential of all clandestine resistance groups, he succeeded in early 1930 in forming the Vietnamese Communist Party—from late 1930 called the Indochinese Communist Party—from a number of competing communist organizations. In May of that year the communists exploited conditions of near starvation over large areas of central Vietnam by staging a broad peasant uprising, during which numerous Vietnamese officials and many landlords were killed, and "Soviet" administrations were set up in several provinces of Annam. It took the French until the spring of 1931 to suppress this movement and, in an unparalleled wave of terror, to reestablish control.

Unlike the dispersed and disoriented leadership of the VNQDD and some smaller nationalist groups, the Indochinese Communist Party recovered quickly from the setback of 1931, relying on cadres trained in the Soviet Union and China. After 1936, when the French extended some political freedoms to the colonies, the party skillfully exploited all opportunities for the creation of legal front organizations, through which it extended its

A 30-year-old Ho Chi Minh addresses delegates of the French Socialist Party in Tours, France, 1920. AFP/Getty Images

influence among intellectuals, workers, and peasants. When political freedoms in French Indochina were again curtailed at the outbreak of World War II, the Communist Party, now a well-disciplined organization, was forced back into hiding.

World War II and Independence

For five years during World War II, Indochina was a French-administered possession of Japan. On Sept. 22, 1940, Jean Decoux, the French governor-general appointed by the Vichy government after the fall of France to the Nazis, concluded an agreement with the Japanese that permitted the stationing of 30,000 Japanese troops in Indochina and the use of all major Vietnamese airports by the Japanese military. The agreement made Indochina the most important staging area for all Japanese military operations in Southeast Asia during the war. The French administration cooperated with the Japanese occupation forces and was ousted only toward the end of the war (in March 1945), when the Japanese began to fear that the French forces might turn against them as defeat approached. After the French had been disarmed, Bao Dai, the last French-appointed emperor of Vietnam, was allowed to proclaim the nominal independence of his country and to appoint a Vietnamese national government at Hue; however, all real power remained in the hands of the Japanese military commanders.

Meanwhile, in May 1941, at Ho Chi Minh's urging, the Communist Party formed a broad nationalist alliance under its leadership. This alliance was called the League for the Independence of Vietnam, which subsequently became known as the Viet Minh. Ho, returning to China to seek assistance, was arrested and imprisoned there by the Nationalist government. After his release he returned to Vietnam and began to cooperate with Allied forces by providing information on Japanese troop movements in Indochina. At the same time, he sought recognition of the Viet Minh as the legitimate representative of Vietnamese nationalist aspirations. When the Japanese surrendered in August 1945, the communist-led Viet Minh ordered a general uprising, and, with no one organized to oppose them, they were able to seize power in Hanoi. Bao Dai, the Vietnamese emperor, abdicated a few days later and declared his fealty to the newly proclaimed Democratic Republic of Vietnam.

The Communist Party had clearly gained the upper hand in its struggle to outmaneuver its disorganized rivals, such as the noncommunist VNQDD. The French, however, were determined to restore their colonial presence in Indochina and, with the aid of British occupation forces, seized control of Cochinchina. Thus, at the beginning of 1946, there were two Vietnams: a communist north and a noncommunist south.

In Focus: Viet Minh

The Viet Nam Doc Lap Dong Minh Hoi (Viet Minh), or League for the Independence of Vietnam, organization led the struggle for Vietnamese independence from French rule. The Viet Minh was formed in China in May 1941 by Ho Chi Minh. Although led primarily by Communists, the Viet Minh operated as a national front organization open to persons of various political persuasions.

In late 1943 members of the Viet Minh, led by Gen. Vo Nguyen Giap, began to infiltrate Vietnam to launch guerrilla operations against the Japanese, who occupied the country during World War II. The Viet Minh forces liberated considerable portions of northern Vietnam, and after the Japanese surrender to the Allies, Viet Minh units seized control of Hanoi and proclaimed the independent Democratic Republic of Vietnam.

The French at first promised to recognize the new government as a free state but failed to do so. On Nov. 23, 1946, at least 6,000 Vietnamese civilians were killed in a French naval bombardment of the port city of Haiphong, and the first Indochina War began. The Viet Minh had popular support and was able to dominate the countryside, while the French strength lay in urban areas. As the war neared an end, the Viet Minh was succeeded by a new organization, the Lien Viet, or Vietnamese National Popular Front. In 1951 the majority of the Viet Minh leadership was absorbed into the Lao Dong, or Vietnamese Workers' Party (later Vietnamese Communist Party), which remained the dominant force in North Vietnam.

Elements of the Viet Minh joined with the Viet Cong against the U.S.-supported government of South Vietnam and the United States in the Vietnam War (or Second Indochina War) of the late 1950s, 1960s, and early 1970s. After the reunification of the country (1976), Viet Minh leaders continued to take an active role in Vietnamese politics.

The First Indochina War

Negotiations between the French and Ho Chi Minh led to an agreement in March 1946 that appeared to promise a peaceful solution. Under the agreement France would recognize the Viet Minh government and give Vietnam the status of a free state within the French Union. French troops were to remain in Vietnam, but they would be withdrawn progressively over five years. For a period in early 1946 the French cooperated with Ho Chi Minh as he consolidated the Viet Minh's dominance over other nationalist groups, in particular those politicians who were backed by the Chinese Nationalist Party.

However, despite tactical cooperation between the French and the Viet Minh, their policies were irreconcilable. While the French aimed to reestablish colonial rule, Hanoi wanted total independence. French intentions were revealed in the decision of Georges-Thierry d'Argenlieu, the high commissioner for Indochina, to proclaim Cochinchina an autonomous republic in June 1946. Further negotiations did not resolve the basic differences between the French and the Viet Minh. In late November 1946 French naval vessels bombarded Haiphong, causing several thousand civilian casualties; the subsequent Viet Minh attempt to overwhelm French troops in Hanoi in December is generally considered to be the beginning of the First Indochina War.

Ho Chi Minh (second from right) *shakes hands with French Premier Georges Bidault* (left), *1946.* Keystone/Hulton Archive/Getty Images

Initially confident of victory, the French long ignored the real political cause of the war—the desire of the Vietnamese people, including their anti-communist leaders, to achieve unity and independence for their country. French efforts to deal with those issues were devious and ineffective. The French reunited Cochinchina with the rest of Vietnam in 1949, proclaiming the Associated State of Vietnam, and appointed the former emperor Bao Dai as chief of state. Most nationalists, however, denounced these maneuvers, and leadership in the struggle for independence from the French remained with the Viet Minh.

Meanwhile, the Viet Minh waged an increasingly successful guerrilla war, aided after 1949 by the new communist government of China. The United States, fearful of the spread of communism in Asia, sent large amounts of aid to the French in the south. The French, however, were shaken by the fall of their garrison at Dien Bien Phu in May 1954 and agreed to negotiate an end to the war with the Viet Minh at an international conference in Geneva.

In Focus: Battle of Dien Bien Phu

The Battle of Dien Bien Phu was a decisive engagement in the First Indochina War. It consisted of a struggle between French and Viet Minh forces for control of a small mountain outpost on the Vietnamese border near Laos. The Viet Minh victory in this battle effectively ended the eight-year-old war between North Vietnam and their former colonizers.

The battle was joined in late 1953 when French forces, who had been rapidly losing ground to the popularly supported Viet Minh, occupied the town of Dien Bien Phu in an attempt to cut the nationalist supply lines into Laos and to maintain a base for forays against enemy forces. Although the Vietnamese quickly cut all the roads into Dien Bien Phu, making it suppliable only by air, the French were confident of their position. They were thus taken by surprise when Giap surrounded the base with 40,000 men and used heavy artillery to break the French lines. Despite heavy U.S. aid, the base was overrun on May 7, 1954.

With French forces in disarray after the battle, the French government sought an end to the fighting; an official settlement was negotiated at an international conference in Geneva. The French sense of national humiliation, particularly acute within the army, had lasting repercussions on French public opinion and contributed—along with later events in Algeria—to the downfall of the French Fourth Republic in 1958.

The Two Vietnams (1954–65)

The agreements concluded in Geneva between April and July 1954 (collectively called the Geneva Accords) were signed by French and Viet Minh representatives and provided for a cease-fire and temporary division of the country into two military zones at latitude 17 °N (popularly called the 17th parallel). All Viet Minh forces were to withdraw north of that line, and all French and Associated State of Vietnam troops were to remain south of it; permission was granted for refugees to move from one zone to the other during a limited time period. An international commission was established, composed of Canadian, Polish, and Indian members under an Indian chairman, to supervise the execution of the agreement.

This agreement left the Democratic Republic of Vietnam (henceforth called North Vietnam) in control of only the northern half of the country. The last of the Geneva Accords—called the Final Declaration—provided for elections, supervised by the commission, to be held throughout Vietnam in July 1956 in order to unify the country. However, because Viet Minh leaders appeared certain to win these elections, and the United States and the leaders in the south would not approve or sign the Final Declaration, the elections were never held.

In the midst of a mass migration of nearly one million people from the north to the south, the two Vietnams began to reconstruct their war-ravaged land. With assistance from the Soviet Union and China, the Hanoi government in the north embarked on an ambitious program of socialist industrialization; they also began to collectivize agriculture in earnest in 1958. In the south a new government appointed by Bao Dai began to build a new country. Ngo Dinh Diem, a Roman Catholic, was named prime minister and succeeded with American support in stabilizing the anticommunist regime in Saigon. He eliminated pro-French elements in the military and abolished the local autonomy of several religious-political groups. Then, in a government-controlled referendum in October 1955, Diem removed Bao Dai as chief of state and made himself president of the Republic of Vietnam (South Vietnam).

Diem's early success in consolidating power did not result in concrete political and economic achievements. Plans for land reform were sabotaged by entrenched interests. With the financial backing of the United States, the regime's chief energies were directed toward building up the military and a variety of intelligence and security forces to counter the still-influential Viet Minh. Totalitarian methods were directed against all who were regarded as opponents, and the favouritism shown to Roman Catholics alienated the majority Buddhist population. Loyalty to the president and his family was made a paramount duty, and Diem's brother, Ngo Dinh Nhu, founded an elitist underground organization to spy on officials, army officers, and prominent local citizens. Diem also refused to participate in the all-Vietnamese elections described in the Final Declaration.

CHAPTER 8

The American War, 1955–74

THE DIEM REGIME AND THE VIET CONG

Leaders in the U.S. capital, Washington, D.C., were surprised and delighted by Diem's initial success. American military and economic aid continued to pour into South Vietnam while American military and police advisers helped train and equip Diem's army and security forces. Beneath the outward success of the Diem regime, however, lay fatal problems. Diem was a poor administrator who refused to delegate authority, and he was pathologically suspicious of anyone who was not a member of his family. His brother and close confidant, Ngo Dinh Nhu, controlled an extensive system of extortion, payoffs, and influence peddling through a secret network called the Can Lao, which had clandestine members in all government bureaus and military units as well as schools, newspapers, and businesses. In the countryside, ambitious programs of social and economic reform had been allowed to languish while many local officials and police engaged in extortion, bribery, and theft of government property. That many of these officials were, like Diem himself, northerners and Roman Catholics further alienated them from the local people.

Diem's unexpected offensive against communist political organizers and propagandists in the countryside in 1955 had resulted in the arrest of thousands and in the temporary disorganization of the communists' infrastructure. By 1957, however, the communists, now called the Viet Cong, had begun a program of terrorism and assassination against government officials and functionaries. The Viet Cong's ranks were soon swelled by many noncommunist Vietnamese who had been alienated by the corruption and intimidation of local officials. Beginning in the spring of 1959, armed bands of Viet Cong were occasionally engaging units of the South Vietnamese army in regular firefights. By that time the Central Committee of the Vietnamese Communist Party, meeting in Hanoi, had endorsed a resolution calling for the use of armed force to overthrow the Diem government. Southerners specially trained in the North as insurgents were infiltrated back into the South along with arms and equipment. A new war had begun.

Despite its American training and weapons, the Army of the Republic of Vietnam, usually called the ARVN, was in many ways ill-adapted to meet the insurgency of the Viet Cong, or VC. Higher-ranking officers, appointed on the basis of their family connections and political reliability, were often apathetic, incompetent, or corrupt—and sometimes all three. The higher ranks of the army were also thoroughly penetrated by Viet Cong agents, who held positions varying from drivers, clerks, and radio operators to senior headquarters officers. With its heavy American-style equipment, the ARVN was principally a road-bound force not well configured to pursuing VC units in swamps or jungles. U.S. military advisers responsible for helping to develop and improve the force usually lacked knowledge of the Vietnamese language, and in any case they routinely spent less than 12 months in the country.

At the end of 1960 the communists in the South announced the formation of the National Liberation Front (NLF), which was designed to serve as the political arm of the Viet Cong and also as a broad-based organization for all those who desired an end to the Diem regime. The Front's regular army, usually referred to as the "main force" by the Americans, was much smaller than Diem's army, but it was only one component of the Viet Cong's so-called People's Liberation Armed Forces (PLAF). At the base of the PLAF were village guerrilla units, made up of part-time combatants who lived at home and worked at their regular occupations during the day. Their function was to persuade or intimidate their neighbours into supporting the NLF, to protect its political apparatus, and to harass the government, police, and security forces with booby traps, raids, kidnappings, and murders. The guerrilla forces also served as a recruiting agency and source of manpower for the other echelons of the PLAF. Above the guerrillas were the local or regional forces, full-time soldiers organized in platoon- or company-sized units who operated within the bounds of a province or region. As members of the guerrilla militia gained experience, they might be upgraded to

In Focus: Viet Cong

The Viet Nam Cong San (Viet Cong), or Vietnamese Communists, were the guerrilla force that, with the support of the North Vietnamese Army, fought against South Vietnam (late 1950s–1975) and the United States (early 1960s–1973). The name is said to have first been used by South Vietnamese Pres. Ngo Dinh Diem to belittle the rebels.

Though beginning in the mid-1950s as a collection of various groups opposed to the government of President Diem, the Viet Cong became in 1960 the military arm of the National Liberation Front (NLF). In 1969 the NLF joined other groups in the areas of South Vietnam that were controlled by the Viet Cong to form the Provisional Revolutionary Government (PRG). The movement's principal objectives were the overthrow of the South Vietnamese government and the reunification of Vietnam.

The early insurgent activity in South Vietnam against Diem's government was initially conducted by elements of the Hoa Hao and Cao Dai religious sects. After 1954 they were joined by former elements of the southern Viet Minh, a Communist-oriented nationalist group. The overwhelming majority of the Viet Cong were subsequently recruited in the south, but they received weapons, guidance, and reinforcements from North Vietnamese Army soldiers who had infiltrated into South Vietnam. During the so-called Tet Offensive of 1968, the Viet Cong suffered devastating losses and their ranks were later filled primarily by North Vietnamese soldiers. For the most part, the Viet Cong fought essentially a guerrilla war of ambush, terrorism, and sabotage; they used small units to maintain a hold on the countryside, leaving the main population centres to government authorities.

Under terms of the agreement reached at the peace negotiations held in Paris in 1971–73, the PRG won acknowledgment of its authority in areas under its control, pending general elections to determine the future of South Vietnam. The peace agreement soon broke down, however, as both the South Vietnamese government and the PRG began trying to improve their military and territorial positions at each other's expense. Following the full-scale North Vietnamese invasion of South Vietnam and the subsequent rapid collapse of the government of South Vietnamese president Nguyen Van Thieu in the spring of 1975, the PRG assumed power as the government of South Vietnam; the following year, when reunification of the country was accomplished, the PRG joined other political groups in forming a National United Front. Real governmental power was subsequently exercised by the Vietnamese Communist Party and its North Vietnamese leadership.

the regional or main forces. These forces were better-equipped and acted as full-time soldiers. Based in remote jungles, swamps, or mountainous areas, they could operate throughout a province (in the case of regional forces) or even the country (in the case of the main force). When necessary, the full-time forces might also reinforce a guerrilla unit or several units for some special operation.

THE U.S. ROLE GROWS

By the middle of 1960 it was apparent that the South Vietnamese army and security forces could not cope with the new threat posed by the Viet Cong. During the last half of 1959, VC-initiated ambushes and attacks on posts averaged well over 100 a month. In the next year 2,500 government functionaries and other real and imagined enemies of the Viet Cong were assassinated. It took some time for the new situation to be recognized in Saigon and Washington. Only after four VC companies had attacked and overrun an ARVN regimental headquarters northeast of Saigon in January 1960 did Americans in Vietnam begin to plan for increased U.S. aid to Diem. They also began to search for ways to persuade Diem to reform and reorganize his government—a search that would prove futile.

To the new administration of U.S. Pres. John F. Kennedy, who took office in 1961, Vietnam represented both a challenge and an opportunity. The Viet Cong's armed struggle against Diem seemed to be a prime example of the new Chinese and Soviet strategy of encouraging and aiding "wars of national liberation" in newly independent nations of Asia and Africa—in other words, helping communist-led insurgencies to subvert and overthrow the shaky new governments of emerging nations. Thus, Kennedy and some of his close advisers believed that Vietnam presented an opportunity to test the United States' ability to conduct a "counterinsurgency" against communist subversion and guerrilla warfare. Kennedy accepted without serious question the so-called domino theory, which held that the fates of all Southeast Asian countries were closely linked and that a communist success in one must necessarily lead to the fatal weakening of the others. A successful effort in Vietnam—in Kennedy's words, "the cornerstone of the free world in Southeast Asia"—would provide to both allies and adversaries evidence of U.S. determination to meet the challenge of communist expansion in the Third World.

Though never doubting Vietnam's importance, the new president was obliged, during much of his first year in office, to deal with far more pressing issues—the construction of the Berlin Wall, conflicts between the Laotian government and the communist-led Pathet Lao, and the humiliating failure of the Bay of Pigs invasion of Cuba. Because of these other, more widely known crises, it seemed to some of Kennedy's advisers all the more important to score some sort of success in Vietnam. Success seemed urgently needed as membership in the NLF continued to climb, military setbacks to the ARVN continued, and the rate of infiltration from the North increased. U.S. intelligence estimated that in 1960 about 4,000 communist cadres infiltrated from the North; by 1962 the total had risen to some 12,900. Most of these men were natives of South Vietnam

U.S. Army chief of staff Gen. Maxwell Taylor (left) *and U.S. Secretary of Defense Robert McNamara* (centre) *meet with Pres. John F. Kennedy* (right) *in the White House, September 1963.* AFP/Getty Images

who had been regrouped to the North after Geneva. More than half were Communist Party members. Hardened and experienced leaders, they provided a framework around which the PLAF could be organized. To arm and equip their growing forces in the South, Hanoi leaders sent crew-served weapons and ammunition in steel-hulled motor junks down the coast of Vietnam and also through Laos via a network of tracks known as the Ho Chi Minh Trail. But most of the firearms for PLAF soldiers actually came from the United States: large quantities of American rifles, carbines, machine guns, and mortars were captured from Saigon's armed forces or simply sold to the Viet Cong by Diem's corrupt officers and functionaries.

Many of the South's problems could be attributed to the continuing incompetence, rigidity, and corruption of the Diem regime, but the South Vietnamese president had few American critics in Saigon or Washington. Instead, the U.S. administration made great efforts to reassure Diem of its support, dispatching Vice Pres. Lyndon B. Johnson to Saigon in May 1961 and boosting economic and military aid.

As the situation continued to deteriorate, Kennedy sent two key advisers, economist W.W. Rostow and former army chief of staff Maxwell Taylor, to Vietnam in the fall of 1961 to assess conditions. The two concluded that the South Vietnamese government was losing the war with the Viet Cong and had neither the will nor the ability to turn the tide on its own. They recommended a greatly expanded program of military assistance, including such items as helicopters and armoured personnel carriers, and an ambitious plan to place American advisers and technical experts at all levels and in all agencies of the Vietnamese government and military. They also recommended the introduction of a limited number of U.S. combat troops, a measure the Joint Chiefs of Staff had been urging as well.

Well aware of the domestic political consequences of "losing" another country to the communists, Kennedy could see no viable exit from Vietnam, but he also

In Focus: Ho Chi Minh Trail

The Ho Chi Minh Trail was an elaborate system of mountain and jungle paths and trails used by North Vietnam to infiltrate troops and supplies into South Vietnam, Cambodia, and Laos during the Vietnam War. The trail was put into operation beginning in 1959, after the North Vietnamese leadership decided to use revolutionary warfare to reunify South with North Vietnam. Accordingly, work was undertaken to connect a series of old trails leading from the panhandle of North Vietnam southward along the upper slopes of the Annamese Cordillera (French: Chaîne Annamitique; Vietnamese: Truong-Son) into eastern Laos and Cambodia and thence into South Vietnam. Starting south of Hanoi in North Vietnam, the main trail veered southwestward to enter Laos, with periodic side branches or exits running east into South Vietnam. The main trail continued southward into eastern Cambodia and then emptied into South Vietnam at points west of Da Lat.

The network of trails and volume of traffic expanded significantly beginning in the 1960s, but it still took more than one month's march to travel from North to South Vietnam using it. Traffic on the trail was little affected by repeated American bombing raids. Efforts were gradually made to improve the trail, which by the late 1960s could accommodate heavy trucks in some sections and was supplying the needs of several hundred thousand regular North Vietnamese troops active in South Vietnam. By 1974, the trail was a well-marked series of jungle roads (some of them paved) and underground support facilities such as hospitals, fuel-storage tanks, and weapons and supply caches. The Ho Chi Minh Trail was the major supply route for the North Vietnamese forces that successfully invaded and overran South Vietnam in 1975.

was reluctant to commit combat troops to a war in Southeast Asia. Instead, the administration proceeded with vigour and enthusiasm to carry out the expansive program of aid and guidance proposed in the Rostow-Taylor report. A new four-star general's position—commander, U.S. Military Assistance Command Vietnam (USMACV)—was established in Saigon to guide the military assistance effort. The number of U.S. military personnel in Vietnam, less than 800 throughout the 1950s, rose to about 9,000 by the middle of 1962.

THE CONFLICT DEEPENS

Buoyed by its new American weapons and encouraged by its aggressive and confident American advisers, the South Vietnamese army took the offensive against the Viet Cong. At the same time, the Diem government undertook an extensive security campaign called the Strategic Hamlet Program. The object of the program was to concentrate rural populations into more defensible positions where they could be more easily protected and segregated from the Viet Cong. The hamlet project was inspired by a similar program in Malaya, where local farmers had been moved into so-called New Villages during a rebellion by Chinese Malayan communists in 1948–60. In the case of Vietnam, however, it proved virtually impossible to tell which Vietnamese were to be protected and which excluded. Because of popular discontent with the compulsory labour and frequent dislocations involved in establishing the villages, many strategic hamlets soon had as many VC recruits inside their walls as outside.

Meanwhile, the Viet Cong had learned to cope with the ARVN's new array of American weapons. Helicopters proved vulnerable to small-arms fire, while armoured personnel carriers could be stopped or disoriented if their exposed drivers or machine gunners were hit. The communists' survival of many military encounters was helped by the fact that the leadership of the South Vietnamese army was as incompetent, faction-ridden, and poorly trained as it had been in the 1950s, despite heavier American assistance. In January 1963 a Viet Cong battalion near the village of Ap Bac in the Mekong delta south of Saigon, though surrounded and outnumbered by ARVN forces, successfully fought its way out of its encirclement, destroying five helicopters and killing about 80 South Vietnamese soldiers and three American advisers. By now some aggressive American newsmen were beginning to report on serious deficiencies in the U.S. advisory and support programs in Vietnam, and some advisers at lower levels were beginning to agree with them; but by now there was also a large and powerful bureaucracy in Saigon that had a deep stake in ensuring that U.S. programs appeared successful. The USMACV commander Paul Harkins and U.S. ambassador Frederick Nolting in particular continued to assure Washington that all was going well.

By the summer of 1963, however, there were growing doubts about the ability of the Diem government to prosecute the war. The behaviour of the Ngo family, always odd, had now become bizarre. Diem's brother Nhu was known to smoke opium daily and was suspected by U.S. intelligence of secretly negotiating with the North. In May 1963 the Ngos became embroiled in a fatal quarrel with the Buddhist leadership. Strikes and demonstrations by Buddhists in Saigon and Hue were met with violence by the army and Nhu's security forces and resulted in numerous arrests. The following month a Buddhist monk, Thich Quang Duc, publicly doused himself with gasoline and set himself ablaze as a protest against Diem's repression. Sensational photographs of that event were on the front pages of major American newspapers the following morning.

By now many students and members of the professional classes in South

Buddhist monk Thich Quang Duc sets himself on fire to protest the repressive regime of South Vietnamese President Ngo Dinh Diem in Saigon, South Vietnam, 1963. Keystone/Hulton Archive/Getty Images

Vietnamese cities had joined the Buddhists. After a series of brutal raids by government forces on Buddhist pagodas in August, a group of South Vietnamese generals secretly approached the U.S. government to determine how Washington might react to a coup to remove Diem. The U.S. reply was far from discouraging, but it was not until November, after further deterioration in Diem's relations with Washington, that the generals felt ready to move. On November 1, ARVN units seized control of Saigon, disarmed Nhu's security forces, and occupied the presidential palace. The American attitude was officially neutral, but the U.S. embassy maintained contact with the dissident generals while making no move to aid the Ngos, who were captured and murdered by the army.

Diem's death was followed by Kennedy's less than three weeks later. With respect to Vietnam, the assassinated president left his successor, Lyndon B. Johnson, a legacy of indecision, half-measures, and gradually increasing involvement. Kennedy had relished Cold War challenges; Johnson did not. A veteran politician and one of the ablest men ever to serve in the U.S. Senate, he had an ambitious domestic legislative agenda that he was determined to fight through Congress. Foreign policy crises would be at best a distraction and at worst a threat to his domestic reforms. Yet Johnson, like Kennedy, was also well aware of the high political costs of "losing" another country to communism. He shared the view of most of his advisers, many of them holdovers from the Kennedy administration, that Vietnam was also a key test of U.S. credibility and ability to keep its commitments to its allies. Consequently, Johnson was determined to do everything necessary to carry on the American commitment to South Vietnam. He replaced Harkins with Gen. William Westmoreland, a former superintendent of the U.S. Military Academy at West Point, and increased the number of U.S. military personnel still further—from 16,000 at the time of Kennedy's death in November 1963 to 23,000 by the end of 1964.

In Focus: The Media and the Vietnam War

Vietnam became a subject of large-scale news coverage only after American combat troops had been committed to the war in the spring of 1965. Prior to that time the number of American newsmen in Indochina had been small, less than two dozen even as late as 1964. At the height of the war, in 1968 there were about 450 accredited journalists of all nationalities in Vietnam. About 60 of these journalists were permanently based in Vietnam reporting for the U.S. wire services, the radio and television networks, and the major newspaper chains and news magazines. USMACV made military transportation readily available to newspeople and some took advantage of this to frequently venture into the field to get their stories first-hand. However many spent most of their time in Saigon and got their stories from Joint U.S. Public Affairs Office daily briefings known as "the five o'clock follies."

The Vietnam conflict was often referred to as the "first television war." Film from Vietnam was flown to Tokyo for quick developing and editing and then flown to the United States. Important stories could be transmitted directly by satellite from Tokyo. Although there was much discussion of the way in which television brought battles right into the living room, most television stories were filmed soon after a battle rather than in the midst of one and many were simply conventional news stories. In any case, most reporting about the war on nightly TV news shows were not film stories fresh from Vietnam but rather brief reports based on wire service dispatches and read by anchormen.

The role of the media in the Vietnam War is a subject of continuing controversy. Some believe that the media played a large role in the U.S. defeat. They argue that the media's tendency toward negative reporting helped to undermine support for the war in the United States while in Vietnam its uncensored coverage provided valuable information to the enemy. Many experts who have studied the role of the media have concluded, however, that prior to 1968 media reporting was generally supportive of the U.S. effort in Vietnam and that the increasingly skeptical and pessimistic tone of reporting after that year may merely have reflected, rather than created, similar feelings among the American public. In any case, American disillusionment with the war a product of many causes of which the media was only one. Political scientist Robert Muller has shown that what most undermined support for the war was simply the level of American casualties. The greater the increase in casualties, the lower the level of public support for the war.

THE GULF OF TONKIN

While Kennedy had at least the comforting illusion of progress in Vietnam (manufactured by Harkins and Diem), Johnson faced a starker picture of confusion, disunity, and muddle in Saigon and of a rapidly growing Viet Cong in the countryside. Those who had expected that the removal of the unpopular Ngos would lead to unity and a more vigorous prosecution of the war were swiftly disillusioned. A short-lived military junta was followed by a shaky dictatorship under Gen. Nguyen Khanh in January 1964.

In Hanoi, communist leaders, believing that victory was near, decided to make a major military commitment to winning the South. Troops and then entire units of the North Vietnamese Army (NVA) were sent south through Laos along the Ho Chi Minh Trail, which was by that time becoming a network of modern roads capable of handling truck traffic. Chinese communist leader Mao Zedong strongly supported the North Vietnamese offensive and promised to supply weapons and technical and logistical personnel. The Soviets, though now openly hostile to China, also decided to send aid to the North.

With the South Vietnamese government in disarray, striking a blow against the North seemed to the Americans to be the only option. U.S. advisers were already working with the South Vietnamese to carry out small maritime raids and parachute drops of agents, saboteurs, and commandos into North Vietnam. These achieved mixed success and in any case were too feeble to have any real impact. By the summer of 1964 the Pentagon had developed a plan for air strikes against selected targets in North Vietnam. The targets were designed both to inflict pain on the North and perhaps retard its support of the war in the South. To make clear the U.S. commitment to South Vietnam, some of Johnson's advisers urged him to seek a congressional resolution granting him broad authority to take action to safeguard U.S. interests in Southeast Asia. Johnson, however, preferred to shelve the controversial issue of Vietnam until after the November election.

However, an unexpected development in August 1964 altered that timetable. On August 2 the destroyer USS *Maddox* was attacked by North Vietnamese torpedo boats while on electronic surveillance patrol in the Gulf of Tonkin. The preceding day, patrol boats of the South Vietnamese navy had carried out clandestine raids on the islands of Hon Me and Hon Nieu just off the coast of North Vietnam, and the North Vietnamese may have assumed that the *Maddox* was involved. In any case, the U.S. destroyer suffered no damage, and the North Vietnamese boats were driven off by gunfire from the *Maddox* and from aircraft based on a nearby carrier.

President Johnson reacted to news of the attack by announcing that the U.S. Navy would continue patrols in the gulf and by sending a second destroyer, the *Turner Joy*, to join the *Maddox*. On the night of August 4 the two ships reported a second attack by torpedo boats. Although the captain of the *Maddox* soon cautioned that evidence for the second incident was inconclusive, Johnson and his advisers chose to believe those who insisted that a second attack had indeed taken place. The president ordered retaliatory air strikes against North Vietnamese naval bases, and he requested congressional support for a broad resolution authorizing him to take whatever action he deemed necessary to deal with future threats to U.S. forces or U.S. allies in Southeast Asia. The measure, soon dubbed the Gulf of Tonkin Resolution, passed the Senate and House overwhelmingly on August 7. Few who voted for the resolution were aware of the doubts concerning the second attack, and even fewer knew of the connection between the North Vietnamese attacks and U.S.-sponsored raids in the North or that the *Maddox* was on an intelligence mission. Although what many came to see as Johnson's deceptions would cause problems later, the immediate result of the president's actions was to remove Vietnam as an issue from the election campaign. In November Johnson was reelected by a landslide.

In Focus: Gulf of Tonkin Resolution

The Gulf of Tonkin Resolution was put before the U.S. Congress by Johnson on Aug. 5, 1964. Johnson's assertion was that this resolution was in reaction to two allegedly unprovoked attacks by North Vietnamese torpedo boats on the destroyers Maddox *and* Turner Joy *of the U.S. Seventh Fleet in the Gulf of Tonkin on August 2 and August 4, respectively. Its stated purpose was to approve and support the determination of the president, as commander in chief, in taking all necessary measures to repel any armed attack against the forces of the United States and to prevent further aggression in the region. It also declared that the maintenance of international peace and security in Southeast Asia was vital to American interests and to world peace.*

Both houses of Congress passed the resolution on August 7, the House of Representatives by 414 votes to nil, and the Senate by a vote of 88 to 2. The resolution served as the principal constitutional authorization for the subsequent vast escalation of the United States' military involvement in the Vietnam War. Several years later, as the American public became increasingly disillusioned with the Vietnam War, many congressmen came to see the resolution as giving the president a blanket power to wage war without congressional approval or oversight. Thus, the resolution was repealed in 1970.

In 1995 Vo Nguyen Giap, who had been North Vietnam's military commander during the Vietnam War, acknowledged the August 2 attack on the Maddox *but denied that the Vietnamese had launched another attack on August 4, as the Johnson administration had claimed at the time.*

THE UNITED STATES ENTERS THE WAR

In the time that passed between the Gulf of Tonkin Resolution and the U.S. presidential election in November 1964, the situation in Vietnam had changed for the worse. Beginning in September, the Khanh government was succeeded by a bewildering array of cliques and coalitions, some of which stayed in power less than a month. In the countryside even the best ARVN units seemed incapable of defeating the main forces of the Viet Cong. The communists were now deliberately targeting U.S. military personnel and bases, beginning with a mortar attack on the U.S. air base at Bien Hoa near Saigon in November.

Many of Johnson's advisers now began to argue for some sort of retaliation against the North. Air attacks against North Vietnam, they argued, would boost the morale of the shaky South Vietnamese and reassure them of continuing American commitment. They would also make Hanoi "pay a price" for its war against Saigon, and they might actually reduce the ability of the North to supply men and matériel for the Viet Cong military effort in the South. Except for Undersecretary of State George Ball, all the president's civilian aides and principal military advisers believed in the efficacy of a bombing campaign; they differed only as to how it should be conducted. The military favoured a short and sharp campaign intended to cripple the North's war-making capabilities. On the other hand, National Security Adviser McGeorge Bundy and Assistant Secretary of Defense John McNaughton argued for a series of graduated air attacks that would become progressively more damaging until the North Vietnamese decided that the cost of waging war in the South was too high. Within the administration, both Ball and Vice Pres. Hubert H. Humphrey warned the president that a major bombing campaign would likely lead only to further American commitment and political problems at home. But Johnson was more concerned with the immediate need to take action in order to halt the slide in Saigon. In mid-February, without public announcement, the United States began a campaign of sustained air strikes against the North that were code-named Rolling Thunder.

Pres. Lyndon B. Johnson (left) *meets in the White House with his Secretary of Defense, Robert S. McNamara* (right), *1963.* Stan Wayman/Time & Life Pictures/Getty Images

The bombing campaign followed the graduated path outlined by Bundy but was steadily expanded to include more targets and more frequent attacks. It was closely directed from the White House in order to avoid provoking the Chinese or Soviets through such actions as attacking ports where Soviet ships might be docked or hitting targets near the Chinese border. Yet it was soon apparent that the bombing would have little direct impact on the struggle in South Vietnam, where the communists appeared to be gaining ground inexorably. By mid-March Westmoreland and the Joint Chiefs of Staff were advising the White House that the United States would have to commit its own troops for combat if it wished to forestall a communist victory in Vietnam. Unhappy memories of the Korean War, where U.S. troops had been bogged down in costly indecisive fighting for three years, had made Johnson and his predecessors reluctant to send soldiers to fight in Asia. However, the choice now confronting the president appeared to be between committing troops or enduring outright defeat.

By June 1965 Westmoreland was predicting the likely collapse of the South Vietnamese army, and he recommended the rapid dispatch of U.S. troops to undertake offensive missions against the Viet Cong and North Vietnamese anywhere in South Vietnam. Secretary of Defense Robert S. McNamara, on a mission to Vietnam in early July, confirmed the need for additional forces. In late July Johnson took the final steps that would commit the United States to full-scale war in Vietnam: he authorized the dispatch of 100,000 troops immediately and an additional 100,000 in 1966. The president publicly announced his decisions at a news conference at the end of July. There was no declaration of war—not even an address to Congress—and no attempt to put the country on a war footing economically. The National Guard and military reserves were not called to active service, even though such a measure had long been part of the military's mobilization plans.

FIREPOWER COMES TO NAUGHT

Although Johnson and his advisers had painstakingly examined the question of committing military forces to Vietnam—how many should be sent and when—they had given little thought to the question of what the troops might do once they arrived. In contrast to the tightly controlled air war in the North, conduct of the ground war in the South was largely left to the leadership of General Westmoreland. Westmoreland commanded all U.S. operations in the South, but he was reluctant to press for a unified U.S. and South Vietnamese command despite the questionable capabilities of many South Vietnamese generals. Instead, the two allies depended on "coordination" and a continuation of the existing advisory relationship, with every

South Vietnamese army unit larger than a company having its complement of U.S. advisers. At the top of the hierarchy, Westmoreland himself served as senior adviser to the chief of the Vietnamese Joint General Staff, Gen. Cao Van Vien. The chronic political instability in Saigon seemed finally to have abated with the installation in February 1965 of a government headed by the army general Nguyen Van Thieu as head of state and air force general Nguyen Cao Ky as prime minister. This arrangement, backed by most of the top military commanders, lasted until 1968, when Ky was eased out of power, leaving Thieu in sole control.

Whatever the status of the South Vietnamese forces, they were clearly relegated to a secondary role as U.S. troops and equipment poured into the country. To support these forces, the Americans constructed an enormous logistical infrastructure that included four new jet-capable air bases with 10,000-foot (3,048 km) runways, six new deepwater ports, 75 tactical air bases, 26 hospitals, and more than 10,000,000 square feet (929,000 sq metres) of warehousing. By the fall of 1965, U.S. Marines and soldiers had clashed with NVA and VC main-force troops in bloody battles on the Batangan Peninsula south of Da Nang and in the Ia Drang valley in the central highlands. The U.S. forces employed their full panoply of firepower, including air strikes, artillery, armed helicopters, and even B-52 bombers, to inflict enormous losses on the enemy. Yet the communists believed they had more than held their own in these battles, and they were encouraged by the fact that they could easily reoccupy any areas they might have lost once the Americans pulled out.

Westmoreland's basic assumption was that U.S. forces, with their enormous and superior firepower, could best be employed in fighting the enemy's strongest units in the jungles and mountains, away from heavily populated areas. Behind this "shield" provided by the Americans, the South Vietnamese army and security forces could take on local Viet Cong elements and proceed with the job of reasserting government control in the countryside. Meanwhile, the regular forces of the Viet Cong and the NVA would continue to suffer enormous casualties at the hands of massive U.S. firepower. Eventually, went the argument, the communists would reach the point where they would no longer be able to replace their losses on the battlefield. Having been ground down on the battlefield, they would presumably agree to a favourable peace settlement.

That point seemed very distant to most Americans as the war continued into 1966 and 1967. Washington declared that the war was being won, but American casualties continued to mount, and much of what the public could see of the war on television appeared confusing if not futile. Because Westmoreland's strategy was based on attrition, one of the ways to measure progress was to track the number of enemy killed. The resultant "body count," which was supposed to be carried

U.S. soldiers on a search-and-destroy patrol in Phuoc Tuy province, South Vietnam, June 1966. U.S. Army photograph

out by troops during or immediately after combat, soon became notorious for inaccuracy and for the tendency of U.S. commanders to exaggerate the figures.

In the provinces just north and east of Saigon, some large-scale operations such as Cedar Falls and Junction City, involving up to a thousand U.S. troops supported by hundreds of sorties by helicopters and fighter-bombers, were mounted to destroy communist base areas and supplies. Though yielding large quantities of captured weapons and supplies, they were ultimately indecisive. The U.S. forces involved in these operations would invariably withdraw when they had completed their sweeps and in due course the Viet Cong and NVA would return. In order to deny the NVA and Viet Cong the use of dense forest to conceal their movements and to hide their supply lines and bases, the U.S. Air Force sprayed millions of gallons of a herbicide called Agent Orange along the Vietnamese border with Laos and Cambodia, in areas northwest of Saigon, and along major waterways. Agent Orange was effective in killing vegetation, but only at the price of causing considerable ecological damage to Vietnam and of exposing thousands of people—both Vietnamese civilians and combatants on both sides of the conflict—to potentially toxic chemicals that would later cause serious, and sometimes fatal, health problems.

Along the DMZ separating North and South Vietnam, the Americans established a string of fortified bases extending from just north of Quang Tri on the South China Sea westward to the Laotian border. These bases were part of a system that also included electronic warning devices, minefields, and infrared detectors designed to check infiltration or outright invasion from the North. The North Vietnamese, pleased to find that the strong-point obstacle system was within range of their artillery, carried out periodic attacks by fire and ground forces against U.S. outposts at Con Thien, Gio Linh, Camp Carroll, and Khe Sanh.

These larger engagements attracted most of the public's attention, but they were not in fact typical of the war in South

In Focus: Agent Orange

Agent Orange is a mixture of herbicides that U.S. military forces sprayed in Vietnam from 1962 to 1971 during the Vietnam War for the dual purpose of defoliating forest areas that might conceal Viet Cong and North Vietnamese forces and destroying crops that might feed the enemy. The defoliant, sprayed from low-flying aircraft, consisted of approximately equal amounts of the unpurified butyl esters of 2,4-dichlorophenoxyacetic acid (2,4-D), and 2,4,5-trichlorophenoxyacetic acid (2,4,5-T). Agent Orange also contained small, variable proportions of 2,3,7,8-tetrachlorodibenzo-p-dioxin—commonly called "dioxin"—which is a by-product of the manufacture of 2,4,5-T and is toxic even in minute quantities. About 13 million gallons of Agent Orange—containing about 375 pounds of dioxin—were dropped on Vietnam. Agent Orange was one of several herbicides used in Vietnam, the others including Agents White, Purple, Blue, Pink, and Green. The names derived from colour-coded bands painted around storage drums holding the herbicides.

Among the Vietnamese, exposure to Agent Orange is considered to be the cause of an abnormally high incidence of miscarriages, skin diseases, cancers, birth defects, and congenital malformations (often extreme and grotesque) dating from the 1970s.

Many U.S., Australian, and New Zealand servicemen who suffered long exposure to Agent Orange in Vietnam later developed a number of cancers and other health disorders. Despite the difficulty of establishing conclusive proof that their claims were valid, U.S. veterans brought a class-action lawsuit against seven herbicide makers that produced Agent Orange for the U.S. military. The suit was settled out of court with the establishment of a $180,000,000 fund to compensate some 250,000 claimants and their families. Separately, the U.S. Department of Veterans Affairs awarded compensation to about 1,800 veterans of the Vietnam conflict.

Vietnam. Most "battles" of the war were sharp, very brief engagements between units of fewer than 200 men. Many of these lasted only a few hours, often only a few minutes, but nevertheless could result in heavy casualties. Overall, communist casualties far outnumbered U.S. casualties, but the North Vietnamese never came close to depleting their manpower as Westmoreland suggested they would. In any case, the communists could, when necessary, ease the pressure on themselves by withdrawing their forces to sanctuaries in nearby Laos, Cambodia, and North Vietnam. Thus, Hanoi, not Washington, largely controlled the tempo of the ground war.

Like the ground war in the South, the air campaign against the North continued to grow in scope and destructiveness but remained indecisive. By the end of 1966, the United States had dropped more bombs on North Vietnam than it had dropped on Japan during World War II and more than it had dropped during the entire Korean War. Yet the bombing seemed to have little impact on the communists' ability to carry on the war. North Vietnam was primarily an agricultural country with few industries to destroy. Many of the necessities of Hanoi's war effort came directly from China and the Soviet Union, which competed with each other to demonstrate support for Ho Chi Minh's "heroic" war against U.S. imperialism. The Soviets provided an estimated 1.8 billion rubles in military and economic aid and sent 3,000 military advisers and technicians along with sophisticated weapons to the North. China spent an estimated $2 billion in assisting Hanoi; at the height of its effort, it had more than 300,000 engineering, medical, and antiaircraft artillery troops in the Democratic Republic of Vietnam. Even when bombing knocked out more than 80 percent of the North's petroleum-storage facilities during the summer of 1966, the Central Intelligence Agency (CIA) reported no discernible shortages of petroleum or disruption of transportation. While the air raids continued, North Vietnam progressively strengthened its air defenses with the help of the latest radars, antiaircraft guns, missiles, and modern jet fighters supplied by the Soviets and Chinese. By the end of 1966 the United States had already lost almost 500 aircraft and hundreds of air crewmen killed or held as prisoners of war.

In Focus: B-52

The B-52, or Stratofortress, was a U.S. long-range heavy bomber. It was designed by the Boeing Company in 1948, first flown in 1952, and first delivered for military service in 1955. Though originally intended to be an atomic-bomb carrier capable of reaching the Soviet Union, it has proved adaptable to a number of missions, and some B-52s are expected to remain in service well into the

21st century. The B-52 has a wingspan of 185 feet (56 metres) and a length of 160 feet 10.9 inches (49 metres). It is powered by eight jet engines mounted under the wings in four twin pods. The plane's maximum speed at 55,000 feet is Mach 0.9 (595 miles, or 957 kilometres, per hour); at only a few hundred feet above the ground, it can fly at Mach 0.5 (375 miles, or 603 kilometres, per hour). It originally carried a crew of six, its sole defensive armament being a remotely controlled gun turret in the tail. In 1991 the gun was eliminated and the crew reduced to five.

Between 1952 and 1962, Boeing built 744 B-52s in a total of eight versions, designated A through H. The B-52A was primarily a test version; it was the B-52B that entered service in the U.S. Strategic Air Command as a long-range nuclear bomber. The C through F versions, their range extended by larger fuel capacity and in-flight refueling equipment, were adapted to carry tons of conventional bombs in their bomb bay and on pylons under the wings. Beginning in 1965, B-52Ds and Fs flying from bases on Guam and Okinawa and in Thailand carried out highly destructive bombing campaigns over North and South Vietnam. The B-52G, also used to attack North Vietnam, was given even greater fuel capacity and was equipped to launch a number of air-to-surface and antiship missiles.

Boeing B-52 Stratofortress, a U.S. high-altitude bomber, dropping a stream of bombs over Vietnam. U.S. Air Force

TET BRINGS THE WAR HOME

By 1967 growing numbers of Americans were becoming increasingly dissatisfied with the war. Some, especially students, intellectuals, academics, and clergymen, opposed the war on moral grounds, pointing out that large numbers of civilians in both the North and the South were becoming the chief victims of the war. War protesters asserted that the United States was in reality supporting a corrupt and oppressive dictatorship in Saigon.

University and college campus protests became common, and youthful picketers sometimes ringed the White House chanting, "Hey, hey, LBJ, how many kids did you kill today?" In October 1967 at least 35,000 demonstrators staged a mass protest outside the Pentagon. Many more Americans, not part of any peace movement, opposed the war because of the increasing American casualties and the lack of evidence that the United States was winning. Still other Americans believed that Johnson was not doing what was necessary to win the war and was obliging the military to fight "with one hand tied behind its back." By the summer of 1967 less than 50 percent of polled citizens said they supported the president's conduct of the war.

In Hanoi the communist leadership was also becoming impatient with the progress of the war. Although pleased with their ability to hold their own against the more numerous and better-armed Americans and their South Vietnamese allies, they were aware that the United States showed no sign of giving up its hopes of victory and indeed had continued to pour more troops into Vietnam. In the summer of 1967 the communists decided on a bold stroke that would cripple the Saigon government and destroy once and for all American expectations of success. Their plan was to launch simultaneous military attacks at cities, towns, and military installations, combined with popular uprisings throughout the country. The "general offensive/general uprising" was scheduled to occur during the Vietnamese lunar New Year festival, or Tet, early in 1968.

To distract attention from their preparations and attract U.S. forces away from the large cities, the communists launched diversionary attacks in October 1967 against the important but isolated town of Dak To in the central highlands and against Loc Ninh on the route to Saigon. Finally, beginning in late January 1968, two North Vietnamese divisions began a prolonged offensive against the Marine base at Khe Sanh, in the northwest corner of South Vietnam near the Laotian border. Like other bases along the DMZ, Khe Sanh was within range of artillery in North Vietnam, and, beginning on January 21, the North Vietnamese unleashed a heavy barrage against it. News reports repeatedly drew comparisons between Khe Sanh and the siege of the French fortress at Dien Bien Phu. Both the president and General Westmoreland were convinced that Khe Sanh was the enemy's main objective and that signs of a communist buildup in the urban areas were merely a diversion.

Exactly the opposite was the case. On January 31, while approximately 50,000 U.S. and South Vietnamese troops were occupied in defending or supporting Khe Sanh and other DMZ bases, the communists launched a sweeping offensive throughout South Vietnam. They attacked 36 of 44 provincial capitals, 64 district capitals, five of the six major cities, and more than two dozen airfields and bases. Westmoreland's Saigon headquarters came under attack, and a VC squad even penetrated the compound of the U.S. embassy. In Hue, the former imperial Vietnamese capital, communist troops seized control of more than half the city and held it for nearly three weeks.

Although taken by surprise, U.S. and South Vietnamese forces struck back quickly against the often poorly coordinated attacks. With the exception of Hue, the communists were unable to hold any town or base for more than a day or two, and their forces suffered extremely heavy casualties. South Vietnamese soldiers, often defending their homes and families, fought surprisingly well, and nowhere did the population rise up to support the Viet Cong. Indeed, so destructive were some communist attacks that many in the local population, while still disliking the Saigon government, became far less supportive of the Viet Cong.

U.S. and South Vietnamese troops may have recovered quickly, but that was not true of Americans at home. The Tet Offensive sent shock waves throughout the United States, startling those who had believed the White House's claims that victory was near and convincing those with doubts that the situation was even worse than they had imagined. Television coverage of the destructive fighting in Saigon and Hue was extensive and graphic and left many with the impression that the United States and its ally were in desperate straits. Many in Washington still expected a major battle at Khe Sanh or further large communist attacks elsewhere.

As criticism of Johnson's leadership by political leaders and the media mounted, the public was shocked to read in a *New York Times* headline story on March 10 that General Westmoreland had requested 206,000 additional troops for Vietnam. This news was widely interpreted as confirmation that the U.S. situation in Vietnam must be dire indeed. In fact, Westmoreland, assessing the Tet attacks as a serious defeat for the communists, wanted the additional troops to deliver a knockout blow against the weakened enemy. He had been encouraged to request the troops by the Joint Chiefs of Staff, who saw this as an opportunity finally to mobilize the reserves and reconstitute a strategic reserve for use in contingencies other than Vietnam. The president turned the request over to his new secretary of defense, Clark Clifford, who had replaced a disillusioned McNamara a few weeks before. Clifford soon decided not only that massive reinforcements were ill-advised but that the entire war effort had to be reassessed.

Primary Document: J. William Fulbright's "The Arrogance of Power" Speech

During televised hearings of the Senate Foreign Relations Committee early in 1966, Chairman J. William Fulbright warned that the war in Vietnam might lead to armed conflict with China. Thus, he urged that the United States halt the bombing of North Vietnam, review the entire military situation, and begin peace talks. The administration paid little heed, and in the speech reprinted here in part, delivered at Johns Hopkins University School of Advanced International Studies on April 21 of that year, Fulbright emphasized the importance of responsible dissent. On June 20 he repeated his warning during his committee's hearings on NATO policy, again declaring that the U.S. could not act as "policeman for the world."

New York Times Magazine, *May 15, 1966: "The Fatal Arrogance of Power."*

The question that I find intriguing is whether a nation so extraordinarily endowed as the United States can overcome that arrogance of power which has afflicted, weakened, and, in some cases, destroyed great nations in the past. The causes of the malady are a mystery but its recurrence is one of the uniformities of history: Power tends to confuse itself with virtue and a great nation is peculiarly susceptible to the idea that its power is a sign of God's favor, conferring upon it a special responsibility for other nations—to make them richer and happier and wiser, to remake them, that is, in its own shining image.

Power also tends to take itself for omnipotence. Once imbued with the idea of a mission, a great nation easily assumes that it has the means as well as the duty to do God's work. The Lord, after all, surely would not choose you as His agent and then deny you the sword with which to work His will. German soldiers in the First World War wore belt buckles imprinted with the words "Gott mit uns." It was approximately under this kind of infatuation—an exaggerated sense of power and an imaginary sense of mission—that the Athenians attacked Syracuse and Napoleon and then Hitler invaded Russia. In plain words, they overextended their commitments and they came to grief.

My question is whether America can overcome the fatal arrogance of power. My hope and my belief are that it can, that it has the human resources to accomplish what few, if any, great nations have ever accomplished before: to be confident but also tolerant and rich but also generous; to be willing to teach but also willing to learn; to be powerful but also wise. I believe that America is capable of all of these things; I also believe it is falling short of them. Gradually but unmistakably we are succumbing to the arrogance of power. In so doing we are not living up to our capacity and promise; the measure of our falling short is the measure of the patriot's duty of dissent . . .

Some of our superpatriots assume that any war the United States fights is a just war, if not indeed a holy crusade, but history does not sustain their view. No reputable historian would deny that the United States has fought some wars which were unjust, unnecessary, or both—I would suggest the War of 1812, the Civil War, and the Spanish-American War as examples. In a historical frame of reference it seems to me logical and proper to question the wisdom of our present military involvement in Asia.

I fail to understand what is reprehensible about trying to make moral distinctions between one war and another—between, for example, resistance to Hitler and intervention in Vietnam.

From the time of Grotius to the drafting of the United Nations Charter, international lawyers have tried to distinguish between "just wars" and "unjust wars." . . .

In the past twenty-five years . . . the Senate's constitutional powers of advice and consent have atrophied into what is widely regarded—though never asserted—to be a duty to give prompt consent with a minimum of advice . . . on Aug. 5, 1964, the Congress received an urgent request from President Johnson for the immediate adoption of a joint resolution regarding Southeast Asia. On August 7, after perfunctory committee hearings and a brief debate, the Congress, with only two senators dissenting, adopted the resolution, authorizing the President "to take all necessary steps, including the use of armed force," against aggression in Southeast Asia.

The joint resolution was a blank check signed by the Congress in an atmosphere of urgency that seemed at the time to preclude debate. Since its adoption, the administration has converted the Vietnamese conflict from a civil war in which some American advisers were involved to a major international war in which the principal fighting unit is an American army of 250,000 men. Each time that senators have raised questions about successive escalations of the war, we have had the blank check of Aug. 7, 1964, waved in our faces as supposed evidence of the overwhelming support of the Congress for a policy in Southeast Asia which, in fact, has been radically changed since the summer of 1964 . . .

I believe that the public hearings on Vietnam, by bringing before the American people a variety of opinions and disagreements pertaining to the war, and perhaps by helping to restore a degree of balance between the executive and the Congress, have done far more to strengthen the country than to weaken it. The hearings have been criticized on the ground that they conveyed an "image" of the United States as divided over the war. Since the country obviously is divided, what was conveyed was a fact rather than an image.

Primary Document: Lyndon B. Johnson's "The Obligation of Power" Speech

By 1966 the controversy caused by the war in Vietnam had produced a serious division within the Democratic Party, with Fulbright leading the attacks by some of his fellow Democrats on the President's policy. At his Johns Hopkins University School of Advanced International Studies address, Fulbright had charged that the U.S. involvement in Vietnam was largely the result of an exercise of executive authority, and had asserted that America was succumbing to "that arrogance of power which has afflicted, weakened, and, in some cases, destroyed great nations in the past." Johnson replied in the following speech at the Woodrow Wilson School of Public and International Affairs of Princeton University, on May 11, 1966.

Vital Speeches of the Day, *June 1, 1966: "The Need for Scholars."*

Now, as we enter the final third of this century, we are engaged again today—yes, once again—with the question of whether democracy can do the job. Many fears of former years no longer seem so relevant. Neither Congress nor our Supreme Court indicate to me any signs of becoming rubber stamps to the executive. Moreover, the executive shows no symptoms of callous indifference to the ills that we must cure if we are to preserve our vitality. State and local governments are more alive and more involved than they were thirty years ago, and our nation's private enterprise has grown many times—many times over—in both size and vitality.

Abroad we can best measure American involvement, whatever our successes and failures, by one simple proposition: not one single country where America has helped mount a major effort to resist aggression, from France, to Greece, to Korea, to Vietnam—not one single country where we have helped today has a government servile to outside interests.

There is a reason for this which I believe goes to the very heart of our society. The exercise of power in this century has meant for all of us in the United States not arrogance but agony. We have used our power not willingly and recklessly ever but always reluctantly and with restraint. Unlike nations in the past with vast power at their disposal, the United States of America has never sought to crush the autonomy of her neighbors. We have not been driven by blind militarism down courses of devastating aggression, nor have we followed the ancient and conceited philosophy of the noble lie that some men are by nature meant to be slaves to others.

As I look upon America this morning from this great platform—this platform of one of her greatest universities—I see instead a nation whose might is not her master but her servant. I see a nation conscious of lessons so recently learned that security and aggression as well as peace and war must be the concerns of our foreign policy; that a great power influences the world just as surely when it withdraws its strength as when it exercises its strength; that aggression must be deterred where possible and met early when undertaken; that the application of military force when it becomes necessary must be for limited purposes and must be tightly controlled.

Surely it is not a paranoiac vision of America's place in the world to recognize that freedom is still indivisible, still has adversaries whose challenge must be answered. Today, of course, as we meet here, that challenge is sternest at the moment in Southeast Asia. Yet there, as elsewhere, our great power is also tempered by great restraint.

What nation has announced such limited objectives or such willingness to remove its military presence once those objectives are secured and achieved? What nation has spent the lives of its sons and vast sums of its fortune to provide the people of a small thriving country the chance to elect the course that we might not ourselves choose?

The aims for which we struggle are aims which in the ordinary course of affairs men of the intellectual world applaud and serve—the principle of choice over coercion, the defense of the weak against the strong and the aggressive, the right—the right—of a young and frail nation to develop free from the interference of her neighbors, the ability of a people however inexperienced and however different and however diverse to fashion a society consistent with their own traditions and values and aspirations.

Other studies, no matter how important, must not now detract the man of learning from the misfortunes of freedom in Southeast Asia. While men may talk of the search for peace and the pursuit of peace, we really know that peace is not something to be discovered suddenly; it's not a thing to be caught and contained. Because peace must be built step by painful patient step. And the building will take the best work of the world's best men and women.

It will take men whose cause is not the cause of one nation but whose cause is the cause of all nations, men whose enemies are not other men but the historic foes of mankind. I hope that many of you will serve in this public service for our world.

DE-ESCALATION, NEGOTIATION, AND VIETNAMIZATION

With the aid of some of the president's other advisers and elder statesmen from the Democratic Party, Clifford succeeded in persuading Johnson that the present number of U.S. troops in Vietnam (about 550,000) should constitute an upper limit and that Johnson, as chief executive, should make a dramatic gesture for peace. In a nationally televised speech on March 31, Johnson announced that he was "taking the first step to de-escalate the conflict" by halting the bombing of North Vietnam (except in the areas near the DMZ). He also announced that the United States was prepared to send representatives to any forum to seek a negotiated end to the war. He followed this surprising declaration with news that he did not intend to seek reelection that year.

Three days later Hanoi announced that it was prepared to talk to the Americans. Discussions began in Paris on May 13 but led nowhere. Hanoi insisted that, before serious negotiations could begin, the United States would have to halt its bombing of the rest of Vietnam. Meanwhile, fighting continued at a high intensity. The communist high command determined to follow the Tet attacks with two more waves in May and August. At the same time, Westmoreland ordered his commanders to "keep maximum pressure" on the communist forces in the South, which he believed had been seriously weakened by their losses at Tet. The result was the fiercest fighting of the war. In the eight weeks following Johnson's speech, 3,700 Americans were killed in Vietnam and 18,000 wounded. The communists were reported by Westmoreland's headquarters as having lost about 43,000. The ARVN's losses were not recorded, but they were usually twice that of the Americans.

In October the Soviets secretly informed Washington that the North Vietnamese would be willing to halt their attacks across the DMZ and begin serious negotiation with the United States and South Vietnam if the United States halted all bombing of the North. Assured by his military advisers that such a halt would not adversely affect the military situation, Johnson announced the cessation of bombing on the last day of October. The bombing halt achieved no breakthrough but rather brought on a period of prolonged bickering between the United States and its South Vietnamese ally about the terms and procedures to govern the talks. By the time South Vietnam joined the talks, Richard M. Nixon had been elected the next U.S. president.

Nixon and his close adviser on foreign affairs, Henry A. Kissinger, recognized that the United States could not win a military victory in Vietnam. Thus, they insisted that the war could be ended only by an "honourable" settlement that would afford South Vietnam a reasonable chance of survival. A hasty American withdrawal, they argued, would undermine U.S. credibility throughout the world. Although public opinion of the war in the United

Primary Document: Lyndon B. Johnson's "Withdrawal Speech"

As 1967 drew to a close it was evident that the Vietnam War was causing serious divisions in the United States. Public disenchantment with the conduct of the war and with the war itself was becoming more widespread. Then on March 31 Pres. Lyndon B. Johnson made an address to the nation on Vietnam policy, in which he announced a cutback in the bombing of North Vietnam and made another offer to start peace negotiations with the Hanoi regime. But the most startling—and totally unanticipated—portion of the speech was his closing announcement that he would not be a candidate for reelection. This statement, coupled with the fact that North Vietnam did accept the offer to begin talks toward a negotiated settlement, radically changed the political picture in the United States in an election year. Portions of President Johnson's address are reprinted below.

Chicago Sun-Times, *April 1, 1968.*

Tonight I want to speak to you on peace in Vietnam and Southeast Asia.

No other question so preoccupies our people. No other dream so absorbs the 250 million human beings who live in that part of the world. No other goal motivates American policy in Southeast Asia.

For years, representatives of our government and others have traveled the world—seeking to find a basis for peace talks. Since last September, they have carried the offer I made public at San Antonio.

It was this: that the United States would stop its bombardment of North Vietnam when that would lead promptly to productive discussions—and that we would assume that North Vietnam would not take military advantage of our restraint.

Hanoi denounced this offer, both privately and publicly. Even while the search for peace was going on, North Vietnam rushed their preparations for a savage assault on the people, the government, and the allies of South Vietnam.

Their attack—during the Tet holidays—failed to achieve its principal objectives. It did not collapse the elected government of South Vietnam or shatter its Army—as the Communists had hoped. It did not produce a "general uprising" among the people of the cities. The Communists were unable to maintain control of any city. And they took very heavy casualties.

But they did compel the South Vietnamese and their allies to move certain forces from the countryside, into the cities. They caused widespread disruption and suffering. Their attacks, and the battles that followed, made refugees of half a million human beings . . .

Tonight, I renew the offer I made last August—to stop the bombardment of North Vietnam. We ask that talks begin promptly and that they be serious talks on the substance of peace. We assume that during those talks Hanoi would not take advantage of our restraint. We are prepared to move immediately toward peace through negotiations . . .

I call upon President Ho Chi Minh to respond positively and favorably to this new step toward peace.

But if peace does not come now through negotiations, it will come when Hanoi understands that our common resolve is unshakable and our common strength is invincible . . .

I believe that a peaceful Asia is far nearer to reality, because of what America has done in Vietnam. I believe that the men who endure the dangers of battle there are helping the entire world avoid far greater conflicts than this one.

The peace that will bring them home will come. Tonight I have offered the first in what I hope will be a series of mutual moves toward peace. I pray that it will not be rejected by the leaders of North Vietnam. I pray that they will accept it as a means by which the sacrifices of their own people may be ended. And I ask your support, my fellow citizens, for this effort to reach across the battlefield toward an early peace . . .

Fifty-two months and ten days ago in a moment of tragedy and trauma, the duties of this office fell upon me. I asked then for "your help and God's" that we might continue America on its course, binding up our wounds, healing our history, moving forward in new unity to clear the American agenda and to keep the American commitment for all our people. United, we have kept that commitment, and united, we have enlarged that commitment.

Through all time to come, America will be a stronger nation, a more just society, a land of greater. opportunity and fulfillment because of what we have done together in these years of unparalleled achievement. Our reward will come in the life of freedom and peace and hope that our children will enjoy through ages ahead. What we won when all our people united must not now be lost in suspicion, distrust, and selfishness or politics among any of our people.

Believing this as I do, I have concluded that I should not permit the presidency to become involved in the partisan divisions that are developing in this political year. With America's sons in the field far away, with America's future under challenge here at home, with our hopes and the world's hopes for peace in the balance every day, I do not believe that I should devote an hour or a day of my time to any duties other than the awesome duties of this office, the presidency of your country.

Accordingly, I shall not seek and I will not accept the nomination of my party for another term as your President. But, let men everywhere know, however, that a strong and a confident, a vigilant America stands ready to seek an honorable peace and stands ready tonight to defend an honored cause, whatever the price, whatever the burden, whatever the sacrifice that duty may require.

Thank you for listening. Goodnight, and God bless all of you.

States made it impossible to commit more troops, Nixon was still confident he could end the war with a favourable settlement. He planned to achieve this through bringing pressure to bear from the Soviets and China, both of whom were eager to improve their relations with the United States, and through the threat of massive force against North Vietnam. To signal to Hanoi that he could still inflict punishment by air, the president decided to act on the proposal of Gen. Creighton Abrams, who had succeeded Westmoreland in July 1969, that the United States bomb the secret communist base areas in Cambodia near the Vietnamese border.

When the communists launched another wave of attacks in South Vietnam in early 1969, Nixon secretly ordered the bombing to proceed. Cambodian premier

Norodom Sihanouk, tired of his uninvited Vietnamese guests, had confidentially approved the attacks, and Hanoi was in no position to complain without revealing its own violation of Cambodia's neutrality. Although elaborate measures had been taken in Washington and Saigon to ensure that the air attacks be kept completely secret, the story broke in the *New York Times* in May of that year. Infuriated by this breach of security, Nixon began a series of measures to plug "leaks" of information; these became part of a system of illegal surveillance and burglary that eventually led to the infamous Watergate scandal of 1972.

In view of the surprisingly good performance of the South Vietnamese army at Tet, and responding to growing pressure in the United States to begin a withdrawal of U.S. troops, the Nixon administration decided to accelerate a program to provide South Vietnam with the high-quality weapons and training that would enable them gradually to take over sole responsibility for fighting the ground war—a program labeled Vietnamization. In June 1969 Nixon announced the withdrawal of 25,000 U.S. troops from Vietnam. In September he announced further troop withdrawals, and by March 1970 he was announcing the phased withdrawal of 150,000 troops over the next year. Abrams protested that the still inexperienced and incompletely trained ARVN could hardly take over the job at such a rapid pace. However, the withdrawals were enormously popular at home, and the White House soon found them politically indispensable.

Though popular at home, the withdrawals lowered the morale of the troops remaining in Vietnam by underlining the apparent pointlessness of the war. By 1970 signs of serious problems in morale and leadership were seemingly everywhere. These signs included increased drug abuse, more frequent and serious racial incidents, and even "fraggings," the murder or deliberate maiming of commissioned and noncommissioned officers by their own troops with fragmentation weapons such as hand grenades. News of the My Lai Massacre, a mass murder by U.S. soldiers of several hundred civilians in Quang Ngai province in 1968, became public at the end of 1969, further undermining convictions about the righteousness of the U.S. military effort in Vietnam. From 1965 to 1973, more than 30,000 U.S. military personnel either in Vietnam or in service related to Vietnam received dishonourable discharges for desertion (though only a small number of desertions actually took place on the battlefield). Another 10,000 deserters were still at large when the United States withdrew from the war in 1973; most of these took advantage of clemency programs offered under Pres. Gerald R. Ford in 1974 and Pres. Jimmy Carter in 1977. Also during the period 1965–73, about half a million men became "draft dodgers," illegally evading conscription into the armed forces or simply refusing to respond to their draft notices.

In Focus: My Lai Massacre

As many as 500 unarmed villagers were massacred by U.S. soldiers in the hamlet of My Lai on March 16, 1968, during the Vietnam War.

My Lai was located in the province of Quang Ngai, an area believed to be a stronghold of the Viet Cong and thus a focus of the U.S. military. After receiving word that Viet Cong were in the hamlet, a company of U.S. soldiers was sent there on a search-and-destroy mission. Although no armed Viet Cong were found, the soldiers nonetheless killed all the elderly men, women, and children they could find; few villagers survived. The incident was initially covered up by high-ranking army officers, but it was later made public by former soldiers. In the ensuing courts-martial, platoon leader Lieutenant William Calley was accused of directing the killings, and in 1971 he was convicted of premeditated murder and sentenced to life in prison; five other soldiers were tried and acquitted. Many, however, believed that Calley had been made a scapegoat, and in 1974 he was paroled. The massacre and other atrocities revealed during the trial divided the U.S. public and contributed to growing disillusionment with the war.

More than 200,000 men were charged with draft evasion and more than 8,000 convicted. Of those convicted, most were either offered clemency by Ford or pardoned by Carter.

THE UNITED STATES NEGOTIATES A WITHDRAWAL

While Vietnamization and troop withdrawals proceeded in Vietnam, the negotiations in Paris remained deadlocked. Kissinger secretly opened separate talks with high-level Vietnamese diplomats, but the two sides remained far apart. The Americans proposed a mutual withdrawal of both U.S. and North Vietnamese forces. However, Hanoi insisted on an unconditional U.S. withdrawal and on the replacement of the U.S.-backed regime of Nguyen Van Thieu by a neutral coalition government. Nixon considered using renewed bombing and a blockade of the North to coerce the communist leadership, but his military and intelligence experts advised him that such actions would not be likely to have a decisive effect. Furthermore, his political advisers worried about the impact of such actions on an American public eager to see continued de-escalation of the war.

Nixon consequently refrained from striking North Vietnam, but he could not resist the opportunity to intervene in Cambodia, where a pro-Western government under General Lon Nol had overthrown Sihanouk's neutralist regime in March 1970. Since that time, the new regime had attempted to force the communists out of their border sanctuaries. The North Vietnamese easily fended off the attacks of the Cambodian army and

Primary Document: Richard M. Nixon's "The Pursuit of Peace in Vietnam" Speech

Within the first month after taking office, Pres. Richard Nixon had decided that the only way to deal with the Vietnam War was through unilateral withdrawal of American combat troops, but not in such a way as to leave South Vietnam vulnerable to an immediate Communist takeover. In a television address to the nation on November 3, the President explained his policy to the public. The heart of it was the "Vietnamization plan" whereby the American withdrawal would be paced to allow for a strengthening of the South Vietnamese forces. Portions of Nixon's address are reprinted here.

Department of State Bulletin, Nov. 24, 1969.

Good evening, my fellow Americans: Tonight I want to talk to you on a subject of deep concern to all Americans and to many people in all parts of the world—the war in Vietnam . . .

Let me begin by describing the situation I found when I was inaugurated on January 20.

—The war had been going on for four years.

—31,000 Americans had been killed in action.

—The training program for the South Vietnamese was behind schedule.

—540,000 Americans were in Vietnam, with no plans to reduce the number.

—No progress had been made at the negotiations in Paris and the United States had not put forth a comprehensive peace proposal.

—The war was causing deep division at home and criticism from many of our friends, as well as our enemies, abroad.

In view of these circumstances there were some who urged that I end the war at once by ordering the immediate withdrawal of all American forces . . .

The defense of freedom is everybody's business—not just America's business. And it is particularly the responsibility of the people whose freedom is threatened. In the previous administration we Americanized the war in Vietnam. In this administration we are Vietnamizing the search for peace.

The policy of the previous administration not only resulted in our assuming the primary responsibility for fighting the war but, even more significantly, did not adequately stress the goal of strengthening the South Vietnamese so that they could defend themselves when we left.

The Vietnamization plan was launched following Secretary [of Defense Melvin R.] Laird's visit to Vietnam in March. Under the plan, I ordered first a substantial increase in the training and equipment of South Vietnamese forces.

In July, on my visit to Vietnam, I changed General Abrams' orders so that they were consistent with the objectives of our new policies. Under the new orders, the primary mission of our troops is to enable the South Vietnamese forces to assume the full responsibility for the security of South Vietnam.

Our air operations have been reduced by over 20 percent.

And now we have begun to see the results of this long-overdue change in American policy in Vietnam:

—After five years of Americans going into Vietnam, we are finally bringing American men home. By December 15, over 60,000 men will have been withdrawn from South Vietnam, including 20 percent of all of our combat forces.

—The South Vietnamese have continued to gain in strength. As a result, they have been able to take over combat responsibilities from our American troops.

Two other significant developments have occurred since this administration took office:

—Enemy infiltration, infiltration which is essential if they are to launch a major attack, over the last three months is less than 20 percent of what it was over the same period last year.

—Most important, United States casualties have declined during the last two months to the lowest point in three years.

Let me now turn to our program for the future.

We have adopted a plan which we have worked out in cooperation with the South Vietnamese for the complete withdrawal of all U.S. combat ground forces and their replacement by South Vietnamese forces on an orderly scheduled timetable. This withdrawal will be made from strength and not from weakness. As South Vietnamese forces become stronger, the rate of American withdrawal can become greater . . .

My fellow Americans, I am sure you can recognize from what I have said that we really only have two choices open to us if we want to end this war:

—I can order an immediate, precipitate withdrawal of all Americans from Vietnam without regard to the effects of that action.

—Or we can persist in our search for a just peace, through a negotiated settlement if possible or through continued implementation of our plan for Vietnamization if necessary—a plan in which we will withdraw all of our forces from Vietnam on a schedule in accordance with our program, as the South Vietnamese become strong enough to defend their own freedom.

I have chosen this second course. It is not the easy way. It is the right way. It is a plan which will end the war and serve the cause of peace, not just in Vietnam but in the Pacific and in the world . . .

I have chosen a plan for peace. I believe it will succeed.

If it does succeed, what the critics say now won't matter. If it does not succeed, anything I say then won't matter.

began to arm and support the Cambodian communist movement, known as the Khmer Rouge. Eager to support Lon Nol and destroy the sanctuaries, Nixon authorized a large sweep into the border areas by a U.S. and South Vietnamese force of 20,000 men. The allies captured enormous quantities of supplies and equipment but failed to trap any large enemy forces. In the United States, news of the Cambodian incursion triggered widespread protest and demonstrations. These became even more intense after National Guard troops opened fire on a crowd of protesters at Kent State University in Ohio, killing four students and wounding several others, on May 4. At hundreds of campuses, students "went on strike." Congress, meanwhile, repealed the Gulf of Tonkin Resolution.

In Focus: Kent State—May 4, 1970

No action of Pres. Richard Nixon's first term aroused such vehement response as the American invasion of Cambodia. Although the public at large seemed to support the venture, the President's April 30 speech proved to be the catalyst that revived the flagging antiwar movement on college and university campuses across the nation. The student disturbances were unprecedented in their ferocity. At Kent State University in Ohio the reaction culminated in a riot on May 2 in which the Reserve Officers' Training Corps (ROTC) building was burned down. The governor declared martial law and sent National Guard troops onto the campus. As the demonstrations continued on Monday, May 4, guardsmen suddenly opened fire on the protesters, killing four students and wounding eleven. The killings stunned the nation and gave greater impetus to a previously planned mass demonstration in Washington, D.C., on May 9. By May 10, 448 colleges and universities were on strike or closed. Official investigations as to exactly what had happened at Kent State were inconclusive, although the case was reopened by the Justice Department in 1973 for further study. The following selection reprints parts of the Report of the President's Commission on Campus Unrest. *The commission, under former Pennsylvania governor William Scranton, issued its report on Sept. 26, 1970.*

The Report of the President's Commission on Campus Unrest, *Washington, D.C., 1970.*

Kent State was a national tragedy. It was not, however, a unique tragedy. Only the magnitude of the student disorder and the extent of student deaths and injuries set it apart from similar occurrences on numerous other American campuses during the past few years. We must learn from the particular horror of Kent State and insure that it is never repeated.

The conduct of many students and nonstudent protestors at Kent State on the first four days of May 1970 was plainly intolerable. We have said in our report, and we repeat: Violence by students on or off the campus can never be justified by any grievance, philosophy, or political idea. There can be no sanctuary or immunity from prosecution on the campus. Criminal acts by students must be treated as such wherever they occur and whatever their purpose. Those who wrought havoc on the town of Kent, those who burned the ROTC building, those who attacked and stoned National Guardsmen, and all those who urged them on and applauded their deeds share the responsibility for the deaths and injuries of May 4.

The widespread student opposition to the Cambodian action and their general resentment of the National Guardsmen's presence on the campus cannot justify the violent and irresponsible actions of many students during the long weekend . . .

The May 4 rally began as a peaceful assembly on the Commons—the traditional site of student assemblies. Even if the Guard had authority to prohibit a peaceful gathering—a question that is at least debatable—the decision to disperse the noon rally was a serious error. The timing and manner of the dispersal were disastrous. Many students were legitimately in the area as they went to and from class. The rally was held during the crowded noontime luncheon period. The rally was peaceful, and there was no apparent impending violence. Only when the Guard attempted to disperse the rally did some students react violently . . .

The National Guardsmen on the Kent State campus were armed with loaded M-1 rifles, high-velocity weapons with a horizontal range of almost two miles. As they confronted the students, all that stood between a guardsman and firing was the flick of a thumb on the safety mechanism, and the pull of an index finger on the trigger. When firing began, the toll taken by these lethal weapons was disastrous . . .

Even if the guardsmen faced danger, it was not a danger that called for lethal force. The 61 shots by 28 guardsmen certainly cannot be justified. Apparently, no order to fire was given, and there was inadequate fire control discipline on Blanket Hill. The Kent State tragedy must mark the last time that, as a matter of course, loaded rifles are issued to guardsmen confronting student demonstrators.

Members of the National Guard in riot gear at a protest over the invasion of Cambodia at Kent State University in Kent, Ohio, May 4, 1970. Time & Life Pictures/Getty Images

By the summer of 1970 the White House was left with little more than Vietnamization and troop withdrawals as a way to end the war, given that Hanoi would not agree to mutual withdrawal. Vietnamization appeared to be proceeding smoothly, and American counterinsurgency experts had moved swiftly after Tet to help the South Vietnamese government to develop programs to root out the Viet Cong's underground government and establish control of the countryside. The Viet Cong, seriously weakened by losses in the 1968–69 offensives, now found themselves on the defensive in many areas. However, the limits of Vietnamization were soon demonstrated. In March 1971 a large ARVN attack into Laos, code-named Lam Son 719 and designed to interdict the Ho Chi Minh Trail, ended in heavy casualties and a disorderly retreat.

In the United States, large-scale demonstrations were now less common, but disillusionment with the war was more widespread than ever. One poll claimed that 71 percent of Americans believed the United States had "made a mistake" in sending troops to Vietnam and that 58 percent found the war "immoral." Discontent was particularly directed toward the selective service system, which had long been seen as unfairly conscripting young men from racial minorities and poor backgrounds while allowing more privileged men to defer conscription by enrolling in higher education. College deferments were limited in 1971, but by that time the military was calling up fewer conscripts each year. Nixon ended all draft calls in 1972, and in 1973 the draft was abolished in favour of an all-volunteer military.

Encouraged by their success in Laos, the Hanoi leadership launched an all-out invasion of the South on March 30, 1972, spearheaded by tanks and supported by artillery. South Vietnamese forces at first suffered staggering defeats, but Nixon, in an operation code-named Linebacker, unleashed U.S. air power against the North, mined Haiphong Harbour (the principal entry point for Soviet seaborne supplies), and ordered hundreds of U.S. aircraft into

In Focus: Pentagon Papers

The Pentagon Papers, which contain a history of the U.S. role in Indochina from World War II until May 1968, were commissioned in 1967 by Johnson's Secretary of Defense Robert S. McNamara. They were turned over (without authorization) to The New York Times *by Daniel Ellsberg, a senior research associate at the Massachusetts Institute of Technology's Center for International Studies.*

The 47-volume history, consisting of approximately 3,000 pages of narrative and 4,000 pages of appended documents, took 18 months to complete. Ellsberg, who worked on the project, had been an ardent early supporter of the U.S. role in Indochina but, by the project's end, had become seriously opposed to U.S. involvement. He felt compelled to reveal the nature of U.S. participation and leaked major portions of the papers to the press.

On June 13, 1971, The New York Times *began publishing a series of articles based on the study, which had been classified as "top secret" by the federal government. After the third daily installment appeared in the* Times, *the U.S. Department of Justice obtained in U.S. District Court a temporary restraining order against further publication of the classified material, contending that further public dissemination of the material would cause "immediate and irreparable harm" to U.S. national-defense interests.*

The Times—*joined by the* Washington Post, *which also was in possession of the documents—fought the order through the courts for the next 15 days, during which time publication of the series was suspended. On June 30, 1971, in what is regarded as one of the most significant prior-restraint cases in history, the U.S. Supreme Court, in a 6–3 decision, freed the newspapers to resume publishing the material. The court held that the government had failed to justify restraint of publication.*

The Pentagon Papers revealed that the Truman administration gave military aid to France in its colonial war against the communist-led Viet Minh, thus directly involving the United States in Vietnam; that in 1954 President Eisenhower decided to prevent a communist takeover of South Vietnam and to undermine the new communist regime of North Vietnam; that President Kennedy transformed the policy of "limited-risk gamble" that he had inherited into a policy of "broad commitment"; that President Johnson intensified covert warfare against North Vietnam and began planning to wage overt war in 1964, a full year before the depth of U.S. involvement was publicly revealed; and that Johnson also ordered the bombing of North Vietnam in 1965 despite the judgment of the U.S. intelligence community that it would not cause the North Vietnamese to cease their support of the Viet Cong insurgency in South Vietnam.

The release of the Pentagon Papers stirred nationwide and, indeed, international controversy because it occurred after several years of growing dissent over the legal and moral justification of intensifying U.S. actions in Vietnam. The disclosures and their continued publication despite top-secret classification were embarrassing to the Nixon administration, especially since Nixon was preparing to seek reelection in 1972. So distressing were these revelations that Nixon authorized unlawful efforts to discredit Ellsberg, efforts that came to light during the investigation of the Watergate scandal.

The papers were subsequently published in book form as The Pentagon Papers *(1971).*

action against the invasion forces and their supply lines. By mid-June the communists' Easter Offensive had ground to a halt.

With the failure of their offensive, Hanoi leaders were finally ready to compromise. The United States had indicated as early as 1971 that it would not insist on the withdrawal of North Vietnamese forces from the South. Now Hanoi signaled in return that it would not insist on replacing Thieu with a coalition government. On the basis of these two concessions, Kissinger and North Vietnamese emissary Le Duc Tho secretly hammered out a complicated peace accord in October 1972. The Saigon government, however, balked at a peace agreement negotiated without its participation or consent and demanded important changes in the treaty. In November (following Nixon's reelection), Kissinger returned to Paris with some 69 suggested changes to the agreement designed to satisfy Thieu. The North Vietnamese responded with anger, then with proposed changes of their own. Nixon, exasperated with what he saw as the North's intransigence and also anxious to persuade Thieu to cooperate, ordered B-52 bombers again to attack

Hanoi. This so-called Christmas bombing was the most intense bombing campaign of the war. After eight days, the North Vietnamese agreed to return to Paris to sign an agreement essentially the same as that agreed upon in October. Thieu, reassured by a massive influx of U.S. military aid and by a combination of promises and threats from Nixon, reluctantly agreed to go along. On Jan. 27, 1973, the Agreement on Ending the War and Restoring Peace in Viet-Nam was signed by representatives of the South Vietnamese communist forces, North Vietnam, South Vietnam, and the United States. A cease-fire would go into effect the following morning throughout North and South Vietnam, and within 60 days all U.S. forces would be withdrawn, all U.S. bases dismantled, and all prisoners of war released. An international force would keep the peace, the South Vietnamese would have the right to determine their own future, and North Vietnamese troops could remain in the South but would not be reinforced. The 17th parallel would remain the dividing line until the country could be reunited by "peaceful means."

Primary Document: Henry Kissinger's "Vietnam Truce Agreement"

During the autumn of 1972 presidential adviser Henry Kissinger conducted negotiations in Paris with Le Duc Tho of North Vietnam to gain a settlement of the Vietnam War. On October 26 Kissinger announced that the negotiations had been successful and that "peace was at hand." But it turned out that the bilateral settlement with Hanoi lacked the approval of South Vietnam, and thus peace was stalemated again. In mid-December Pres. Richard Nixon ordered saturation bombing of North Vietnam. By the end of the month the bombing was ordered stopped, and the Paris peace talks were scheduled to resume. On Jan. 15, 1973, the President ordered a halt to all military action against North Vietnam because progress was being made in Paris. On January 23, in a televised address to the nation, Nixon announced that Kissinger and Le Duc Tho had initialed an agreement to end the fighting. Details of the agreement were explained by Kissinger in a nationally televised news conference on January 24. Portions of the news conference clarifying the main points of the truce are reprinted here. In addition to the agreement, there were several protocols relating to such matters as the return of American prisoners, implementation of an international control commission, cease-fire regulations, institution of a joint military commission, and the removal of mines from Haiphong Harbor.

Department of State Bulletin, *Feb. 12, 1973.*

Ladies and gentlemen: The President last evening presented the outlines of the agreement, and by common agreement between us and the North Vietnamese we have today released the texts. And I am here to explain, to go over briefly, what these texts contain and how we got there, what we have tried to achieve in recent months, and where we expect to go from here.

Let me begin by going through the agreement, which you have read.

The agreement, as you know, is in nine chapters. The first affirms the independence, sovereignty, unity, and territorial integrity, as recognized by the 1954 Geneva agreements on Vietnam, agreements which established two zones divided by a military demarcation line.

Chapter II deals with the cease-fire. The cease-fire will go into effect at seven o'clock, Washington time, on Saturday night. The principal provisions of chapter II deal with permitted acts during the cease-fire and with what the obligations of the various parties are with respect to the cease-fire.

Chapter II also deals with the withdrawal of American and all other foreign forces from Vietnam within a period of 60 days. And it specifies the forces that have to be withdrawn. These are, in effect, all military personnel and all civilian personnel dealing with combat operations. We are permitted to retain economic advisers, and civilian technicians serving in certain of the military branches.

Chapter II further deals with the provisions for resupply and for the introduction of outside forces. There is a flat prohibition against the introduction of any military force into South Vietnam from outside of South Vietnam, which is to say that whatever forces may be in South Vietnam from outside South Vietnam, specifically North Vietnamese forces, cannot receive reinforcements, replacements, or any other form of augmentation by any means whatsoever. With respect to military equipment, both sides are permitted to replace all existing military equipment on a one-to-one basis under international supervision and control . . .

Chapter III deals with the return of captured military personnel and foreign civilians, as well as with the question of civilian detainees within South Vietnam.

This, as you know, throughout the negotiations presented enormous difficulties for us. We insisted throughout that the question of American prisoners of war and of American civilians captured throughout Indochina should be separated from the issue of Vietnamese civilian personnel detained, partly because of the enormous difficulty of classifying the Vietnamese civilian personnel by categories of who was detained for reasons of the civil war and who was detained for criminal activities, and secondly, because it was foreseeable that negotiations about the release of civilian detainees would be complex and difficult and because we did not want to have the issue of American personnel mixed up with the issues of civilian personnel in South Vietnam.

This turned out to be one of the thorniest issues, that was settled at some point and kept reappearing throughout the negotiations. It was one of the difficulties we had during the December negotiations.

As you can see from the agreement, the return of American military personnel and captured civilians is separated in terms of obligation, and in terms of the time frame, from the return of Vietnamese civilian personnel.

The return of American personnel and the accounting of missing in action is unconditional and will take place within the same time frame as the American withdrawal.

The issue of Vietnamese civilian personnel will be negotiated between the two Vietnamese parties over a period of three months, and as the agreement says, they will do their utmost to resolve this question within the three-month period.

So I repeat, the issue is separated, both in terms of obligation and in terms of the relevant time frame, from the return of American prisoners, which is unconditional.

We expect that American prisoners will be released at intervals of two weeks or 15 days in roughly equal installments. We have been told that no American prisoners are held in Cambodia. American prisoners held in Laos and North Vietnam will be returned to us in Hanoi. They will be received by American medical evacuation teams and flown on American airplanes from Hanoi to places of our own choice, probably Vientiane.

There will be international supervision of both this provision and of the provision for the missing in action. And all American prisoners will, of course, be released, within 60 days of the signing of the agreement. The signing will take place on January 27 in two installments, the significance of which I will explain to you when I have run through the provisions of the agreement and the associated protocols.

Chapter IV of the agreement deals with the right of the South Vietnamese people to self-determination. Its first provision contains a joint statement by the United States and North Vietnam in which those two countries jointly recognize the South Vietnamese people's right to self-determination, in which those two countries jointly affirm that the South Vietnamese people shall decide for themselves the political system that they shall choose and jointly affirm that no foreign country shall impose any political tendency on the South Vietnamese people.

The other principal provisions of the agreement are that in implementing the South Vietnamese people's right to self-determination, the two South Vietnamese parties will decide, will agree among each other, on free elections, for offices to be decided by the two parties, at a time to be decided by the two parties. These elections will be supervised and organized first by an institution which has the title of National Council for National Reconciliation and Concord, whose members will be equally appointed by the two sides, which will operate on the principle of unanimity, and which will come into being after negotiation between the two parties, who are obligated by this agreement to do their utmost to bring this institution into being within 90 days.

Leaving aside the technical jargon, the significance of this part of the agreement is that the United States has consistently maintained that we would not impose any political solution on the people of South Vietnam. The United States has consistently maintained that we would not impose a coalition government or a disguised coalition government on the people of South Vietnam . . .

The next chapter deals with the reunification of Vietnam and the relationship between North and South Vietnam. In the many negotiations that I have conducted over recent weeks, not the least arduous was the negotiation conducted with the ladies and gentlemen of the press, who constantly raised issues with respect to sovereignty, the existence of South Vietnam as a political entity, and other matters of this kind . . .

Chapter VI deals with the international machinery, and we will discuss that when I talk about the associated protocols of the agreement.

Chapter VII deals with Laos and Cambodia. Now, the problem of Laos and Cambodia has two parts. One part concerns those obligations which can be undertaken by the parties signing the agreement—that is to say, the three Vietnamese parties and the United States—those measures that they can take which affect the situation in Laos and Cambodia. A second part of the situation in Laos has to concern the nature of the civil conflict that is taking place within Laos and Cambodia and the solution of which, of course, must involve as well the two Laotian parties and the innumerable Cambodian factions.

Let me talk about the provisions of the agreement with respect to Laos and Cambodia and our firm expectations as to the future in Laos and Cambodia.

The provisions of the agreement with respect to Laos and Cambodia reaffirm, as an obligation to all the parties, the provisions of the 1954 agreement on Cambodia and of the 1962 agreement on Laos, which affirm the neutrality and right to self-determination of those two countries. They are therefore consistent with our basic position with respect also to South Vietnam.

In terms of the immediate conflict, the provisions of the agreement specifically prohibit the use of Laos and Cambodia for military and any other operations against any of the signatories of the Paris agreement or against any other country. In other words, there is a flat prohibition against the use of base areas in Laos and Cambodia.

There is a flat prohibition against the use of Laos and Cambodia for infiltration into Vietnam or, for that matter, into any other country.

Finally, there is a requirement that all foreign troops be withdrawn from Laos and Cambodia, and it is clearly understood that North Vietnamese troops are considered foreign with respect to Laos and Cambodia.

Now, as to the conflict within these countries which could not be formally settled in an agreement which is not signed by the parties of that conflict, let me make this statement, without elaborating it: It is our firm expectation that within a short period of time there will be a formal cease-fire in Laos which in turn will lead to a withdrawal of all foreign forces from Laos, and, of course, to the end of the use of Laos as a corridor of infiltration.

Secondly, the situation in Cambodia, as those of you who have studied it will know, is somewhat more complex because there are several parties headquartered in different countries. Therefore, we can say about Cambodia that it is our expectation that a de facto cease-fire will come into being over a period of time relevant to the execution of this agreement.

Our side will take the appropriate measures to indicate that it will not attempt to change the situation by force. We have reason to believe that our position is clearly understood by all concerned parties, and I will not go beyond this in my statement.

Chapter VIII deals with the relationship between the United States and the Democratic Republic of Vietnam.

As I have said in my briefings on October 26 and on December 16 and as the President affirmed on many occasions, the last time in his speech last evening, the United States is seeking a peace that heals. We have had many armistices in Indochina. We want a peace that will last.

And therefore it is our firm intention in our relationship to the Democratic Republic of Vietnam to move from hostility to normalization, and from normalization to conciliation and cooperation. And we believe that under conditions of peace we can contribute throughout Indochina to a realization of the humane aspirations of all the people of Indochina. And we will, in that spirit, perform our traditional role of helping people realize these aspirations in peace.

Chapter IX of the agreement is the usual implementing provision.

THE FALL OF SOUTH VIETNAM

On March 29, 1973, the last U.S. military unit left Vietnam. By that time the communists and South Vietnamese were already engaged in what journalists labeled the "postwar war." Both sides alleged, more or less accurately, that the other side was continuously violating the terms of the peace agreements. The United States maintained its program of extensive military aid to Saigon, but the president's ability to influence events in Vietnam was being sharply curtailed. As Nixon's personal standing crumbled under the weight of Watergate revelations, Congress moved to block any possibility of further military action in Vietnam. In the summer of 1973 Congress passed a measure prohibiting any U.S. military operations in or over Indochina after August 15.

The following year saw a discernible pattern of hostilities: lower levels of

Primary Document: Henry Kissinger's "The Evacuation of Vietnam" News Conference

On April 30, 1975, the South Vietnamese government collapsed and surrendered to North Vietnam. The long Vietnam War had finally ended. Cambodia had already fallen thirteen days earlier, and Laos was soon to follow. In the days before Saigon's collapse, the United States conducted a massive evacuation project to bring out most of the Americans who were still there, as well as thousands of South Vietnamese who felt they would be endangered by the Communist takeover. On April 29 Secretary of State Henry Kissinger held a news conference explaining the evacuation and answering reporters' questions on the future of American foreign policy. Portions of the news conference are reprinted here.

Weekly Compilation of Presidential Documents, *May 5, 1975.*

Ladies and gentlemen, when the President spoke before the Congress, he stated as our objective the stabilization of the situation in Vietnam.

We made clear at that time, as well as before many Congressional hearings, that our purpose was to bring about the most controlled and the most humane solution that was possible and that these objectives required the course which the President had set.

Our priorities were as follows: We sought to save the American lives still in Vietnam; we tried to rescue as many South Vietnamese that had worked with the United States for 15 years, in reliance on our commitments, as we possibly could; and, we sought to bring about as humane an outcome as was achievable under the conditions that existed.

Over the past 2 weeks, the American personnel in Vietnam have been progressively reduced. Our objective was to reduce at a rate that was significant enough so that we would finally be able to evacuate rapidly, but which would not produce a panic which might prevent anybody from getting out.

Our objective was also to fulfill the human obligation which we felt to the tens of thousands of South Vietnamese who had worked with us for over a decade.

Finally, we sought through various intermediaries to bring about as humane a political evolution as we could.

By Sunday evening, the personnel in our mission had been reduced to 950, and there were 8,000 South Vietnamese to be considered in a particularly high-risk category—between five and eight thousand. We do not know the exact number.

On Monday evening Washington time, around 5 o'clock, which was Tuesday morning in Saigon, the airport in Tan Son Nhut was rocketed and received artillery fire.

The President called an NSC meeting. He decided that if the shelling stopped by dawn Saigon time, we would attempt to operate with fixed-wing aircraft from Tan Son Nhut airport for one more day to remove the high-risk South Vietnamese, together with all the Defense Attaché's Office [DAO], which was located near the Tan Son Nhut airport. He also ordered a substantial reduction of the remaining American personnel in South Vietnam.

I may point out that the American personnel in Saigon was divided into two groups; one with the Defense Attaché's Office, which was located near the Tan Son Nhut airport; the second one, which was related to the Embassy and was with the United States mission in downtown Saigon.

The shelling did stop early in the morning on Tuesday, Saigon time, or about 9 PM last night, Washington time. We then attempted to land C-130s, but found that the population at the airport had got out of control and had flooded the runways. It proved impossible to land any more fixed-wing aircraft.

The President thereupon ordered that the DAO personnel, together with those civilians that had been made ready to be evacuated, be moved to the DAO compound which is near Tan Son Nhut airport. And at about 11 o'clock last night, he ordered the evacuation of all Americans from Tan Son Nhut and from the Embassy as well.

This operation has been going on all day which, of course, is night in Saigon, under difficult circumstances. And the total number of those evacuated numbers about 6,500—we will have the exact figures for you tomorrow—of which about a thousand are Americans.

Our Ambassador has left, and the evacuation can be said to be completed.

In the period since the President spoke to the Congress, we have therefore succeeded in evacuating all of the Americans who were in South Vietnam, losing the two Marines last night to rocket fire and two pilots today on a helicopter.

We succeeded in evacuating something on the order of 55,000 South Vietnamese, and we hope that we have contributed to a political evolution that may spare the South Vietnamese some of the more drastic consequences of a political change. But this remains to be seen; this last point remains to be seen.

As far as the Administration is concerned, I can only underline the point made by the President. We do not believe that this is a time for recrimination. It is a time to heal wounds, to look at our international obligations, and to remember that peace and progress in the world has depended importantly on American commitment and American convictions and that the peace and progress of our own people is closely tied to that of the rest of the world.

combat and casualties, but unimpeded warfare along the never-defined zones of control of the South Vietnamese government and the communists. Hundreds of Vietnamese continued to lose their lives each day after the fighting was supposed to have stopped. By the summer of 1974 Nixon had resigned in disgrace, Congress had cut military and economic aid to Vietnam by 30 percent, and the Lon Nol regime in Cambodia appeared close to defeat. Thieu's government, corrupt and inefficient as ever, now faced enormous difficulties with inflation, unemployment, apathy, and an enormous desertion rate in the army. After an easy success at Phuoc Long, northeast of Saigon, in December 1974–January 1975, the Hanoi leaders believed that victory was near. In early March the North Vietnamese launched the first phase of what was expected to be a two-year offensive to secure South Vietnam. As it happened, the South's government and army collapsed in less than two months. Thousands of ARVN troops retreated in disorder, first from the central highlands and then from Hue and Da Nang. Gerald R. Ford, who had succeeded Nixon as U.S. president, pleaded in vain with Congress for additional military aid that might at least raise Saigon's morale. But members of Congress, like most of their constituents, were ready to wash their hands of a long and futile war. On April 21 Thieu resigned and flew to Taiwan. On April 30 what remained of the South Vietnamese government surrendered unconditionally, and NVA tank columns occupied Saigon without a struggle. The remaining Americans escaped in a series of frantic air- and sealifts with Vietnamese friends and coworkers. A military government was instituted, and on July 2, 1976, the country was officially united as the Socialist Republic of Vietnam with its capital in Hanoi. Saigon was renamed Ho Chi Minh City. The 30-year struggle for control over Vietnam was over.

CHAPTER 9

POLITICAL LEADERS OF THE VIETNAM WAR

The following brief biographies of major political leaders from French Indochina, North Vietnam, South Vietnam, United Vietnam, Cambodia, and the United States concentrate on their actions in the period leading up to and during the Vietnam War.

FRENCH INDOCHINA

PAUL DOUMER

(b. March 22, 1857, Aurillac, France—d. May 6, 1932, Paris)

Paul Doumer was the 13th president of the French Third Republic. His term was cut short by an assassin's bullet.

In 1889 Doumer was elected as a Radical deputy from the Yonne *département,* and his reputation as a fiscal expert led to his appointment (1895) as minister of finance in the Cabinet of Léon Bourgeois. Unsuccessful in his efforts to introduce a national income tax, he was appointed governor general of Indochina the following year.

Doumer was one of the most active and, from the French point of view, effective governors general of Indochina. Unlike many of his predecessors and successors he occupied his post for a relatively sustained period (1897–1902) and had clearly defined aims. His most important achievements were to strengthen the hold of the governor general over the administrators at the head of the various components of Indochina and to place the colonial economy on a sound basis. While this latter development was welcomed by the French, it involved rigorous imposition of taxes on the local population, which caused deep resentment.

Doumer returned to the Chamber of Deputies in 1902 and then moved to the Senate (1912) as representative of Corsica. In 1903 he wrote *L'Indochine française* and in 1906 *Le Livre de mes fils* ("The Book of My Sons"). From 1927 to 1931 he was president of the Senate and chairman of the important budget commission. In addition, he served as finance minister in the Aristide Briand cabinets of January 1921 to January 1922 and December 1925 to March 1926.

Doumer's election to the presidency on May 13, 1931, was popularly received and he successfully weathered ministerial crises caused by the deaths of André Maginot and Briand. However, he was fatally shot by a Russian anarchist, Pavel Gorgulov, the following year.

Jean Decoux

(b. 1884, Bordeaux, France—d. Oct. 21, 1963, Paris)

Jean Decoux was governor-general of French Indochina for the provisional (Vichy) French government during World War II (1940–45). His reforms, which were designed to undermine Japanese influence in the area, unwittingly helped lay the groundwork for Vietnamese nationalist resistance to French rule after the war.

Decoux was promoted to rear admiral in 1935 and became vice admiral and commander in chief of French naval forces in East Asia in 1939. He became governor-general of Indochina on July 20, 1940, soon after France's capitulation to Nazi Germany. Within two weeks he received demands from the Japanese for permission to send troops through Tonkin (now northern Vietnam) in order to block Allied supply routes to China and for use of Indochinese air bases to facilitate Japan's conquest of China. Loyal to France and resolved to preserve its colonial prestige, Decoux cabled for assistance to Vichy. The government there advised him to submit to the Japanese demands, and on September 20 he concluded a treaty that opened the harbour of Haiphong to the Japanese and gave them the right to station their troops in Tonkin.

Although the Japanese allowed Decoux and his French administration to remain in nominal control of the mundane affairs of state, he was not permitted to do anything that conflicted with their interests. In the face of Japanese threats of invasion, he mobilized Indochina's natural resources and manpower for the Japanese war effort late in 1941. Meanwhile, he worked to promote understanding and to improve social relations between the Indochinese people and the French colonists. He set up youth groups and other organizations that later opposed the reimposition of the French colonial regime.

Decoux installed Vietnamese in civil-service posts, with salaries equal to those of Frenchmen, and established an advisory Franco-Vietnamese grand federal council, with twice as many Vietnamese nationals as Frenchmen represented. The council had little real power, but many of its Vietnamese officials later attained administrative posts under the Viet Minh's independent government.

Initially a strict Vichy supporter, Decoux switched his loyalties to the Free French under Gen. Charles de Gaulle toward the end of the war and sought to undermine Japanese occupation forces. He was arrested by the Japanese on March 9, 1945, after their invasion of Indochina.

After the war he was imprisoned by the French for two years for collaborating with the discredited Vichy government and abetting the Japanese war effort.

Bao Dai

(b. Oct. 22, 1913, Vietnam, French Indochina—d. Aug. 1, 1997, Paris, France)

Bao Dai was the last reigning emperor of Vietnam (1926–45).

The son of Emperor Khai Dinh, a vassal of the French colonial regime, and a concubine of peasant ancestry, Nguyen Vinh Thuy was educated in France and spent little of his youth in his homeland. He succeeded to the throne in 1926 and assumed the title Bao Dai ("Keeper of Greatness"). He initially sought to reform and modernize Vietnam but was unable to win French cooperation.

During World War II the French colonial regime exercised a firm control over

An undated photograph of former Korean emperor Bao Dai (left) *some time before he abdicated to Ho Chi Minh after the latter established the Republic of Vietnam in 1945.* AFP/Getty Images

Bao Dai until the Japanese *coup de force* of March 1945, which swept away French administration in Indochina. The Japanese considered bringing back the aging Prince Cuong De from Japan to head a new quasi-independent Vietnamese state, but they finally allowed Bao Dai to remain as an essentially powerless ruler. When the Viet Minh seized power in their revolution of August 1945, Ho Chi Minh and his colleagues judged that there was symbolic value to be gained by having Bao Dai linked to them. The Viet Minh asked Bao Dai to resign and offered him an advisory role as "Citizen Prince Nguyen Vinh Thuy." Finding that the Viet Minh accorded him no role, and distrustful of the French, Bao Dai fled to Hong Kong in 1946. There he led a largely frivolous life, making appeals against French rule.

In 1949 the French accepted the principle of an independent Vietnam but retained control of its defense and finance. Bao Dai agreed to return to Vietnam in these circumstances in May 1949, and in July he became temporary premier of a tenuously unified and nominally independent Vietnam. Reinstalled as sovereign, Bao Dai continued his pleasure-seeking ways and became generally known as the "Playboy Emperor." He left the affairs of state to his various pro-French Vietnamese appointees, until October 1955 when a national referendum called for the country to become a republic. Bao Dai retired and returned to France to live.

NORTH VIETNAM

Phan Boi Chau

(b. 1867, Nghe An province, northern Vietnam—d. Sept. 29, 1940, Hue, Vietnam, French Indochina)

Phan Boi Chau was a dominant personality of early Vietnamese resistance movements, whose impassioned writings and tireless schemes for independence earned him the reverence of his people as one of Vietnam's greatest patriots.

Phan Boi Chau was the son of a poor scholar who stressed education and preparation for the mandarin examinations, the only means to success in the traditional bureaucracy. By the time he received his doctorate in 1900 Chau had become a firm nationalist.

In 1903 he wrote *Luu cau huyet le tan thu* ("Ryukyu's Bitter Tears"), an allegory equating Japan's bitterness at the loss of the Ryukyu Islands with the Vietnamese loss of independence. With fellow revolutionaries he formed the Duy Tan Hoi ("Reformation Society") in 1904 and secured the active support of Prince Cuong De, thus presenting to the people an alliance of royalty and resistance.

In 1905 Chau moved his resistance movement to Japan, and in 1906 he met the Chinese revolutionary Sun Yat-sen. His plans to place Cuong De on the throne of Vietnam resulted in a meeting in 1906 with the prince and the Vietnamese reformer Phan Chau Trinh. A Franco-Japanese understanding forced Chau, the Vietnamese students he had brought to Japan, and Cuong De to leave Japan in 1908–09. By 1912 Chau had reluctantly given up his monarchist scheme. He reorganized the resistance movement in Guangzhou, China, under the name Viet Nam Quang Phuc Hoi ("Vietnam Restoration Society"). The organization launched a plan to assassinate the French governor-general of Indochina, but the plan failed. Chau was imprisoned in Guangzhou from 1914 to 1917; during his confinement he wrote *Nguc trung thu* ("Prison Notes"), a short autobiography.

Upon his release, Chau studied Marxist doctrine and resumed his resistance to the French. In June 1925 he was seized and taken to Hanoi, but hundreds of Vietnamese protested against his arrest. The French pardoned him and offered him a civil service position that he refused.

Ho Chi Minh

(b. May 19, 1890, Hoang Tru, Vietnam, French Indochina—d. Sept. 2, 1969, Hanoi, Viet.)

Ho Chi Minh was the founder of the Indochinese Communist Party (1930) and its successor, the Viet Minh (1941), and president from 1945 to 1969 of the Democratic Republic of Vietnam (North Vietnam). As the leader of the Vietnamese nationalist movement for nearly three decades, Ho was one of the prime movers of the post-World War II anticolonial movement in Asia and one of the most influential communist leaders of the 20th century.

In 1938 Ho returned to China and stayed for a few months with Mao Zedong at Yen-an. When France was defeated by Germany in 1940, Ho and his lieutenants, Vo Nguyen Giap and Pham Van Dong, plotted to use this turn of events to advance their own cause. About this time he began to use the name Ho Chi Minh ("He Who Enlightens"). Crossing over the border into Vietnam in January 1941, the trio and five comrades organized in May the Viet Nam Doc Lap Dong Minh Hoi (League for the Independence of Vietnam), or Viet Minh; this gave renewed emphasis to a peculiarly Vietnamese nationalism.

The new organization was forced to seek help in China from the government of Chiang Kai-shek. But Chiang distrusted Ho as a Communist and had him arrested. Ho was then imprisoned in China for 18 months, during which time he wrote his famed *Notebook from Prison* (a collection of short poems written in classic Chinese, a mixture of melancholy, stoicism, and a call for revolution). His friends obtained his release by an arrangement with Chiang Fa-k'uei, a warlord in South China, agreeing in return to support Chiang's interests in Indochina against the French.

In 1945 two events occurred that paved the way to power for the Vietnamese revolutionaries. First, the Japanese completely overran Indochina and imprisoned or executed all French officials. Six months later the United States dropped the atomic bomb on Hiroshima, and the Japanese were totally defeated. Thus, the two strongest adversaries of the Viet Minh and Ho Chi Minh were eliminated.

Ho Chi Minh seized his opportunity. Within a few months he contacted U.S. forces and began to collaborate with the Office of Strategic Services (OSS; a U.S. undercover operation) against the Japanese. Further, his Viet Minh guerrillas fought against the Japanese in the mountains of South China.

At the same time, commandos formed by Vo Nguyen Giap, under Ho's direction, began to move toward Hanoi, the Vietnamese capital, in the spring of 1945. After Japan's surrender to the Allies, they entered Hanoi on August 19. Finally, on September 2, before an enormous crowd gathered in Ba Dinh Square, Ho Chi Minh declared Vietnam independent, using words ironically reminiscent of the U.S. Declaration of Independence: "All men are born equal: the Creator has given us inviolable rights, life, liberty, and happiness . . . !"

All obstacles were not removed from the path of the Viet Minh, however. According to the terms of an Allied agreement, Chiang Kai-shek's troops were supposed to replace the Japanese north of the 16th parallel. More significantly, France, now liberated from Nazi occupation and under the leadership of Charles de Gaulle, did not intend to simply accept the fait accompli of an independent Vietnam and attempted to reassert its control in the region. On October 6 the French general Jacques Leclerc landed in Saigon, followed a few days later by a strong armoured division. Within three months, he had control of South Vietnam. Ho had to choose between continuing the fight or negotiating. He chose negotiations, but not without preparing for an eventual transition to war.

Ho Chi Minh's strategy was to get the French to make the Chinese in the north withdraw and then to work for a treaty with France in which recognition of independence, evacuation of Leclerc's forces, and reunification of the country would be assured. Negotiations began in late October 1945, but the French refused to speak of independence, and Ho was caught in a stalemate. In March the deadlock was broken: on his side, Ho Chi Minh allowed parties other than the Viet Minh to be included in the new government, in an attempt to gain a wider base of support for the demands made on the French; at the same time, the French sent a diplomatic mission to China to obtain the evacuation of the Chinese soldiers. This was done, and some of Leclerc's troops were also removed from Haiphong, in the north. Having secured the withdrawal of the Chinese, Ho signed an agreement with the French on March 6. According to its terms, Vietnam was recognized as a "free state with its own government, army, and finances," but it was integrated into a French Union in which Paris continued to play the key role. Twelve days later, Leclerc entered Hanoi with a few battalions, which were to be confined to a restricted area.

The agreement was unsatisfactory to extremists on both sides, and Ho Chi Minh went to France for a series of conferences (June to September 1946) and concluded a second agreement with the French government. But the peace was broken by an incident at Haiphong (Nov. 20–23, 1946) when a French cruiser opened fire on the town after a clash between French and Vietnamese soldiers. Almost 6,000 Vietnamese were killed, and hope for an amicable settlement ended. Sick and disillusioned, Ho Chi Minh was not able to oppose demands for retaliation by his more militant followers, and the First Indochina War began on December 19.

After a few months, Ho, who had sought refuge in a remote area of North Vietnam, attempted to reestablish contact with Paris, but the terms he was offered were unacceptable. In 1948 the French offered to return the former Annamese (Vietnamese) emperor Bao Dai, who had abdicated in favour of the revolution in August 1945. These terms were more favourable than those offered to Ho Chi Minh two years earlier, because the French were now attempting to weaken the Viet Minh by supporting the traditional ruling class in Vietnam. But this policy was not successful. The Viet Minh army, commanded by Giap, was able to contain the French and Bao Dai's forces with guerrilla tactics and terrorism, and by the end of 1953 most of the countryside was under Viet Minh control, with the larger cities under a virtual state of siege. The French were decisively defeated at Dien Bien Phu on May 7, 1954, and had no choice but to negotiate.

From May to July 21, 1954, representatives of eight countries—with Vietnam represented by two delegations, one composed of supporters of Ho Chi Minh, the other of supporters of Bao Dai—met in Geneva to find a solution. They concluded with an agreement according to which Vietnam was to be divided at the 17th parallel until elections, scheduled for 1956, after which the Vietnamese would establish a unified government.

It is difficult to assess Ho's role in the Geneva negotiations. He was represented by Pham Van Dong, a faithful associate. The moderation exhibited by the Viet Minh in accepting a partition of the country and in accepting control of less territory than they had conquered during the war follows the pattern established by the man who had signed the 1946 agreements with France. But this flexibility, which was also a response to pressures exerted by the Russians and Chinese, did not achieve everything for the Viet Minh. Hanoi lost out because the elections that were to guarantee the country's reunification were postponed indefinitely by the United States and by South Vietnam, which was created on a de facto basis at this time.

North Vietnam, where Ho and his associates were established, was a poor country, cut off from the vast agricultural areas of the south. Its leaders were forced to ask for assistance from their larger Communist allies, China and the Soviet Union. In these adverse conditions Ho Chi Minh's regime became repressive and rigidly totalitarian. Attempted agricultural reforms in 1955–56 were conducted with ignorant brutality and repression. "Uncle" Ho, as he had become known to the North Vietnamese, was able to preserve his immense popularity, but he abandoned a kind of humane quality that had distinguished some of his previous revolutionary activities despite ruthless purges of Trotskyists and bourgeois nationalists in 1945–46.

The old statesman had better luck in the field of diplomacy. He traveled to Moscow and Beijing (1955) and to New Delhi and Jakarta (1958), skillfully maintaining a balance between his powerful Communist allies and even, at the time of his journey to Moscow in 1960, acting as a mediator between them. Linked by old habit, and perhaps by preference, to the Soviet Union, but aware of the seminal role China had played in the revolution in Asia, preoccupied with using his relations with Moscow to lessen China's influence in Asia, and, above all, careful to assert Vietnamese rights, Ho Chi Minh skillfully maintained a balance between the two Communist giants. When the war was resumed, he obtained an equal amount of aid from both.

Beginning about 1959, North Vietnam again became involved in war. Guerrillas, popularly known as the Viet Cong, were conducting an armed revolt against the U.S.-sponsored regime of Ngo Dinh Diem in South Vietnam. Their leaders, veterans of the Viet Minh, appealed to North Vietnam for aid. In July 1959, at a meeting of the central committee of Ho Chi Minh's Lao Dong (Workers' Party), it was decided that the establishment of socialism in the North was linked with the unification with the South. This policy was confirmed by the third congress of the Lao Dong, held shortly thereafter in Hanoi. During the congress, Ho Chi Minh ceded his position as the party's secretary-general to Le Duan. He remained chief of state, but, from this point on, his activity was largely behind-the-scenes. Ho certainly continued to have enormous influence in the government, which was dominated by his old followers Pham Van Dong, Truong Chinh, Vo Nguyen Giap, and Le Duan, but he was less actively involved, becoming more and more a symbol to the people. His public personality, which had never been the object of a cult comparable to that of Joseph Stalin, Mao, or even Josip Broz Tito, is best symbolized by his popular name, Uncle Ho. He stood for the essential unity of the divided Vietnamese family.

This role, which he played with skill, did not prevent him from taking a position in the conflict ravaging his country, especially after American air strikes against the North began in 1965. On July 17, 1966, he sent a message to the people ("nothing is as dear to the heart of the

Vietnamese as independence and liberation") that became the motto of the North Vietnamese cause. On Feb. 15, 1967, in response to a personal message from U.S. Pres. Lyndon Johnson, he announced: "We will never agree to negotiate under the threat of bombing." Ho lived to see only the beginning of a long round of negotiations before he died in September 1969. The removal of this powerful leader undoubtedly damaged chances for an early settlement.

Pham Hung

(b. June 11, 1912, Vinh Long province, Vietnam, French Indochina—d. March 10, 1988, Ho Chi Minh City [formerly Saigon], Viet.)

Pham Hung served briefly as prime minister (1987–88) of Vietnam and was the first southern Vietnamese to reach the highest level of the Communist Party Central Committee, the Politburo.

Hung, an early follower of Ho Chi Minh, joined the Revolutionary Youth League soon after his expulsion from secondary school and helped form Ho's Indochinese Communist Party (1930). Hung was arrested by the French colonial authorities in 1931 and sentenced to death, but his sentence was commuted to life imprisonment at Poulo Condore on the prison island of Con Son. He was freed during the 1945 uprising in which Ho's forces gained control of northern Vietnam. He held key posts in the Communist Party in southern Vietnam until the defeat of France in 1954 and the subsequent legal division of the country, after which he entered the Politburo in North Vietnam.

As chairman of the Central Office of South Vietnam from 1967, Hung directed Viet Cong guerilla warfare and coordinated the 1968 Tet Offensive. He was the political commissar during the 1975 capture of Saigon (later Ho Chi Minh City), and the next year he was named a deputy prime minister in the first unified government. He served as interior minister and commander of the internal security force (1980–87) until government reformers chose him to replace Prime Minister Pham Van Dong.

Le Duc Tho

(b. Oct. 14, 1911, Nam Ha province, Viet.—d. Oct. 13, 1990, Hanoi)

Le Duc Tho was a Vietnamese politician and corecipient in 1973 (with Henry Kissinger) of the Nobel Prize for Peace, which he declined.

Le Duc Tho was one of the founders of the Indochinese Communist Party in 1930. For his political activities he was imprisoned by the French in 1930–36 and 1939–44. After his second release he returned to Hanoi in 1945 and helped lead the Viet Minh, the Vietnamese independence organization, as well as a revived communist party called the Vietnam Workers' Party. He was the senior Viet Minh official in southern Vietnam until the Geneva Accords of 1954. From 1955 he was a member of the Politburo of the Vietnam Workers' Party, or the Communist Party of Vietnam, as it was renamed in 1976. During the Vietnam War Tho oversaw the Viet Cong insurgency that began against the South Vietnamese government in the late 1950s. He carried out most of his duties during the war while in hiding in South Vietnam.

Tho is best known for his part in the cease-fire of 1973, when he served as special adviser to the North Vietnamese delegation to the Paris Peace Conferences in 1968–73. He eventually became his delegation's principal spokesman, in which capacity he negotiated the cease-fire agreement that led to the withdrawal of the last American troops from South Vietnam. It was for this accomplishment that he was awarded the Nobel Peace Prize. Tho oversaw the North Vietnamese offensive that overthrew the South Vietnamese government in 1975, and he played a similar role in the first stages of Vietnam's invasion of Cambodia in 1978. He remained a member of the Politburo until 1986.

SOUTH VIETNAM

Ngo Dinh Diem

(b. Jan. 3, 1901, Quang Binh province, northern Vietnam—d. Nov. 2, 1963, Cho Lon, South Vietnam)

Ngo Dinh Diem served as president, with dictatorial powers, of South Vietnam from 1955 until his assassination.

Diem was born into one of Vietnam's noble families. His ancestors in the 17th century had been among the first Vietnamese converts to Roman Catholicism. He was on friendly terms with the Vietnamese imperial family in his youth, and in 1933 he served as the emperor Bao Dai's minister of the interior. However, he resigned that same year in frustration at French unwillingness to countenance his legislative reforms. Relinquishing his titles and decorations, he spent the next 12 years living quietly in Hue. In 1945 Diem was captured by the forces of Ho Chi Minh, who invited him to join his independent government in the North, hoping that Diem's presence would win Catholic support. But Diem rejected the proposal and went into self-imposed exile, living abroad for most of the next decade.

In 1954 Diem returned at Bao Dai's request to serve as prime minister of a U.S.-backed government in South Vietnam. After defeating Bao Dai in a government-controlled referendum in October 1955, he ousted the emperor and made himself president of the newly declared Republic of Vietnam (South Vietnam). Diem refused to carry out the Geneva Accords, which had called for free elections to be held throughout Vietnam in 1956 in order to establish a national government. With the south torn by dissident groups and political factions, Diem established an autocratic regime that was staffed at the highest levels by members of his own family.

With U.S. military and economic aid, he was able to resettle hundreds of thousands of refugees from North Vietnam in the south, but his own Catholicism and the preference he showed for fellow Roman Catholics made him unacceptable to Buddhists, who were an overwhelming majority in South Vietnam. Diem never fulfilled his promise of land reforms, and during his rule, Communist influence and appeal grew among southerners as the Communist-inspired Viet Cong launched an increasingly intense guerrilla war against his government. The military tactics Diem used against the insurgency were heavy-handed and ineffective and only served to deepen his government's unpopularity and isolation.

South Korean President Ngo Dinh Diem (centre) *watches an agricultural show, 1955. An assassination attempt had been made on Diem just minutes before this photograph was taken.* Keystone/Hulton Archive/Getty Images

Diem's imprisoning and killing of hundreds of Buddhists, who he alleged were abetting Communist insurgents, finally persuaded the United States to withdraw its support from him. Diem's generals assassinated him during a coup d'état.

Nguyen Khanh
(b. 1927)

Nguyen Khanh participated in a successful coup d'état against Diem in 1963 and served briefly as president of South Vietnam in 1964.

Khanh served in the French colonial army until 1954 and rose through the ranks of the Vietnamese army to become chief of staff to Gen. Duong Van Minh. He joined Minh and other high military officials in assassinating Diem on Nov. 1, 1963, and led a countercoup against Minh in 1964. Khanh administered the government of South Vietnam in January–October 1964. His regime was undermined by several coups; he himself resigned once. After Gen. Nguyen Cao Ky took control of the government in February 1965, Khanh was named roving ambassador but was, in effect, exiled to the United States.

Nguyen Van Thieu

(b. April 5, 1923, Tri Thuy, Ninh Thuan province, Vietnam, French Indochina—d. Sept. 29, 2001, Boston, Mass., U.S.)

Nguyen Van Thieu was president of the Republic of Vietnam (South Vietnam) from 1967 until the republic fell to the forces of North Vietnam in 1975.

The son of a small landowner, Thieu joined the communist-oriented Viet Minh in 1945 but later fought for the French colonial regime against the Viet Minh. In 1954 he was put in charge of the Vietnamese National Military Academy and, after 1956, continued to serve under the regime of Ngo Dinh Diem in South Vietnam. Thieu played an important part in a successful coup against Diem in 1963. In 1965 he became chief of state in a military government headed by Premier Nguyen Cao Ky. In 1967 he was elected president under a new constitution promulgated in that year. He was reelected without opposition in 1971.

Thieu's emergence coincided with the beginning of major U.S. intervention in the war against the Viet Cong insurgents and North Vietnam. Despite criticism of the authoritarian nature of his regime, he retained the support of the United States throughout the administrations of the U.S. presidents Johnson and Nixon. He continued to consolidate his power after the peace agreements of 1973 (in which his government was a somewhat reluctant participant) and the withdrawal of U.S. troops from South Vietnam.

Communist gains in South Vietnam's northern provinces early in 1975 prompted Thieu to recall troops to defend Saigon. Badly managed, the retreat turned into a rout, allowing communist forces to surround the capital. After resisting for several days, Thieu was persuaded that his resignation might permit a negotiated settlement of the war. On April 21, 1975, in a speech denouncing the United States, he resigned in favour of his vice president, Tran Van Huong, and shortly afterward left the country. He went first to Taiwan and later to England, taking up residence in Surrey, before settling in the United States.

Nguyen Cao Ky

(b. Sept. 8, 1930, Son Tay, Vietnam, French Indochina)

Nguyen Cao Ky was a South Vietnamese military and political leader known for his flamboyant manner and militant policies.

A member of the French forces that opposed the Vietnamese liberation movement, Ky joined the South Vietnamese Air Force after the nation was partitioned in 1954. He attracted much attention because of his vehement anticommunism, as well as his bravado, and was highly favoured by U.S. advisers in Vietnam. As a result he was named commander of South Vietnam's air force after the 1963 overthrow of the Diem government. With U.S. aid, Ky soon built up a fighting force of 10,000 men.

In June 1965 Ky, together with Thieu and Minh, led a military coup in unseating the government of Premier Phan Huy Quat. As the head of that triumvirate, Ky provoked widespread opposition to his authoritarian policies. In 1967 the top military leaders reached an agreement by which Thieu would run for president and Ky for vice president of a new regime. Unhappy with his new position, Ky became an outspoken critic of Thieu's administration. In 1971 he attempted to oppose Thieu for the presidency but was forced to remove himself as a candidate and returned to the air force. Upon the fall of South Vietnam in April 1975, Ky fled to the United States.

UNIFIED VIETNAM

Le Duan

(b. April 7, 1908, Quang Tri province [now Binh Tri Thien province], Vietnam, French Indochina—d. July 10, 1986, Hanoi, Viet.)

Le Duan was a Vietnamese communist politician.

Le Duan was a founding member of the Indochinese Communist Party in 1930. Twice imprisoned by the French, he joined the Viet Minh and attained an influential position on the Central Committee of Ho's new Republic of Vietnam in Hanoi in 1945. After Vietnam's division in 1954, Le Duan was put in charge of establishing an underground Communist Party organization in South Vietnam. He thus oversaw the creation in 1962 of the People's Revolutionary Party, a crucial component of the National Liberation Front.

Upon Ho's death in 1969, Le Duan, as first secretary to the Vietnam Workers' Party, assumed party leadership—a position that he retained after the party's reorganization as the Vietnamese Communist Party in 1976. At that time, his official title became secretary-general. After the end of the Vietnam War in 1975, Le Duan led the party through a difficult period that witnessed the formal reunification of Vietnam, the Vietnamese invasion of Cambodia, and the country's break with China and the expulsion of much of its ethnic Chinese community. Vietnam under Le Duan entered into a close alliance with the Soviet Union and became a member of Comecon (Council for Mutual Economic Assistance).

Nguyen Van Linh

(b. July 1, 1915, near Hanoi, Vietnam, French Indochina—d. April 27, 1998, Ho Chi Minh City (formerly Saigon), Viet.)

Nguyen Van Linh was a secretive Vietnamese guerrilla leader who operated under a number of aliases for many years before assuming a public political role after the Vietnam War ended. He served as general secretary of the Vietnamese Communist Party from 1986 to 1991 and during his time in office initiated a program of *doi moi* (renovation) and free-market reforms that encouraged international investment and helped free the country from its economic isolation. Nguyen Van Linh began his fight against French colonial rule when he was 14 and at 15 was imprisoned for his activities. Upon his release in 1936, he joined the Indochinese Communist Party and resumed his anti-French efforts, and he was jailed again from 1941 to 1945. He advanced in the party ranks, and after the division of the country following the French withdrawal, he became an underground leader in South Vietnam. With the fall of the government of the south and the reunification of Vietnam, Nguyen Van Linh became party chief in Saigon; he was promoted to the party's Politburo the following year. He was dropped from the Politburo in 1982 but was reinstated in 1985, and in December 1986 he became party leader. Following his retirement from office in 1991, he remained an adviser to the party. Nguyen Van Linh later expressed regret over some of his reforms, claiming that they had led to corruption and exploitation.

Vo Van Kiet

(b. Nov. 23, 1922, Trung Hiep, Vietnam, French Indochina—d. June 11, 2008, Singapore)

Vo Van Kiet was Vietnam's prime minister (1991–97) and a strong advocate of *doi moi*, the economic plan that encouraged entrepreneurial initiative and foreign investment. Under this policy he pushed for free-market reform and helped free the country from its economic isolation. Kiet fought in the French Indochina War as a member (1945–54) of the Viet Minh and later in the Vietnam War with the Viet Cong (1958–75). As Communist Party chief (1976–82) of Ho Chi Minh City, Kiet was charged with instituting socialist reforms in the city, but he favoured more gradual change and supported free enterprise. The party replaced him (1982), and he was transferred to Hanoi. In spite of his disagreements with the ruling Communist Party, Kiet was elected prime minister in 1991. During his time in office, he expanded diplomatic ties with foreign countries, and in 1995 he restored diplomatic relations between Vietnam and the U.S. Kiet also encouraged the Hanoi government to reconcile with dissidents, to listen to the opinions of opponents, and to support a free press. Even after resigning from office in 1997, Kiet remained a vocal critic of the Communist Party and its shortcomings. He retired from his position as adviser to the party's Central Committee in 2001.

CAMBODIA

Norodom Sihanouk

(b. Oct. 31, 1922, Phnom Penh, Cambodia, French Indochina)

Norodom Sihanouk was twice king of Cambodia (1941–55 and 1993–2004) and also served as prime minister, head of state, and president. He attempted to steer a neutral course for Cambodia in its civil and foreign wars of the late 20th century.

Sihanouk was, on his mother's side, the grandson of King Sisowath Monivong (reigned 1927–41), whom he succeeded to the throne at age 18. At the time Cambodia was a French protectorate, and Sihanouk wielded little power. However, near the end of World War II, the occupying Japanese encouraged the young king to declare Cambodia's independence from France. When French military forces moved back into the region, Sihanouk decided to wait until France's retreat from Indochina, which occurred in 1954. He founded the Sangkum Reastr Niyum ("People's Socialist Community") in January 1955, won a referendum in February approving its program, and on March 2 abdicated in favour of his father, Norodom Suramarit, becoming the new monarch's prime minister, foreign minister, and subsequently permanent representative to the United Nations. Five years later, after the death of his father (April 3, 1960), he accepted the role of head of state (June 13).

Sihanouk steered a neutralist course in his foreign policy. In return for a North Vietnamese pledge to respect Cambodia's frontiers, he allowed Vietnamese communists to operate covertly from bases inside eastern Cambodia. He subsequently rejected U.S. aid and assistance, relying on his immense popularity with the Cambodian people to keep radicals of both the right and the left under control. Under Sihanouk's benign rule, Cambodia experienced 15 years of fragile peace and mild prosperity while much of Southeast Asia was in a state of upheaval.

However, Sihanouk's maintenance of Cambodian neutrality in the Vietnam War ended in 1970 when he was ousted in a U.S.-supported coup led by Gen. Lon Nol. He then lived in Beijing as the titular head of a government-in-exile.

Following the Khmer Rouge takeover of Cambodia in 1975, Sihanouk returned home, only to be put under house arrest; under dictator Pol Pot, a four-year reign of terror ensued during which more than one million Cambodians were killed. Sihanouk was released in January 1979 because the Khmer Rouge regime was falling to Vietnamese military forces and needed an advocate in the United Nations. After denouncing the Vietnamese invasion, he dissociated himself from the Khmer Rouge. From residences in China and North Korea, Sihanouk became president of an uneasy coalition government-in-exile made up of the three principal anti-Vietnamese Khmer forces—the Khmer Rouge, the anticommunist Khmer People's National Liberation Front, and Sihanouk's neutralist party. He retained his role as resistance leader until 1991, when he was elected president of Cambodia's Supreme National Council, an interim administrative body.

In September 1993, following UN-sponsored elections the previous May,

Cambodia's National Assembly voted to restore the monarchy, and Sihanouk once again became king. His son, Norodom Ranariddh, served as first prime minister until 1997, when he was overthrown in a coup by Hun Sen, who nevertheless left Sihanouk on the throne.

In later years Sihanouk retreated from politics to work as a filmmaker and composer. He abdicated on Oct. 7, 2004, and his son Norodom Sihamoni, chosen to succeed him, was crowned king on October 29.

Lon Nol

(b. Nov. 13, 1913, Prey Vêng, Cambodia—d. Nov. 17, 1985, Fullerton, Calif., U.S.)

Lon Nol deposed Prince Norodom Sihanouk (1970), which involved Cambodia in the Indochina war and ended in the takeover (1975) of the country by the communist Khmer Rouge.

Lon Nol entered the French colonial service in 1937 and became a magistrate, then a provincial governor and head of the national police (1951). He joined the army in 1952 and fought against intruding Vietnamese communist guerrillas in Cambodia as an area commander. After again serving as a provincial governor, he became Cambodian army chief of staff (1955) and commander in chief (1960) under the country's leader, Prince Norodom Sihanouk. He was deputy premier (1963), minister of defense (1968–69), and twice premier (1966–67 and from 1969) under Sihanouk.

Lon Nol was a prime architect of the coup in March 1970 that overthrew Sihanouk, and he became the most prominent leader in the new government, serving as its premier until 1972. Abandoning Sihanouk's policy of neutrality in the Indochina war, Lon Nol established close ties with the United States and South Vietnam, permitting their forces to operate on Cambodian territory. On March 10, 1972, he assumed total power over Cambodia and installed himself as president two days later. In the meantime, the communist Khmer Rouge movement was gathering strength in the Cambodian countryside, despite a U.S. air campaign against the insurgents. On April 1, 1975, with Khmer Rouge communist guerrillas only a few miles from the capital, Lon Nol left the country and settled in the United States, where he died in 1985.

Pol Pot

(b. May 19, 1925, Kompong Thom province, Cambodia—d. April 15, 1998, near Anlong Veng, along the Cambodia-Thailand border)

Pol Pot was the Khmer political leader whose totalitarian regime (1975–79) imposed severe hardships on the Cambodian people. His radical communist government forced the mass evacuations of cities, killed or displaced millions of people, and left a legacy of brutality and impoverishment.

The son of a landowning farmer, Saloth Sar was sent at age 5 or 6 to live with an older brother in Phnom Penh, where he was educated. A mediocre student, he failed the entrance examinations for high school and so instead studied carpentry for a year at a technical school in Phnom Penh. In 1949 he went to Paris on a scholarship to study radio electronics. There he became involved with the French Communist Party and joined a group of young left-wing Cambodian nationalists who later became his fellow leaders in the Khmer Rouge. In France he spent more time on revolutionary activities than on his studies. His scholarship was cut short after he failed examinations, and he returned to Phnom Penh in 1953.

Pol Pot taught at a private school in Phnom Penh from 1956 to 1963, when he left the capital because his communist ties were suspected by the police. By 1963 he had adopted his revolutionary pseudonym, Pol Pot. He spent the next 12 years building up the Communist Party that had been organized in Cambodia in 1960, and he served as the party's secretary. An opponent of the Sihanouk government and of the military government of Gen. Lon Nol, he led the Khmer Rouge guerrilla forces in their overthrow of Lon Nol's regime in 1975. Pol Pot was prime minister of the new Khmer Rouge government from 1976 until he was overthrown by invading Vietnamese in January 1979. It is estimated that from 1975 to 1979, under the leadership of Pol Pot, the government caused the deaths of more than one million people from forced labour, starvation, disease, torture, or execution while carrying out a program of radical social and agricultural reforms.

Following the Vietnamese invasion of his country, Pol Pot withdrew to bases in Thailand to lead the Khmer Rouge forces against the new Hanoi-supported government in Phnom Penh, which refused to consider peace negotiations as long as he remained at the head of the party. Although ostensibly removed from the military and political leadership of the Khmer Rouge in 1985, he remained a guiding force in the organization, which continued its guerrilla campaign into the 1990s, though with diminishing intensity. By 1997 the Khmer Rouge were in deep decline, their ranks riddled by desertions and factionalism. In June of that year Pol Pot was forcibly ousted from the organization's leadership and placed under house arrest by his colleagues, and in July he was convicted of treason. Pol Pot died of natural causes in 1998.

UNITED STATES

John F. Kennedy

(b. May 29, 1917, Brookline, Mass., U.S.—d. Nov. 22, 1963, Dallas, Texas)

John F. Kennedy was the 35th president of the United States (1961–63). He faced a number of foreign crises, especially in Cuba and Berlin, but managed to secure

John F. Kennedy being sworn in as U.S. president, January 20, 1961. Encyclopædia Britannica, Inc.

such achievements as the Nuclear Test-Ban Treaty and the Alliance for Progress. He was assassinated while riding in a motorcade in Dallas.

Kennedy was the youngest man and the first Roman Catholic ever elected to the presidency of the United States. His administration lasted 1,037 days. From the onset he was concerned with foreign affairs. In his memorable inaugural address, he called upon Americans "to bear the burden of a long twilight struggle . . . against the common enemies of man: tyranny, poverty, disease, and war itself."

The Soviet premier, Nikita Khrushchev, thought he had taken the young president's measure when the two leaders met in Vienna in June 1961. Khrushchev ordered a wall built between East and West Berlin and threatened to sign a separate peace treaty with East Germany. The president activated National Guard and reserve units, and Khrushchev backed down on his separate peace threat. Kennedy then made a

U.S. President John F. Kennedy signing the Nuclear Test-Ban Treaty, October 7, 1963. National Archives and Records AdministrationInc.

dramatic visit to West Berlin, where he told a cheering crowd, "Today, in the world of freedom, the proudest boast is 'Ich bin ein [I am a] Berliner.' " In October 1962 a buildup of Soviet short- and intermediate-range nuclear missiles was discovered in Cuba. Kennedy demanded that the missiles be dismantled; he ordered a "quarantine" of Cuba—in effect, a blockade that would stop Soviet ships from reaching that island. For 13 days nuclear war seemed near; then the Soviet premier announced that the offensive weapons would be withdrawn. Ten months later Kennedy scored his greatest foreign triumph when Khrushchev and Prime Minister Harold Macmillan of Great Britain joined him in signing the Nuclear Test-Ban Treaty. Yet Kennedy's commitment to combat the spread of communism led him to escalate American involvement in the conflict in Vietnam, where he sent not just supplies and financial assistance, as President Eisenhower had, but 15,000 military advisers as well.

Henry Cabot Lodge

(b. July 5, 1902, Nahant, Mass., U.S.—d. Feb. 27, 1985, Beverly, Mass.)

Henry Cabot Lodge was a U.S. senator and diplomat who ran unsuccessfully for the vice presidency of the United States in 1960.

He was the grandson of Sen. Henry Cabot Lodge (1850–1924) and a member of a politically dedicated family that included six U.S. senators and a governor of Massachusetts. Lodge began his career in politics, after several years as a journalist, with two terms as a Republican in the Massachusetts legislature (1933–36), followed by service in the U.S. Senate (1937–44, 1947–52). He lost his Senate seat in 1952 to Rep. John F. Kennedy. In that year he had been active in promoting the presidential candidacy of Dwight D. Eisenhower, who subsequently appointed Lodge permanent U.S. representative to the United Nations.

In July 1960 he was nominated for the vice presidency on the unsuccessful Republican ticket headed by Nixon. Lodge served as U.S. ambassador to South Vietnam (1963–64, 1965–67), and as such he was the main channel of communication between Washington and the South Vietnamese leadership. After expressing his belief to President Kennedy that the war could not be won while Diem remained in power, Lodge, along with agents of the CIA, notified a cadre of South Vietnamese generals that the United States would make no move to oppose an attempted coup. In November 1963 the plot was carried to fruition, and Diem was deposed. In spite of assurances to Lodge that the lives of Diem and his brother, Ngo Dinh Nhu, would be spared, both were killed during the takeover. Lodge was later named ambassador to West Germany (1968–69), and he was chief negotiator at the talks in Paris on peace in Vietnam (1969). He then served as special envoy to the Vatican (1970–77).

Walt Rostow

(b. Oct. 7, 1916, New York, N.Y., U.S.—d. Feb. 13, 2003, Austin, Texas)

Walt Rostow, as an adviser to presidents Kennedy and Johnson, advocated an ever-increasing American commitment to the Vietnam War. He was a Rhodes scholar who taught at several prestigious universities in the U.S. and Britain and became well known with the publication of *The Stages of Economic Growth: A Non-Communist Manifesto* (1960). Kennedy hired Rostow in 1961 as his deputy special assistant for national security affairs. Rostow chaired the State Department's policy planning council from 1961 to 1966, when he became Johnson's special assistant for national security affairs (the post later known as national security adviser). Even after most other government officials had become convinced that the Vietnam War was unwinnable, Rostow consistently pushed for its escalation, convinced that the U.S. was winning and that the war was necessary so that economic modernization could take place in Southeast Asia.

Maxwell Taylor

(b. Aug. 26, 1901, Keytesville, Mo., U.S.—d. April 19, 1987, Washington, D.C.)

Maxwell Taylor was a U.S. Army officer and pioneer in airborne warfare in Europe during World War II.

A 1922 graduate of the United States Military Academy at West Point, New York, Taylor went on to study at the Command and General Staff School, Fort Leavenworth, Kansas, and at the Army War College in Washington, D.C. Taylor assisted in the organization of the U.S. Army's first airborne division, the 82nd, early in World War II and was its artillery commander during the Sicilian and Italian campaigns. At great personal risk, he passed through enemy lines 24 hours before the Allied invasion of Italy (1943) to confer with Italian leaders about the possibility of conducting an airborne assault on Rome. In March 1944, just prior to the Normandy Invasion, he took command of the 101st Airborne Division. He joined its parachute assault before dawn on D-Day (June 6, 1944) and led the division in the disastrous Arnhem operation in The Netherlands (September 1944). Taylor's division gained wide fame for its defense of Bastogne during the Battle of the Bulge late in 1944.

After the war Taylor was superintendent of West Point (1945–49). As commanding general of the Eighth Army in 1953, Taylor directed United Nations forces in Korea during the closing phases of the Korean War. He then served as army chief of staff (1955–59), in which post he was an early advocate of the strategic doctrine of "flexible response," which emphasized the maintenance of conventional infantry forces as a prudent wartime alternative to the all-out use of nuclear weapons. He was appointed chairman of the Joint Chiefs of Staff in 1962 by Kennedy, to whom he was a trusted adviser. Two years later he became

Maxwell Taylor, 1944. National Archives, Washington, D.C.

U.S. ambassador to South Vietnam, which at that time was being given increasing military support by the United States. He resigned that post in July 1965 but served as a special consultant (1965–69) to President Johnson.

Lyndon B. Johnson

(b. Aug. 27, 1908, Gillespie county, Texas, U.S.—d. Jan. 22, 1973, San Antonio, Texas)

Lyndon B. Johnson was the 36th president of the United States (1963–69). A moderate Democrat and vigorous leader in the United States Senate, Johnson was elected vice president in 1960 and acceded to the presidency in 1963 upon Kennedy's assassination. During his administration he signed into law the Civil Rights Act (1964), the most comprehensive civil rights legislation since the Reconstruction era, initiated major social service programs, and bore the brunt of national opposition to his vast expansion of American involvement in the Vietnam War.

In the tempestuous days after the assassination of John F. Kennedy on

President Lyndon B. Johnson talking with Martin Luther King, Jr., in the Oval Office at the White House, Washington, D.C., 1963. Yoichi Okamoto/Lyndon B. Johnson Library Photo

Nov. 22, 1963, Johnson helped to calm national hysteria and ensure continuity in the presidency. In early August 1964, after North Vietnamese gunboats allegedly attacked U.S. destroyers in the Gulf of Tonkin near the coast of North Vietnam without provocation, Johnson ordered retaliatory bombing raids on North Vietnamese naval installations and, in a televised address to the nation, proclaimed, "We still seek no wider war." Two days later, at Johnson's request, Congress overwhelmingly passed the Gulf of Tonkin Resolution, which authorized the president to take "all necessary measures to repel any armed attack against the forces of the United States and to prevent further aggression." In effect, the measure granted Johnson the constitutional authority to conduct a war in Vietnam without a formal declaration from Congress. Although there were contradictory reports about the "engagement" in the gulf—about which side did what, if anything, and when—Johnson never discussed them with the public.

Despite his campaign pledges not to widen American military involvement in Vietnam, Johnson soon increased the number of U.S. troops in that country and expanded their mission. In February 1965, after an attack by Viet Cong guerrillas on a U.S. military base in Pleiku, Johnson ordered "Operation Rolling Thunder," a series of massive bombing raids on North Vietnam intended to cut supply lines to North Vietnamese and Viet Cong fighters in the South; he also dispatched 3,500 Marines to protect the border city of Da Nang. Fifty thousand additional troops were sent in July, and by the end of the year the number of military personnel in the country had reached 180,000. The number increased steadily over the next two years, peaking at about 550,000 in 1968.

As each new American escalation met with fresh enemy response and as no end to the combat appeared in sight, the president's public support declined steeply. American casualties gradually mounted, reaching nearly 500 a week by

Lyndon B. Johnson, c. 1963. White House Collection

the end of 1967. Moreover, the enormous financial cost of the war, reaching $25 billion in 1967, diverted money from Johnson's cherished Great Society programs and began to fuel inflation. Beginning in 1965, student demonstrations grew larger and more frequent and helped to stimulate resistance to the draft. From 1967 onward, antiwar sentiment gradually spread among other segments of the population, including liberal Democrats, intellectuals, and civil rights leaders, and by 1968 many prominent political figures, some of them former supporters of the president's Vietnam policies, were publicly calling for an early negotiated settlement of the war. As his popularity sank to new lows in 1967, Johnson was confronted by demonstrations almost everywhere he went. It pained him to hear protesters, especially students—whom he thought would venerate him for his progressive social agenda—chanting, "Hey, hey, LBJ, how many kids did you kill today?" To avoid the demonstrations, he eventually restricted his travels, becoming a virtual "prisoner" in the White House.

Creighton Abrams, U.S. commander in South Vietnam, speaking as Pres. Lyndon B. Johnson (centre) and his advisers listen, 1968. U.S. Department of Defense

On Jan. 23, 1968, an American intelligence-gathering vessel, the USS *Pueblo*, was seized by North Korea; all 80 members of the crew were captured and imprisoned. Already frustrated by the demands of the Vietnam War, Johnson responded with restraint but called up 15,000 navy and air force reservists and ordered the nuclear-powered aircraft carrier USS *Enterprise* to the area. The *Pueblo* crew was held for 11 months and was freed only after the United States apologized for having violated North Korean waters; the apology was later retracted.

To make matters worse, only one week after the seizure of the *Pueblo*, the Tet Offensive by North Vietnamese and Viet Cong forces in South Vietnam embarrassed the Johnson administration and shocked the country. Although the attack was a failure in military terms, the news coverage—including televised images of enemy forces firing on the U.S. embassy in Saigon, the South Vietnamese capital—completely undermined the administration's claim that the war was being won and added further to Johnson's nagging "credibility gap."

Meanwhile, Senator Eugene McCarthy declared his candidacy for the Democratic presidential nomination, an unprecedented affront to a sitting president, and Robert Kennedy announced his own candidacy soon thereafter. On March 31, 1968, Johnson startled television viewers with a national address that included three announcements: that he had just ordered major reductions in the bombing of North Vietnam, that he was requesting peace talks, and that he would neither seek nor accept his party's renomination for the presidency.

In January 1973, less than one week before all the belligerents in Vietnam signed an agreement in Paris to end the war, Johnson suffered a heart attack and died. He was buried at the place he felt most at home: his ranch.

George Ball

(b. Dec. 21, 1909, Des Moines, Iowa, U.S.—d. May 26, 1994, New York, N.Y.)

George Ball was undersecretary of state (1961-66) in the Kennedy and Johnson administrations. He vociferously objected to increasing U.S. troop involvement in Vietnam and warned both presidents that the United States could not win a guerrilla war. His prophetic counsel was ignored, however, and U.S. involvement escalated from 400 "advisers" to more than 500,000 ground troops.

Ball joined the Kennedy administration as undersecretary of state for economic affairs but was soon elevated to undersecretary of state and advised Kennedy during the 1962 Cuban missile crisis. Ball resigned in 1966 to return to his law practice but served as the U.S. ambassador to the United Nations in 1968. His dovish views on Vietnam became known with the publication in 1971 of the sensitive Pentagon Papers.

McGeorge Bundy

(b. March 30, 1919, Boston, Mass., U.S.—d. Sept. 16, 1996, Boston)

McGeorge Bundy was one of the main architects of U.S. foreign policy in the administrations of presidents Kennedy and Johnson.

Bundy supported Kennedy for president in 1960 and in 1961 was made special assistant for national security affairs, a post he retained in the Johnson administration. Under Johnson, Bundy was a forceful advocate of expanding the United States' involvement in the Vietnam War. In February 1965, after visiting South Vietnam, he wrote a crucial memorandum calling for a policy of "sustained reprisal," including air strikes, against North Vietnam if it did not end its guerrilla war against the South Vietnamese government. Later, however, after he had left government service, he advised Johnson against further escalation of the war.

Hubert H. Humphrey

(b. May 27, 1911, Wallace, S.D., U.S.—d. Jan. 13, 1978, Waverly, Minn.)

Hubert H. Humphrey was the 38th vice president of the United States (1965–69). He served in the Democratic administration of President Johnson and was himself a presidential candidate of the Democratic Party in 1968. A liberal leader in the United States Senate (1949–65; 1971–78), he built his political base on a Democrat-Farmer-Labor coalition reminiscent of the Populist Movement.

When he became vice president under Johnson, Humphrey's earlier reputation as a glib and sometimes abrasive "do-gooder" was supplanted by a more conservative image, especially after he defended American participation in the Vietnam War, and he was often vilified by left-wing opponents of the Johnson administration.

Following Johnson's withdrawal from the 1968 presidential election, Humphrey sought the Democratic nomination. Although the party was deeply divided, Humphrey captured the nomination at a tumultuous convention in Chicago but trailed far behind Republican Richard M. Nixon in the polls. His fortunes began to reverse at the end of September, when he announced his plans to halt the bombing campaign in North Vietnam if he were elected. Rising steadily in the polls throughout October, he eventually lost by only 510,000 votes, one of the slimmest margins in any U.S. presidential election. Many observers concluded that he would have won the election had it been held a week later.

Robert S. McNamara

(b. June 9, 1916, San Francisco, Calif., U.S.—d. July 6, 2009, Washington, D.C.)

Robert S. McNamara was U.S. secretary of defense from 1961 to 1968. He revamped Pentagon operations and played a major role in the nation's military involvement in Vietnam.

In 1960 McNamara joined the Kennedy administration as secretary of defense. In his new post he successfully gained control of Pentagon operations and the military bureaucracy, encouraged the modernization of the armed forces, restructured budget procedures, and cut costs by refusing to spend money on what he believed were unnecessary or obsolete weapons systems. McNamara was also at the centre of a drive to alter U.S. military strategy from the "massive retaliation" of the Eisenhower years to a "flexible response," emphasizing counterinsurgency techniques and second-strike nuclear-missile capability.

McNamara initially supported the deepening military involvement of the United States in Vietnam. On visits to South Vietnam in 1962, 1964, and 1966, the secretary publicly expressed optimism that the National Liberation Front and its North Vietnamese allies would soon abandon their attempt to overthrow the U.S.-backed Saigon regime. He became the government's chief spokesman for the day-to-day operations of the war and acted as Pres. Lyndon B. Johnson's principal deputy in the war's prosecution.

As early as 1965, however, McNamara had begun to question the wisdom of U.S. military involvement in Vietnam, and by 1967 he was openly seeking a way to launch peace negotiations. He initiated a full-scale investigation of the American commitment to Vietnam (later published as *The Pentagon Papers*), came out in opposition to continued bombing of North Vietnam (for which he lost influence in the Johnson administration), and in February 1968 left the Pentagon to become president of the World Bank until 1981. McNamara publicly criticised the 2003 invasion of Iraq under the administration of Pres. George W. Bush. McNamara died at his Washington, D.C., home on July 6, 2009. He was 93.

Robert S. McNamara, 1967. Yoichi R. Okamoto, The Lyndon Baines Johnson Library and Museum/National Archives and Records Administration

Clark Clifford

(b. Dec. 25, 1906, Fort Scott, Kan., U.S.—d. Oct. 10, 1998, Bethesda, Md.)

Clark Clifford was a knowledgeable and savvy adviser to four U.S. Democratic presidents and as such served a number of public and private interests.

Clifford began work as an attorney. During World War II he enlisted in the navy and served as an aide to President Truman. Clifford was Kennedy's attorney while the latter was still a senator, and Kennedy continued to seek his advice during his campaign and presidency. Clifford returned to government in 1968 to become Johnson's secretary of defense, a post that he occupied for less than a year. One significant action during his brief tenure was to advise the president to commence action to end the war in Vietnam. His guidance was also sought by Pres. Jimmy Carter, who consulted Clifford regarding difficulties involving his budget director.

J. William Fulbright

(b. April 9, 1905, Sumner, Mo., U.S.—d. Feb. 9, 1995, Washington, D.C.)

J. William Fulbright was the American senator who initiated the international exchange program for scholars known as the Fulbright scholarship. He is also known for his vocal and articulate criticism of U.S. military involvement in South Vietnam during his tenure as chairman of the Senate Foreign Relations Committee.

The American public came to know Fulbright best for his probing, articulate opposition to the Vietnam War, despite the fact that he initially supported U.S. involvement. Indeed, as an old friend and former Senate colleague of President Johnson, Fulbright had shepherded the Gulf of Tonkin Resolution through the Senate. In 1966, however, his committee held televised hearings on U.S. military involvement in Southeast Asia, from which he emerged as a leading proponent for an end to the U.S. bombing of North Vietnam and for peace talks to settle the Vietnamese conflict.

Eugene McCarthy

(b. March 29, 1916, Watkins, Minn., U.S.—d. Dec. 10, 2005, Washington, D.C.)

Eugene McCarthy was a U.S. senator. His entry into the 1968 race for the Democratic presidential nomination ultimately led Johnson to drop his bid for reelection.

In 1958 McCarthy was elected to the Senate, where he remained a relatively unknown figure nationally until Nov. 30, 1967. On that day, he announced his intention to challenge Johnson in the Democratic presidential primaries. Although in 1964 he had supported the Gulf of Tonkin Resolution (which gave the president broad powers to wage the Vietnam War), by 1967 McCarthy had become an outspoken critic of the war. At first McCarthy's challenge was not taken seriously, but his candidacy soon attracted the growing numbers of Democrats who opposed further American involvement in the Vietnam War. After the Minnesota senator, with his trenchant wit and scholarly, understated manner, captured 42 percent of the vote in the New Hampshire primary in March 1968, Johnson made the dramatic announcement of his withdrawal from the race. McCarthy went on to sweep three primaries but then lost four of the next five to Senator Robert F. Kennedy. Following Kennedy's assassination, McCarthy lost the nomination at the convention in Chicago to Humphrey, who had declined to run in the primaries.

Robert F. Kennedy

(b. Nov. 20, 1925, Brookline, Mass., U.S.—d. June 6, 1968, Los Angeles, Calif.)

Robert F. Kennedy. U.S. News & World Report Magazine; photograph, Warren K. Leffler/Library of Congress, Washington, D.C. (digital file no. 03685u)

Robert F. Kennedy was the U.S. attorney general and adviser during the administration of his brother Pres. John F. Kennedy (1961–63). Later U.S. senator (1965–68), he was assassinated while campaigning for the presidential nomination.

Robert Kennedy first came into national prominence in 1953, when he was an assistant counsel to the Senate Permanent Subcommittee on Investigations, headed by Joseph R. McCarthy. In 1957 he was chief counsel to the Senate select committee conducting investigations into labour racketeering, which led to his long-standing feud with James R. Hoffa of the Teamsters Union. Kennedy resigned from the committee staff in 1960 to conduct his brother's campaign for the U.S. presidency and was subsequently appointed (1961) attorney general in the Cabinet of President Kennedy.

On Nov. 22, 1963, his brother was assassinated in Dallas, Texas. Robert Kennedy continued to serve as attorney general until he resigned in September 1964. In November 1964 he was elected U.S. senator from New York. Within two years Kennedy had established himself as a major political figure in his own right. He became the chief spokesman for liberal Democrats and a critic of Johnson's Vietnam policy. On March 16, 1968, he announced his candidacy for the presidency. By June 4 he had won five out of six presidential primaries, including one that day in California. Shortly after midnight on June 5 he spoke to his followers in Los Angeles' Ambassador Hotel. As he left through a kitchen hallway he was fatally wounded by a Palestinian immigrant, Sirhan Bishara Sirhan. Robert Kennedy was buried near his brother at Arlington National Cemetery.

Richard M. Nixon

(b. Jan. 9, 1913, Yorba Linda, Calif., U.S.—d. April 22, 1994, New York, N.Y.)

Richard M. Nixon was the 37th president of the United States (1969–74). Faced with almost certain impeachment for his role in the Watergate scandal, Nixon became the first American president to resign from office. He was also vice president (1953–61) under Eisenhower.

Nixon won the Republican nomination for president in 1968 by putting together a coalition that included Southern conservatives led by Senator Strom Thurmond of South Carolina. Nixon campaigned on a vague platform promising an honourable peace in Vietnam—Nixon said that he had a "secret plan" to end the war—the restoration of law and order in the cities, a crackdown on illegal drugs, and an end to the draft. Democratic Party nominee Hubert H. Humphrey, who as Johnson's vice president was heavily burdened by the latter's unpopular Vietnam policies, called for an end to the bombing of North Vietnam as "an acceptable risk for peace." Johnson himself halted the bombing on October 31, less than one week before the election, in preparation for direct negotiations with Hanoi. Had he taken this step earlier, Humphrey might have won the election, as polls showed him gaining rapidly on Nixon in the final days of the campaign. Nixon won the election by a narrow margin, 31.7 million popular votes to Humphrey's nearly 30.9 million; the electoral vote was 301 to 191.

Aiming to achieve "peace with honor" in the Vietnam War, Nixon gradually reduced the number of U.S. military personnel in Vietnam. Under his policy of "Vietnamization," combat roles were transferred to South Vietnamese troops, who nevertheless remained heavily dependent on American supplies and air support. At the same time, however, Nixon resumed the bombing of North Vietnam (suspended by President Johnson in October 1968) and expanded the air and ground war to neighbouring Cambodia and Laos. In the spring of 1970, U.S. and South Vietnamese forces attacked North Vietnamese sanctuaries in Cambodia, which prompted widespread protests in the United States; one of these demonstrations—at Kent State University on May 4, 1970—ended tragically when soldiers of the Ohio National Guard fired

Richard M. Nixon, 1969. U.S. Department of Defense

into a crowd of about 2,000 protesters, killing four and wounding nine.

After intensive negotiations between National Security Adviser Henry Kissinger and North Vietnamese Foreign Minister Le Duc Tho, the two sides reached an agreement in October 1972, and Kissinger announced, "Peace is at hand." But the South Vietnamese raised objections, and the agreement quickly broke down. An intensive 11-day bombing campaign of Hanoi and other North Vietnamese cities in late December was followed by more negotiations, and a new agreement was finally reached in January 1973 and signed in Paris. It included an immediate cease-fire, the withdrawal of all American military personnel, the release of all prisoners of war, and an international force to keep the peace.

Henry Kissinger

(b. May 27, 1923, Fürth, Ger.)

Henry Kissinger, as adviser for national security affairs and secretary of state, was a major influence in the shaping of foreign policy from 1969 to 1976 under presidents Nixon and Ford. In 1973 he was jointly awarded the Nobel Prize for Peace with Le Duc Tho of North Vietnam for their efforts to negotiate a peaceful settlement of the Vietnam War.

In December 1968 Kissinger was appointed by President Nixon as assistant for national security affairs. He eventually came to serve as head of the National Security Council (1969–75) and as secretary of state (September 1973–Jan. 20, 1977).

Henry Kissinger (left) meeting with Chinese Premier Zhou Enlai, 1972. White House Photo

Kissinger soon emerged as an influential figure in the Nixon administration. His major diplomatic achievements involved China, the Soviet Union, Vietnam, and the Middle East. He developed a policy of warmer U.S. relations with the Soviet Union, détente, which led to the Strategic Arms Limitation Talks (SALT) in 1969. He established the pro-Pakistan policy in the India-Pakistan war of late 1971, helped negotiate the SALT I arms agreement with the Soviet Union (signed 1972), and developed a rapprochement between the United States and the People's Republic of China (1972), the first official U.S. contact with that nation since the Chinese Communists had come to power.

Although he originally advocated a hard-line policy in Vietnam and helped engineer the U.S. bombing of Cambodia (1969–70), Kissinger later played a major role in Nixon's Vietnamization policy—the disengagement of U.S. troops from South Vietnam and their replacement by South Vietnamese forces. On Jan. 23, 1973, after months of negotiations with the North Vietnamese government in

Paris, he initialed a cease-fire agreement that both provided for the withdrawal of U.S. troops and outlined the machinery for a permanent peace settlement between the two Vietnams. For this apparent resolution of the Vietnam conflict, Kissinger shared the 1973 Nobel Prize for Peace with the North Vietnamese negotiator, Le Duc Tho (who refused the honour).

Dean Rusk

(b. Feb. 9, 1909, Cherokee county, Ga., U.S.—d. Dec. 20, 1994, Athens, Ga.)

Dean Rusk was U.S. secretary of state during the Kennedy and Johnson administrations. He became a target of antiwar hostility as he consistently defended the United States' participation in the Vietnam War.

During World War II, Rusk served Gen. Joseph W. Stilwell as deputy chief of staff for the China-Burma-India theatre. After the war he held positions in both the state and war departments. In March 1950 he became assistant secretary of state for Far Eastern affairs, a position in which he was involved in U.S. prosecution of the Korean War. Rusk supported the war, but he disagreed with MacArthur's advocacy of expanding the fighting into China.

Rusk was president of the Rockefeller Foundation from 1952 to 1960. In 1961 he became secretary of state under President Kennedy. Within a year he faced crises in Cuba, Indochina, and Berlin. Rusk's characteristically cool and reticent personality, however, contributed to the State Department's reduced role in national policy making.

Rusk was retained as secretary of state in the Johnson administration following Kennedy's assassination. From 1964 to 1968 he consistently defended the United States' military involvement in Vietnam, making himself a target of growing antiwar sentiment in the country. His longtime opposition to the diplomatic recognition of Communist China confirmed his image as an inflexible stalwart of the Cold War.

George McGovern

(b. July 19, 1922, Avon, S.D., U.S.)

George McGovern was a U.S. senator and an unsuccessful reformist Democratic candidate for the presidency in 1972. He campaigned on a platform advocating an immediate end to the Vietnam War and for a broad program of liberal social and economic reforms at home.

As chairman of a Commission on Party Structure and Delegate Selection prior to the Democratic National Convention in 1972, McGovern helped enact party reforms that gave increased representation to minority groups at the convention. Supported by these groups, he won the presidential nomination but alienated many of the more traditional elements in the Democratic Party. McGovern was unable to unify the party sufficiently to offer an effective challenge to the incumbent Republican president,

Nixon, who defeated him by an overwhelming margin.

Gerald R. Ford

(b. July 14, 1913, Omaha, Neb., U.S.—d. Dec. 26, 2006, Rancho Mirage, Calif.)

Gerald R. Ford was the 38th president of the United States (1974–77), who, as 40th vice president, succeeded to the presidency upon Nixon's resignation under the process decreed by the Twenty-fifth Amendment to the Constitution. This made Ford the country's only chief executive who was not elected as either president or vice president. His first act upon assuming office was to grant his predecessor "a full, free, and absolute pardon."

On the day of Nixon's resignation Ford took the oath of office and became president, stating, "Our long national nightmare is over." He retained the foreign and domestic policy staffs of the Nixon administration, including Secretary of State Henry Kissinger.

During the final days of the Vietnam War, in March 1975, Ford ordered an airlift of some 237,000 anticommunist Vietnamese refugees from Da Nang, most of whom were taken to the United States. Two months later, after the seizure by Cambodia of the American cargo ship *Mayaguez*, Ford declared the event an "act of piracy" and sent the Marines to seize the ship. They succeeded, but the rescue operation to save the 39-member crew resulted in the loss of 41 American lives and the wounding of 50 others.

Gerald R. Ford. Courtesy Gerald R. Ford Library

In a close contest at the Republican convention in August 1976, Ford won his party's nomination. That fall Ford became the first incumbent president to agree to public debates with a challenger—Jimmy Carter, the Democratic nominee. Ford ran substantially behind from the beginning of the campaign, owing in large part to negative fallout from the Nixon pardon but also to the general public's perception of his ineptitude. His decisions in office had often seemed to be those of

Kissinger and the others left over from the Nixon administration; sometimes, as those made during the *Mayaguez* incident, they seemed simply ill-considered. He misspoke on many occasions, notably declaring in a debate with Jimmy Carter, "There is no Soviet domination of Eastern Europe" and "I don't believe that the Poles consider themselves dominated by the Soviet Union," which journalist William F. Buckley, Jr., called "the ultimate Polish joke." Ford was defeated in the November 1976 election by a popular vote of 40.8 million to 39.1 million and an electoral vote of 297 to 240.

John Kerry

(b. Dec. 11, 1943, Denver, Colo., U.S.)

John Kerry was the Democratic Party's nominee for president in 2004.

After graduating from Yale University in 1966, Kerry enlisted in the U.S. Navy and served in the Vietnam War as an officer of a gunboat in the Mekong delta. By the time he returned from Vietnam in 1969, he had achieved the rank of lieutenant and had been honoured with a Silver Star, a Bronze Star, and three Purple Hearts.

Concluding his military service in 1970, he questioned the purpose and execution of the war and was a cofounder of the Vietnam Veterans of America and a spokesperson for the Vietnam Veterans Against the War. In this role he gained national attention in 1971 when he testified before the Senate Foreign Relations Committee. In 1982 he was elected lieutenant governor of Massachusetts, and in 1984 he won election to the U.S. Senate. He was reelected three times (1990, 1996, and 2002).

John Kerry, 2004. Sharon Farmer

As senator, Kerry, along with Republican Senator John McCain of Arizona, was known for helping to normalize relations with Vietnam by clearing up the status of American veterans declared POW/MIA (prisoner of war or missing in action).

John McCain. Courtesy Office of U. S. Senator John McCain

JOHN MCCAIN

(b. Aug. 29, 1936, Panama Canal Zone)

John McCain is a veteran of the Vietnam War and was the Republican Party's nominee for president in 2008.

McCain served in the U.S. Navy as a ground-attack pilot. In 1967, during the Vietnam War, McCain was nearly killed in a severe accidental fire aboard the aircraft carrier USS *Forrestal*, then on active duty in the Gulf of Tonkin.

Later that year McCain's plane was shot down over Hanoi, and, badly injured, he was captured by the North Vietnamese. In captivity he endured torture and years of solitary confinement. When his father was named commander of all U.S. forces in the Pacific in 1968, the North Vietnamese, as a propaganda ploy, offered early release to the younger McCain. However, McCain refused unless every American captured before him was also freed. Finally released in 1973, he received a hero's welcome home as well as numerous service awards, including the Silver Star and the Legion of Merit.

CHAPTER 10

Military Commanders of the Vietnam War

The following brief biographies of major military commanders concentrate on their actions during the Vietnam War.

VO NGUYEN GIAP

(b. 1912, An Xa, Vietnam, French Indochina)

Vo Nguyen Giap was a Vietnamese military and political leader whose perfection of guerrilla as well as conventional strategy and tactics led to the Viet Minh victory over the French (and to the end of French colonialism in Southeast Asia) and later to the North Vietnamese victory over South Vietnam and the United States.

The son of an ardent anticolonialist scholar, Giap as a youth began to work for Vietnamese autonomy. He attended the same high school as Ho Chi Minh, the Communist leader, and while still a student in 1926 he joined the Tan Viet Cach Menh Dang, the Revolutionary Party of Young Vietnam. In 1930, as a supporter of student strikes, he was arrested by the French Sûreté and sentenced to three years in prison, but he was paroled after serving only a few months. He studied at the Lycée Albert-Sarraut in Hanoi, where in 1937 he received a law degree. Giap then became a professor of history at the Lycée Thanh Long in Hanoi, where he converted many of his fellow teachers and students to his political views. In 1938 he married Minh Thai, and together they worked for the Indochinese Communist Party. When in 1939 the party was prohibited, Giap escaped to China, but his wife and sister-in-law were captured by the French police. His sister-in-law was guillotined; his wife received a life sentence and died in prison after three years.

In 1941 Giap formed an alliance with Chu Van Tan, guerrilla leader of the Tho, a minority tribal group of northeastern Vietnam. Giap hoped to build an army that would drive out the French and support the goals of the Viet Minh. With Ho Chi Minh, Giap marched his forces into Hanoi in August 1945, and in September Ho announced the independence of Vietnam, with Giap in command of all police and internal security forces and commander in chief of the armed forces. Giap sanctioned the execution of many non-Communist nationalists, and he censored nationalist newspapers to conform to Communist Party directives. In the French Indochina War, Giap's brilliance as a military strategist and tactician led to his winning the decisive battle at Dien Bien Phu on May 7, 1954, which brought the French colonialist regime to an end.

Gen. Vo Nguyen Giap visits a victory monument at the former Dien Bien Phu battlefield in April 2004 to commemorate his Vietnamese troops' defeat of French forces fifty years before. AFP/Getty Images

On the division of the country in July, Giap became deputy prime minister, minister of defense, and commander in chief of the armed forces of North Vietnam. He subsequently led the military forces of the north to eventual victory in the Vietnam War, compelling the Americans to leave the country in 1973 and bringing about the fall of South Vietnam in 1975. From 1976, when the two Vietnams were reunited, to 1980 Giap served as Vietnam's minister of national defense; he also became a deputy prime minister in 1976. He was a full member of the Politburo of the Vietnamese Communist Party until 1982.

VAN TIEN DUNG

(b. May 1, 1917, Co Nhue, Vietnam, French Indochina—d. March 17, 2002, Hanoi)

Van Tien Dung was one of North Vietnam's greatest war heroes—a peasant soldier who rose to become commander in chief of the North Vietnamese army and lead the final Ho Chi Minh Campaign that captured and occupied Saigon, South Vietnam, in 1975. As a young man, Dung was arrested by French colonial authorities for his Communist Party activities, but he escaped from prison and in 1947 joined Giap's High Command staff. Despite his lack of military training and limited battlefield experience, Dung proved to be an able logistic planner. He was named chief of staff of the People's Army of Vietnam in 1953 and succeeded Giap as commander in chief in 1975. After the reunification of Vietnam, he served (1980–87) as defense minister.

TRAN VAN TRA

(b. 1918, Quang Ngai province, Vietnam, French Indochina—d. April 20, 1996, Ho Chi Minh City [formerly Saigon], Viet.)

Tran Van Tra proved to be an able commander in the Vietnam War by leading communist raids on Saigon both during the Tet Offensive of 1968 and during the city's capture in 1975.

Raised in southern Vietnam, he began his military career in the late 1930s fighting against the French in the Viet Minh resistance movement. Following the Geneva Accords of 1954 that partitioned the country, he assumed various posts in the North Vietnamese army. In 1963 he was sent back to the south, where he led Viet Cong guerrillas against U.S. and South Vietnamese forces. Although he scored many battlefield victories and was appointed military head of the underground communist government in South Vietnam, he often clashed with party leaders over wartime strategy. He returned briefly to Hanoi in the mid-1970s to help plan the final assault on Saigon, in which he was the frontline commander. Dismayed at the lack of official credit he and other generals from South Vietnam received following the war, he wrote a personal account of the conflict, which was censored upon its publication in 1982. Despite falling from favour in Hanoi, Tra retained his influence among former army officials, with whom in 1987 he organized a war veterans association. The group was vocal in its opposition to government policies and was banned in 1990.

WILLIAM WESTMORELAND

(b. March 26, 1914, Spartanburg county, S.C., U.S.—d. July 18, 2005, Charleston, S.C.)

William Westmoreland commanded U.S. forces in the Vietnam War from 1964 to 1968, a period during which American involvement increased from several thousand troops to more than 500,000.

Westmoreland served in the Korean War and in 1955 was promoted to major general, becoming at age 42 the youngest man to have achieved that rank in the U.S. Army. Westmoreland became a full general in 1964. In Vietnam he implemented a strategy of attrition, using overwhelming firepower to try to kill enemy troops at a rate faster than they could be replaced. Though he employed search-and-destroy tactics, massive aerial bombing campaigns, napalm, and the defoliant Agent

Gen. William C. Westmoreland (right) *inspects a 9th infantry division's Mekong Delta base camp near Long Thanh, Vietnam, 1966.* Hulton Archive/Getty Images

Orange—all to devastating effect—the communist forces of North Vietnam and their Viet Cong allies in South Vietnam remained determined to unite their country under communist rule. Senior officials in Johnson's administration and a growing number of ordinary citizens began to see the war as unwinnable, and Westmoreland was recalled to Washington and given the post of army chief of staff. He retired in 1972.

CREIGHTON WILLIAMS ABRAMS, JR.

(b. Sept. 14, 1914, Springfield, Mass., U.S.—d. Sept. 4, 1974, Washington, D.C.)

Creighton Williams Abrams, Jr., was commander (1968–72) of all U.S. forces in Vietnam during the latter stages of the Vietnam War.

In April 1967 Abrams, by then a four-star general and vice chief of staff of the army, was named deputy to Westmoreland, who was at that time the head of the U.S. Military Assistance Command, Vietnam. On July 2, 1968, after Westmoreland was appointed army chief of staff, Abrams succeeded him as top commander of all U.S. forces in the Vietnam theatre. In this position he implemented Nixon's Vietnamization policy, overseeing a reduction of U.S. combat troops from more than 500,000 to fewer than 30,000 and also directing an intensive training program for the army of South Vietnam. He was in charge of the U.S.-South Vietnamese incursion into Cambodia in 1970. In 1972 he was appointed army chief of staff in Washington, D.C., where he implemented the transition to an all-volunteer force. He died of cancer while in office and was buried at Arlington National Cemetery, Virginia. The U.S. Army's main battle tank, the M-1 Abrams, is named in his honour.

CHAPTER 11

Journalists and Antiwar Activists of the Vietnam War

A number of American journalists and antiwar activists had a noticeable effect on the perception of the war by the American public. The following brief biographies of some of these individuals concentrate on their activities during the Vietnam War.

DAVID HALBERSTAM

(b. April 10, 1934, New York, N.Y., U.S.—d. April 23, 2007, Menlo Park, Calif.)

David Halberstam received a Pulitzer Prize in 1964 for his penetrating coverage of the Vietnam War as a staff reporter (1960–67) for the *New York Times*.

After earning a bachelor's degree in journalism from Harvard University (1955), Halberstam worked as a reporter for the *Daily Times Leader* in West Point, Miss., and for the *Nashville Tennessean* (now the *Tennessean*) before joining the *New York Times*. While his reporting on Vietnam initially supported U.S. involvement there, *The Making of a Quagmire* (1965) reflected a growing disillusionment with the war, and its title became a byword for intractable military operations. Halberstam's examination of power resulted in three volumes that were viewed loosely as a trilogy: *The Best and the*

Brightest (1972) chronicled the military failings of the United States during the Vietnam War; *The Powers That Be* (1979) reviewed the impact that the media had on history; and *The Reckoning* (1986) scrutinized the auto industry.

WALTER CRONKITE

(b. Nov. 4, 1916, St. Joseph, Mo., U.S.—d. July 17, 2009, New York, N.Y.)

Walter Cronkite was an American journalist and pioneer of television news programming. He was the longtime anchor of the *CBS Evening News with Walter Cronkite* (1962–81), for which he reported on many of the most historic events of the latter half of the 20th century.

In 1962 Cronkite attained the position he would become most famous for: anchorman of the *CBS Evening News*. Soon after Cronkite took over from his predecessor Douglas Edwards, the then 15-minute broadcast was expanded to 30 minutes, making it the first half-hour nightly news show on American network television. From the anchor chair of the *CBS Evening News with Walter Cronkite*, he reported on the most traumatic and triumphant moments of American life in the 1960s, from the assassination of President John F. Kennedy in 1963 to the Apollo Moon landing in 1969. The influence of Cronkite's reporting is perhaps best illustrated by his commentary on the Vietnam War. In 1968 he left the anchor desk to report from Vietnam on the aftermath of the Tet Offensive. Upon his return Cronkite departed from his usual objectivity, declaring that the war could end only in a protracted stalemate. President Lyndon B. Johnson told his staff, "If I've lost Cronkite, I've lost Middle America," and some held that Johnson's decision not to run for reelection that year was a direct result of Cronkite's reporting.

CBS news anchor Walter Cronkite reports from Vietnam on the Tet offensive for a CBS special news report, 1968. CBS Photo Archive/Hulton Archive/Getty Images

Cronkite continued in his position at CBS through the 1970s, reporting on the decade's most memorable events, including the Watergate scandal, the resignation of President Richard M. Nixon, and the historic peace negotiations between Egyptian Pres. Anwar el-Sādāt and Israeli Prime Minister Menachem Begin. His avuncular mien and adherence to journalistic integrity—exemplified by his sign-off line, "And that's the way it is"—endeared him to the American public, and a 1973 poll named him "the most trusted man in America." After a long illness, Cronkite died at the age of 92, at his home in New York City.

JOAN BAEZ

(b. Jan. 9, 1941, Staten Island, N.Y., U.S.)

Joan Baez was an American folk singer and political activist who interested young audiences in folk music during the 1960s. Despite the inevitable fading of the folk music revival, Baez continued to be a popular performer into the 21st century. By touring with younger performers throughout the world and staying politically engaged, she reached a new audience both in the United States and abroad. Her sense of commitment and unmistakable voice continued to win acclaim.

An active participant in the 1960s protest movement, Baez made free concert appearances for UNESCO, civil rights organizations, and anti-Vietnam War rallies. In 1964 she refused to pay federal taxes that went toward war expenses, and she was jailed twice in 1967. The following year she married David Harris, a leader in the national movement to oppose the draft who served nearly two years in prison for refusing to comply with his draft summons (they divorced in 1973). Baez was in Hanoi in December 1972, delivering Christmas presents and mail to American prisoners of war, when the United States targeted the North Vietnamese capital with the most intense bombing campaign of the war. The title track of her 1973 album *Where Are You Now, My Son?* chronicled the experience; it was a 23-minute spoken word piece, punctuated with sound clips that Baez had recorded during the bombing. Throughout the years, she remained deeply committed to social and political causes, lending her voice to many concerts for a variety of causes.

JANE FONDA

(b. Dec. 21, 1937, New York, N.Y., U.S.)

Jane Fonda was an American motion-picture actress also noted for her political activism.

In the 1970s and 1980s Fonda was active on behalf of left-wing political causes. She was an outspoken opponent of the Vietnam War who journeyed to Hanoi in 1972 to denounce the U.S. bombing campaigns there. During that trip she visited with the crew of North Vietnamese air defense battery, and photographs of Fonda in the seat of an antiaircraft gun were widely circulated. Her actions led to Fonda's being branded

"Hanoi Jane" (recalling World War II's Tokyo Rose). In 1988 she apologized to American veterans of the Vietnam War in a televised interview with Barbara Walters, saying that some of her behaviour in Hanoi was "thoughtless and careless."

ABBIE HOFFMAN

(b. Nov. 30, 1936, Worcester, Mass., U.S.—d. April 12, 1989, New Hope, Pa.)

Abbie Hoffman was an American political activist and founder of the Youth International Party (Yippies).

Hoffman was active in the American civil rights movement before turning his energies to protesting the Vietnam War and the American economic and political system. His acts of protest blurred the line between political action and guerrilla theatre, and they utilized absurdist humour to great effect. In August 1967 Hoffman and a dozen confederates disrupted operations at the New York Stock Exchange by showering the trading floor with dollar bills. In October of that year he led a crowd of more than 50,000 antiwar protesters in an attempt to levitate the Pentagon and exorcise the evil spirits that he claimed resided within.

Hoffman's ethic was codified with the formal organization of the Yippies in January 1968. Later that year Hoffman secured his place as a countercultural icon when he joined thousands of protesters outside the Democratic Party's national convention in Chicago. Before the demonstrations degenerated into a street battle between police and protesters, Hoffman and Yippie cofounder Jerry Rubin unveiled Pigasus, a boar hog that would serve as the Yippies' presidential candidate in 1968. These exploits, among others, led to Hoffman's being named a defendant in the so-called Chicago Seven trial (1969), in which he was convicted of crossing state lines with intent to riot at the Democratic convention; the conviction was later overturned.

CHAPTER 12

Vietnam Unified, 1974–

THE SOCIALIST REPUBLIC

Although the establishment of the Socialist Republic of Vietnam in 1976 had officially reunified the country, Vietnam at peace faced formidable problems. In the South alone, millions of people had been made homeless by the war, and more than one-seventh of the population had been killed or wounded; the costs in the North were probably as high or higher. Plans to reconstruct the country called for the expansion of industry in the North and of agriculture in the South. Within two years of the communist victory, however, it became clear that Vietnam would face major difficulties in realizing its goals.

Hanoi had been at war for more than a generation—indeed, Ho Chi Minh had died in 1969—and the bureaucracy was poorly trained to deal with the problems of peacetime economic recovery. The government encountered considerable resistance to its policies, particularly in the huge metropolis of Saigon (renamed Ho Chi Minh City in 1976), where members of the commercial sector—many of whom were ethnic Chinese—sought to avoid cooperating in the new socialist economic measures and resisted assignment to "new economic zones" in the countryside. During the late 1970s the country also suffered major floods and drought that severely reduced food production. When the regime suddenly announced a program calling for the socialization of industry and agriculture in the South in early 1978, hundreds of thousands of people (mainly ethnic Chinese) fled the country on foot or by boat.

These internal difficulties were compounded by problems in foreign affairs. Perhaps unrealistically, the regime decided to pursue plans to form a close alliance with new revolutionary governments in neighbouring Laos and Cambodia (Kampuchea). Such plans risked incurring not only the hostility of the United States but also that of China, which had its own interests in those countries. As Sino-Vietnamese relations soured, Hanoi turned to Moscow and signed a treaty of friendship and cooperation with the Soviet Union. In the meantime, relations with the revolutionary Democratic Kampuchea (Khmer Rouge) government in Cambodia rapidly deteriorated when it refused Hanoi's offer of a close relationship among the three countries that once formed French Indochina. Savage border fighting culminated in a Vietnamese invasion of Cambodia in December 1978. The Khmer Rouge were dislodged from power, and a pro-Vietnamese government was installed in Phnom Penh.

Khmer Rouge forces now took refuge in isolated areas of the country and began a guerrilla war of resistance against the new government, the latter backed by some 200,000 Vietnamese troops. In the meantime, China launched a brief but fierce punitive invasion along the Sino-Vietnamese border in early 1979 in response to Vietnamese actions in Cambodia. During the month-long war the Chinese destroyed major Vietnamese towns and inflicted heavy damage in the frontier zone, but they also suffered heavy casualties from the Vietnamese defenders.

Vietnam was now nearly isolated in the world. Apart from the protégé regime in Phnom Penh and the government of Laos, which also depended heavily on Vietnamese aid for its survival, the country was at odds with the rest of its regional neighbours. The member states of the Association of Southeast Asian Nations (ASEAN) opposed the Vietnamese occupation of Cambodia and joined with China in supporting guerrilla resistance forces represented by the Khmer Rouge and various noncommunist Cambodian groups. An economic trade embargo was imposed on Vietnam by the United States and most other Western countries. Only the Soviet Union and its allies in eastern Europe stood by Vietnam.

Under such severe external pressure, Vietnam suffered continuing economic difficulties. The cost of stationing troops in Cambodia and of maintaining a strong defensive position along the Chinese border was especially heavy. To make matters worse, the regime encountered continuing problems in integrating the southern provinces into a socialist economy. In the early 1980s the government announced a number of reforms to spur the economy. Then, following the death of veteran party chief Le Duan in 1986 and his succession by the pro-reform Nguyen Van Linh, the party launched a

In Focus: Khmer Rouge

Khmer Rouge was a radical communist movement that ruled Cambodia from 1975 to 1979 after winning power through a guerrilla war. It was purportedly set up in 1967 as the armed wing of the Communist Party of Kampuchea.

Cambodia's communist movement originated in the Khmer People's Revolutionary Party, which was formed in 1951 under the auspices of the Viet Minh of Vietnam. The party's largely French-educated Marxist leaders eventually renamed it the Communist Party of Kampuchea. By the late 1950s the party's members were engaged in clandestine activities against the government of Prince Norodom Sihanouk. However, for many years they made little headway against Sihanouk from their bases in remote jungle and mountain areas, partly because of Sihanouk's own popularity among the peasants whom the communists sought to incite to rebellion.

After a right-wing military coup toppled Sihanouk in 1970, the Khmer Rouge entered into a political coalition with him. Thus, the Khmer Rouge finally began attracting increased support in the Cambodian countryside, a trend that was accelerated by the destructive U.S. bombing campaigns over Cambodia in the early 1970s. By this time the Khmer Rouge were also receiving substantial aid from North Vietnam, which had withheld its support during the years of Sihanouk's rule.

In a civil war that continued for nearly five years from 1970, the Khmer Rouge gradually expanded the areas of the Cambodian countryside under their control. Finally, in April 1975, Khmer Rouge forces mounted a victorious attack on the capital city of Phnom Penh and established a national government to rule Cambodia. The military leader of the Khmer Rouge, Pol Pot, became the new government's prime minister. The Khmer Rouge's rule over the next four years was marked by some of the worst excesses of any Marxist government in the 20th century, during which as many as 1.5 million Cambodians died and many of the country's professional and technical class were exterminated.

The Khmer Rouge government was overthrown in 1979 by invading Vietnamese troops, who installed a puppet government propped up by Vietnamese aid and expertise. The Khmer Rouge retreated to remote areas and resumed guerrilla warfare, this time operating from bases near the border with Thailand and obtaining aid from China. In 1982 they formed a fragile coalition (under the nominal leadership of Sihanouk) with two noncommunist Khmer groups opposed to the Vietnamese-backed central government. The Khmer Rouge was the strongest partner in this coalition, which carried on guerrilla warfare until 1991. The Khmer Rouge opposed the United Nations–sponsored peace settlement of 1991 and the multiparty elections in 1993, and they continued guerrilla warfare against the noncommunist coalition government formed after those elections.

Isolated in the remote western provinces of the country and increasingly dependent on gem smuggling for their funding, the Khmer Rouge suffered a series of military defeats and grew weaker from year to year. In 1995 many of their cadres accepted an offer of amnesty from the Cambodian government, and in 1996 one of their leading figures, Ieng Sary, defected along with several thousand guerrillas under his command and signed a peace agreement with the government. The disarray within the organization intensified in 1997, when Pol Pot was arrested by other Khmer Rouge leaders and sentenced to life imprisonment. Pol Pot died in 1998 and soon afterward the surviving leaders of the Khmer Rouge defected or were imprisoned.

program of sweeping economic and institutional renovation (*doi moi*). Actual implementation, however, did not begin until 1988, when a deepening economic crisis and declining support from the Soviet Union compelled the government to slash spending, court foreign investment, and liberalize trade. Other policies essentially legalized free market activities that the government had previously tried to limit or suppress.

PROBLEMS OF MODERNIZATION

These measures stabilized the economy, but the sudden collapse of communist rule in eastern Europe and disintegration of the Soviet Union left Vietnam completely isolated. Having begun removing its armed forces from Cambodia in 1985, Vietnam completed withdrawal in September 1989 and intensified efforts to improve relations with its neighbours. A peace conference in Paris formally ended the Cambodian conflict in 1991 and provided United Nations supervision until elections could be held in 1993. The Cambodian settlement removed a key obstacle to normalizing relations with China, Japan, and Europe. The Vietnamese agreement to help the United States determine the fate of Americans missing in action encouraged the United States to lift the embargo in 1994 and establish diplomatic relations with Hanoi in 1995. Admission to membership in ASEAN in July 1995 symbolized Vietnam's full acceptance into the family of nations.

The return of peace and stability to the region allowed Vietnam to concentrate on the economic reforms begun in the late 1980s. The government took a pragmatic approach, responding flexibly to domestic realities while seeking ideas from diverse international sources. Major components of reform included instituting a relatively liberal foreign investment law, decollectivizing agriculture, ending fixed prices and subsidies, and significantly reducing the number of state-owned enterprises. Results were on the whole favourable. The output of food staples per capita, after a half century of decline, increased sufficiently for Vietnam to become a sizeable exporter of rice in 1989. Job creation in the private sector made up for job losses in the public sector. Foreign investment spurred growth in crude oil production, light manufacturing, and tourism. Vietnam also redirected its trade in a remarkably short period of time from ex-communist countries to such new partners as Hong Kong, Singapore, South Korea, Taiwan, and Japan. Growth in the gross domestic product (GDP) averaged nearly 8 percent annually through the 1990s.

With success, however, came a weakening of commitment to further change and renewed concern about preserving Vietnam's "socialist orientation." One consequence was the continued prominence in the economy of state-owned enterprises, fewer than half of which were profitable but which accounted for nearly one-third of GDP. Leaders also worried that the corruption, inequality, and materialism

In Focus: The POW-MIA Controversy

On Jan. 27, 1973, the Paris Peace Accords were signed, officially bringing to an end the American war in Vietnam. One of the prerequisites for and provisions of the treaty was the return of all American prisoners of war (POWs). On February 12 the first of 595 U.S. military and civilian POWs were released in Hanoi and flown directly to Clark Air Force Base in the Philippines. In the 1974 State of the Union address, Nixon told the American people that "all our troops have returned from Southeast Asia—and they have returned with honor." But many Americans had started questioning whether in fact all POWs had been released. The Vietnam POW issue soon became a major controversy, prompting congressional investigations, partisan politics, the production of major motion pictures, and the formation of a number of POW and MIA (missing in action) organizations.

The uproar over POWs caused the Senate to form the Senate Select Committee on POW/MIA Affairs. Senator John Kerry, a veteran of the war, was appointed chairman. The controversy was fed by reported live sightings and photographs of Americans held in captivity. Investigations revealed that the photographs were phony, and the sightings could not be verified. No credible evidence has ever been provided to substantiate the existence of American POWs in Vietnam. This, however, is not a definitive answer. The POW issue remained a significant public concern for a number of reasons. It is argued that it was used to renege on Nixon's promise of billions of dollars of economic assistance to Vietnam; as a political tool to preclude the formalization of relations with Vietnam; as an election issue to gain the support of the families of servicemen missing in action, veterans, and the active military; and as a welfare system for the families of personnel missing in action.

The POW/MIA issue in Vietnam is unique for a number of reasons. The Vietnam War was the first war lost by the United States. As a consequence, after the war it was impossible to search the battlefields for remains. Because the country was never occupied, it was impossible to search the prisons and cemeteries. Additionally, Vietnam shared a common border with China and had close ties with the former Soviet Union, which resulted in unknown numbers of POWs being taken to China and possibly the Soviet Union. Much of Vietnam is covered with dense jungle. The geography, terrain, and climate make it exceedingly difficult to find and recover remains. These factors damaged the recovery efforts and precluded a comprehensive, accurate accounting. However, on July 11, 1995, the administration of U.S. Pres. Bill Clinton extended diplomatic recognition to Vietnam, which gave Americans greater access to the country.

In 1973, when the last known American POWs were released, more than 2,500 U.S. servicemen were designated missing in action. As of August 2004, more than 1,800 servicemen still were unaccounted for. The U.S. Department of Defense lists 687 American POWs returned alive from the Vietnam War. North Vietnam acknowledged that 55 Americans died in captivity. POWs in the Hanoi prison system endeavored to maintain a registry of captive Americans. They concluded that at least 766 American POWs entered the system. POWs were initially held in four prisons in Hanoi and six facilities within 50 miles of the city. The "Hanoi Hilton" was the largest prison. No POW ever escaped from Hanoi.

More than 80 percent of the POWs held in North Vietnam were aircrew personnel, with 332 from the U.S. Air Force, 146 from the U.S. Navy, and 26 from the U.S. Marine Corps. POWs held in

North Vietnam were used for propaganda, psychological warfare, and negotiating purposes. POWs were tortured, isolated, and psychologically abused in violation of the 1949 Geneva Convention to which North Vietnam was a signatory. Some POWs were paraded before reporters and foreign visitors and forced to confess to war crimes against the people of Vietnam. Others resisted torture and refused to comply. The Pentagon made no effort to court-martial those individuals who cooperated with the enemy, with the one exception of Robert Garwood, who did not return to the United States until 1979. However, most POWs served with honour and dignity. Because the average aviator was older and more mature, more highly trained, and better educated than the average soldier in Vietnam, they faired much better in captivity. Army Special Forces Captain Floyd James Thompson, who was captured on March 26, 1964, was the longest-held POW. Navy Lt. Everett Alvarez, who was shot down Aug. 5, 1964, was the first pilot captured. Air Force Colonel John Flynn was the highest-ranking POW.

associated with the new market economy could undermine support for the party. In 1991, Nguyen Van Linh yielded the party's chairmanship to Do Muoi, a cautious, consensus-seeking politician. Although a new constitution enacted in 1992 was seen as a step toward loosening party control of the government, the party remained unwilling to share power with noncommunist elements. Muoi's replacement, Le Kha Phieu, chosen in 1997 after months of bitter factional infighting, lacked both the power and the determination to accelerate the pace of reform. Internal opposition to further liberalization caused Vietnam in 1999 to decide, after years of negotiation, not to sign a trade agreement with the United States that would have also secured membership in the World Trade Organization (WTO). In the face of relentless globalization, Vietnam was threatened by paralysis on account of its reluctance to reform its political institutions.

Impatience with government corruption and slowing economic growth (exacerbated by the Asian economic crisis of the late 1990s) catalyzed large-scale demonstrations early in the 21st century. The demonstrations, in turn, ultimately contributed to the senior party leaders' decision to replace Le Kha Phieu with Nong Duc Manh in April 2001. The new party leader immediately took steps to curb corruption, and to integrate Vietnam more fully into the global economy. Once again, the country's GDP experienced a surge of growth. Trade negotiations with the United States were rekindled, and an accord was signed later that year. At the end of 2006, Vietnam ratified the accession agreement to become the WTO's 150th member in January 2007.

CHAPTER 13

Vietnam and the Cold War

"America's Suicide Attempt"

As the Vietnam War began to recede into the past, the entire episode, from a neutral perspective, increasingly came to seem incredible. That the most powerful and wealthy nation on earth should undertake 15 years of wasting conflict against a tiny state 10,000 miles (16,093 km) from its shores—and lose—almost justifies the historian Paul Johnson's phrase "America's suicide attempt." Yet the destructive and futile U.S. engagement in Southeast Asia was a product of a series of trends that had been maturing since World War II. The early Cold War gave rise to U.S. leadership in the containment of Communism. Decolonization then thrust the United States into a role described by advocate and critic alike as "the world's policeman"—protector and benefactor of the weak new governments of the Third World. The potential of guerrilla insurgency, demonstrated in Josip Broz Tito's resistance to the Nazis and especially in the postwar victories of Mao Zedong, the Viet Minh, and Fidel Castro, made it the preferred mode for revolutionary action around the world. The emerging nuclear stalemate alerted Washington to the need to prepare for fighting limited (sometimes called "brushfire") wars sponsored by the Soviet Union or China through proxies in the Third World. In this era of Khrushchevian and Maoist assertiveness the United States could not allow any of its client states to fall to a Communist "war of national liberation" lest it lose prestige and credibility to Moscow and Beijing. Finally, the "domino theory," to the effect that the fall of one country would inexorably lead to the communization of its neighbours, magnified the importance of even the smallest state and guaranteed that sooner or later the United States would become entangled under the worst possible conditions. One or even all of the assumptions under which the United States became involved in Vietnam may have been faulty, but very few in the government and the public questioned them until long after the country was committed.

By 1961, Ngo Dinh Diem's fledgling government in South Vietnam was receiving more U.S. aid per capita than any other country except Laos and South Korea. Authoritative reports detailed both the Viet Cong's campaign of terror against government officials in the south and widespread discontent over Diem's corrupt and imperious rule. In the face of both Nikita Khrushchev's renewed vow to support wars of national liberation and Charles de Gaulle's warning ("I predict you will sink step by step into a bottomless military and political quagmire"), John F. Kennedy chose Vietnam as a test case for American theories of state building and counterinsurgency. He approved a proposal by Walt Rostow and Gen. Maxwell Taylor to assign advisers to every level of Saigon's government and military, and the number of Americans in Vietnam grew from 800 to 11,000 by the end of 1962.

Primary Document: John F. Kennedy's "A Long Twilight Struggle" Speech

In many speeches, notably the following address delivered at the University of Washington on Nov. 16, 1961, President Kennedy emphasized that America did not have unlimited power to control the world. He warned that those people who sought easy answers, who demanded either peace at any price or total victory, who saw the alternatives as being either "Red or dead," were equally wrong and that their solutions would be equally disastrous. The only sane and effective foreign policy in a nuclear age was one that combined willingness to negotiate and to compromise with a determination to defend basic values.

Bulletin, *Dec. 4, 1961: "Diplomacy and Defense: A Test of National Maturity."*

We increase our arms at a heavy cost, primarily to make certain that we will not have to use them. We must face up to the chance of war if we are to maintain the peace. We must work with certain countries lacking in freedom in order to strengthen the cause of freedom. We find some who call themselves neutrals who are our friends and sympathetic to us, and others who call themselves neutral who are unremittingly hostile to us. And as the most powerful defender of freedom on earth, we find ourselves unable to escape the responsibilities of freedom and yet unable to exercise it without restraints imposed by the very freedoms we seek to protect. We cannot, as a free nation, compete with our adversaries in tactics of terror, assassination, false promises, counterfeit mobs, and crises.

We cannot, under the scrutiny of a free press and public, tell different stories to different audiences, foreign, domestic, friendly, and hostile.

We cannot abandon the slow processes of consulting with our allies to match the swift expediencies of those who merely dictate to their satellites. We can neither abandon nor control the international organization in which we now cast less than 1 percent of the vote in the General Assembly. We possess weapons of tremendous power, but they are least effective in combating the weapons most often used by freedom's foes: subversion, infiltration, guerrilla warfare, and civil disorder. We send arms to other peoples—just as we can send them the ideals of democracy in which we believe—but we cannot send them the will to use those arms or to abide by those ideals.

And while we believe not only in the force of arms but in the force of right and reason, we have learned that reason does not always appeal to unreasonable men, that it is not always true that "a soft answer turneth away wrath," and that right does not always make might.

In short we must face problems which do not lend themselves to easy or quick or permanent solutions. And we must face the fact that the United States is neither omnipotent or omniscient, that we are only 6 percent of the world's population, that we cannot impose our will upon the other 94 percent of mankind, that we cannot right every wrong or reverse each adversity, and that therefore there cannot be an American solution to every world problem . . .

If vital interests under duress can be preserved by peaceful means, negotiations will find that out. If our adversary will accept nothing less than a concession of our rights, negotiations will find that out. And if negotiations are to take place, this nation cannot abdicate to its adversaries the task of choosing the forum and the framework and the time . . .

In short, we are neither "warmongers" nor "appeasers," neither "hard" nor "soft." We are Americans, determined to defend the frontiers of freedom by an honorable peace if peace is possible, but by arms if arms are used against us. And if we are to move forward in that spirit, we shall need all the calm and thoughtful citizens that this great university can produce, all the light they can shed, all the wisdom they can bring to bear.

It is customary, both here and around the world, to regard life in the United States as easy. Our advantages are many. But more than any other people on earth, we bear burdens and accept risks unprecedented in their size and their duration, not for ourselves alone but for all who wish to be free. No other generation of free men in any country has ever faced so many and such difficult challenges—not even those who lived in the days when this university was founded in 1861.

This nation was then torn by war. This territory had only the simplest elements of civilization. And this city had barely begun to function. But a university was one of their earliest thoughts, and they summed it up in the motto that they adopted: "Let there be light." What more can be said today regarding all the dark and tangled problems we face than: Let there be light.

Ho Chi Minh's North Vietnamese considered the struggle against Diem and his American sponsors merely the next phase of a war that had begun against the Japanese and had continued against the French. Their determination to unify Vietnam and conquer all of Indochina was the principal dynamic behind the conflict. The total number of Communist troops in the South grew by recruitment and infiltration from some 7,000 in 1960 to more than 100,000 by 1964. Most were guerrilla militiamen who served also as local party cadres. Above them were the Viet Cong (formally the National Liberation Front, or NLF), deployed in regional military units, and units of the People's Army of North Vietnam (PAVN) entering the South along the Ho Chi Minh Trail. U.S. Special Forces tried to counter Communist control of the countryside with a "strategic hamlet" program, a tactic used with success by the British in Malaya. Diem instituted a policy of relocating the rural population of South Vietnam in order to isolate the Communists. The program caused widespread resentment, while Diem's persecution of local Buddhist sects provided a rallying point for protests. When Buddhist monks resorted to dramatic self-immolation in front of Western news cameras, Kennedy secretly instructed Ambassador Henry Cabot Lodge to approve a military coup. On Nov. 1, 1963, Diem was overthrown and murdered.

South Vietnam then underwent a succession of coups d'état that undermined all pretense that the United States was defending democracy. The struggle was thenceforth viewed in Washington as a military effort to buy time for state building and the training of the South Vietnamese army (Army of the Republic of Vietnam; ARVN). When two American destroyers exchanged fire with a North Vietnamese torpedo boat 8 miles (12.8 km) off the North's coast in August 1964 (an event whose occurrence was later disputed), Congress passed the Gulf of Tonkin Resolution authorizing the president to take whatever measures he deemed necessary to protect American lives in Southeast Asia. Lyndon B. Johnson held off on escalating the war during the 1964 electoral campaign but in February 1965 ordered sustained bombing of North Vietnam and sent the first U.S. combat units to the South. By June, U.S. troops in Vietnam numbered 74,000.

The Soviet Union reacted to American escalation by trying to reconvene the Geneva Conference and bring pressure to bear on the United States to submit to the peaceful reunification of Vietnam. China bluntly refused to encourage a negotiated settlement and insisted that the U.S.S.R. help North Vietnam by pressuring the United States elsewhere. The Soviets, in turn, resented Beijing's assertion of leadership in the Communist world and had no desire to provoke new crises with Washington. The North Vietnamese were caught in the middle; Ho's ties were to Moscow, but geography obliged him to favour Beijing. Hence North Vietnam joined in boycotting the March 1965

Communist conference in Moscow. The Soviets, however, dared not ignore the Vietnam War lest they confirm Chinese accusations of Soviet "revisionism."

THE CONDUCT AND COST OF THE WAR

Meanwhile, the United States slid ineluctably into the quagmire predicted by de Gaulle. U.S. forces reached a peak of 543,000 men in 1969. (Australia, New Zealand, Thailand, and the Philippines also sent small contingents, and South Korea contributed 50,000 men.) The U.S. strategy was to employ mobility, based on helicopters, and firepower to wear down the enemy by attrition at minimal cost in U.S. lives.

The war of attrition on the ground, like the bombing in the North, was designed less to destroy the enemy's ability to wage war than to demonstrate to the enemy that he could not win and to bring him to the bargaining table. But stalemate suited Hanoi, which could afford to wait, while it was anathema to the Americans. Johnson's popularity fell steadily. Most Americans favoured more vigorous prosecution to end the war, but a growing number advocated withdrawal. Antiwar dissent grew and spread and overlapped with sweeping and violent demands for social change. The American foreign policy consensus that had sustained containment since the 1940s was shattered by Vietnam. In retrospect, Johnson's attempt to prevent the war from disturbing his own domestic program was vain, and his strategic conception was grounded in folly and hubris. He and his advisers had no clear notion of what the application of American force was supposed to achieve. It was merely assumed to be invincible.

Hanoi understood that the classic Maoist strategy of isolating cities by revolutionizing the countryside was inapplicable to Vietnam because the cities could still hold out with foreign support. Accordingly, in mid-1967 the North Vietnamese Politburo approved a plan for urban attacks throughout South Vietnam. Gen. Vo Nguyen Giap insisted, however, that NLF guerrillas, not PAVN units, be risked. The expectation was that direct attacks on cities would undercut American claims of pacification and magnify domestic American dissent. On Jan. 30, 1968 (the Tet holiday, during which many ARVN troops were home on leave), an estimated 84,000 Communist troops infiltrated South Vietnamese cities, attacked government installations, and even penetrated the American embassy in Saigon. The Tet Offensive was carried out at a terrible cost to Communist strength, but American press reports turned the offensive into a psychological defeat for the United States. Instead of ordering a counterattack, Johnson removed himself from the 1968 presidential campaign, ordered a bombing halt, and pledged to devote the rest of his administration to the quest for peace. Negotiations began in Paris, but the rest of the year was spent bickering over procedural issues.

For more than 25 years after 1941 the United States had maintained an unprecedented depth of involvement in world affairs. In 1968 Vietnam finally forced Americans to face the limits of their resources and will. Whoever succeeded Johnson would have little choice but to find a way to escape from Vietnam and reduce American global responsibilities.

DÉTENTE AS REALISM

After eight years in the shadow of Dwight D. Eisenhower and eight more years out of office, Richard M. Nixon brought to the presidency in 1969 rich experience as an observer of foreign affairs and shrewd notions about how to prevent the American retreat from global commitments from turning into a rout. In broad outlines, the Nixon strategy included a phased withdrawal of ground forces from Vietnam, a negotiated settlement saving the Saigon regime, détente with the U.S.S.R., resumption of relations with mainland China, and military support for selected regional powers that permitted them to take over as local "policemen" in lieu of direct American involvement. In a period of just four years, 1969–72, the United States abandoned once-unshakable Cold War attitudes toward the Communist nations, while scaling back its own exposure in response to the Sino-Soviet split, imminent Soviet strategic parity, and the economic and psychological constraints on U.S. action stemming from the new American imperative of "no more Vietnams." Nixon believed that his own record as an anti-Communist and tough negotiator would quiet conservative opposition to détente, while liberals would find themselves outflanked on their own peace issue. In both ends and means American foreign policy evinced a new realism in stark contrast to the "pay any price, bear any burden" mentality of the Kennedy–Johnson years. In his inaugural address Nixon spoke instead of an "era of negotiation."

Détente, however, was not meant to replace the abiding postwar American strategy of containment. Rather, it was meant to be a less confrontational method of containing Communist power through diplomatic accords and a flexible system of rewards and punishments by which Washington might moderate Soviet behaviour. Journalists dubbed this tactic "linkage" insofar as the United States would link positive inducements (arms control, technology transfers, grain sales) to expected Soviet reciprocity in other areas (restraint in promoting revolutionary movements). Nixon had no illusions that U.S.–Soviet competition would disappear, but he expected that this carrot-and-stick approach would establish rules of the game and recognized spheres of influence. Pulling the Soviets into a network of agreements, and thus giving them a stake in the status quo, would create a stable structure of peace. Finally, expanding economic and cultural ties might even serve to open up Soviet society.

By 1971, Leonid Brezhnev, now established as the new Soviet leader, was ready to welcome American overtures for a variety of reasons. In 1968 relations with the eastern European satellites had flared up again when leaders of the Czechoslovakian Communist party under Alexander Dubček initiated reforms promoting democratization and free speech. A wave of popular demonstrations added momentum to liberalization during this "Prague Spring" until, on August 20, the U.S.S.R. led neighbouring Warsaw Pact armies in a military invasion of Czechoslovakia. Dubček was ousted and the reforms undone. The ostensible justification for this latest Soviet repression of freedom in its empire came to be known as the Brezhnev Doctrine: "Each of our parties is responsible not only to its working class and its people, but also to the international working class, the world Communist movement." The U.S.S.R. asserted its right to intervene in any Communist state to prevent the success of "counterrevolutionary" elements. Needless to say, the Chinese were fearful that the Brezhnev Doctrine might be applied to them. In 1969 they accused the U.S.S.R. of "social imperialism" and provoked hundreds of armed clashes on the borders of Xinjiang and Manchuria. Soviet forces arrayed against China, already raised from 12 weak divisions in 1961 to 25 full ones, now grew to 55 divisions backed by 120 SS-11 nuclear missiles. In August 1969 a Soviet diplomat had carefully inquired about the likely American reaction to a Soviet nuclear strike against China. In sum, the need to repair the Soviet image in the wake of the Prague Spring and the fear of dangerous relations with Beijing and Washington at the same time, as well as the chronic Soviet need for agricultural imports and access to superior Western technology, were all powerful incentives for seeking détente.

From a longer perspective, however, détente had been the strategy of the U.S.S.R. ever since 1956 under the rubric "peaceful coexistence." Brezhnev repeated Khrushchev's assertion that Soviet nuclear parity took the military leverage from the hands of the bourgeois world, forcing it to accept the legitimate interests of other states, to treat the U.S.S.R. as an equal, and to acquiesce in the success of "progressive" and revolutionary struggle. Détente was thus for the Soviets a natural expression of the new correlation of forces, a means of guiding the weakened Americans through the transition to a new phase of history—and was certainly not meant to preserve the status quo or liberalize the U.S.S.R. One Western proponent of détente described the Soviet conception of it as a way "to make the world safe for historical change" and pointed out the implicit double standard—i.e., that it was admissible for the U.S.S.R. to continue the struggle against the capitalist world during détente but a contradiction for the Western powers to struggle against Communism. From the Marxist point of view, however, this was merely another reflection of objective reality: Now that nuclear balance was a fact, greater weight accrued to conventional military strength and popular political action, each of which strongly favoured the Socialist bloc.

The contrasting U.S. and Soviet conceptions of détente would eventually scotch the hopes placed in it on both sides. From 1969 to 1972, however, those differences were not yet apparent, while the immediate incentives for a relaxation of tensions were irresistible.

SCALING BACK U.S. COMMITMENTS

The first indications of a new American sense of limits in foreign policy were in the economic sphere. Since World War II the global market economy had rested on the Bretton Woods monetary system, based on a strong American dollar tied to gold. Beginning in 1958 the United States began to run annual foreign-exchange deficits, resulting partly from the costs of maintaining U.S. forces overseas. For this reason, and because their own exports benefitted from an artificially strong dollar, the Europeans and Japanese tolerated the U.S. gold drain and used their growing fund of "Eurodollars" to back loans and commerce. By the mid-1960s de Gaulle began to criticize the United States for exploiting its leadership role to "export its inflation" to foreign holders of dollars. The Johnson administration's Vietnam deficits then added the prospect of internal American inflation. By 1971 the American economic situation warranted emergency measures. Nixon imposed wage and price controls to stem inflation, and Secretary of the Treasury John Connally abruptly suspended the convertibility of dollars to gold. The dollar was allowed to float against undervalued currencies like the deutsche mark and yen, in consequence of which foreign holders of dollars took sharp losses and foreign exporters faced stiffer competition from American goods. New agreements in December 1971 stabilized the dollar at a rate 12 percent below Bretton Woods, but the United States had sorely tried allied loyalty.

The American retreat from an overextended financial position and insistence that its allies share the burden of stabilizing the U.S. balance of payments was the economic analog to the Nixon Doctrine in military affairs. The new president enunciated this doctrine in an impromptu news conference on Guam during his July 1969 trip to welcome home the Apollo 11 astronauts from the Moon. Nixon announced that the United States would no longer send Americans to fight for Asian nations but would confine itself to logistical and economic support: "Asian hands must shape the Asian future." In accord with this effort to shift more of the burden of containment to threatened peoples themselves, Nixon planned to assist regional pro-Western powers like Iran in becoming bulwarks of stability by providing them with sophisticated American weapons.

Before the Nixon Doctrine could be credible, however, the president had to extricate the United States from Vietnam. In March 1969 he outlined a policy of Vietnamization, comprising a phased withdrawal of American ground troops and additional material and advisory support to make the ARVN self-sufficient. Nixon also hoped to enlist the Soviets in the cause of peace, but Moscow had less influence over Hanoi than he imagined and could not afford to be seen as appeasing the United States. Nixon then shifted to a subtler approach—long-term pressure on Hanoi combined with better relations with both Communist giants. Late in 1969 secret talks began in Paris between Henry Kissinger, Nixon's adviser for national security, and the North Vietnamese Politburo member Le Duc Tho. At the same time, however, Nixon stepped up pressure on the North. When the anti-Communist general Lon Nol overthrew Prince Sihanouk in Cambodia in March 1970, Nixon acceded to the U.S. Army's long-standing desire to destroy Communist sanctuaries inside that country. The U.S.-ARVN operation fell short of its promise and provoked protests at home and abroad. Despite public disfavour and congressional attempts to limit such actions, Nixon ordered continued secret American bombing inside Cambodia and also supported an ARVN operation into Laos to cut the Ho Chi Minh Trail.

THE OPENING TO CHINA AND *OSTPOLITIK*

The linchpin of Nixon's strategy for a settlement in Vietnam was détente with Moscow and Beijing. He was known as a firm supporter of the Nationalist regime on Taiwan, but he had softened his stance against mainland China before taking office. In 1969 he moved to signal Beijing through the good offices of de Gaulle and Yahya Khan of Pakistan. Direct contacts, conducted through the Chinese embassy in Warsaw, were broken off after the 1970 U.S.-ARVN attacks on Cambodia, but Nixon and Kissinger remained hopeful. The Cultural Revolution ended in a serious power struggle in the Chinese leadership. Army commander Lin Biao opposed relations with the United States but died when his plane crashed in unclear circumstances. Zhou Enlai and Mao (presumably) contemplated the value of an American counterweight to the Soviets, concessions on the status of Taiwan, and technology transfers. The Nixon Doctrine also promised to remove the obnoxious U.S. military presence in Asia.

The Pakistani channel bore fruit in December 1970, when Yahya Khan returned from Beijing with an invitation for an American envoy to discuss Taiwan. The following April the Chinese made the surprising public gesture of inviting an American table tennis team to the championship tournament in Beijing. This episode of "Ping-Pong diplomacy" was followed by a secret trip to Beijing by Kissinger. Kissinger's talks with Zhou and Mao yielded an American promise to remove U.S. forces from Taiwan in return for Chinese support of a negotiated settlement in Vietnam. The Chinese also agreed to a presidential visit in February 1972. The American people's long-latent fascination with China immediately revived, and Nixon's trip was a sensation.

Primary Document: The Shanghai Communique

Probably the most notable and surprising achievement of Pres. Richard Nixon's first term was his visit to China in February 1972. The visit had been arranged through the mediation of National Security Adviser Henry Kissinger on a secret trip to Beijing in July 1971 to meet with Chinese Premier Zhou Enlai. But there had been hints earlier in the year of a thaw in the relations between the two nations. On March 15, 1971, the president had announced a discontinuation of the travel ban to China, thus enabling the U.S. table tennis team to visit there in April. And on April 14 he relaxed the trade embargo that had been in effect for a quarter of a century. The following selection is from the joint communique issued at Shanghai on Feb. 27, 1972, at the end of the president's visit.

Department of State Bulletin, *March 20, 1972.*

During the visit, extensive, earnest and frank discussions were held between President Nixon and Premier Chou En-lai on the normalization of relations between the United States of America and the People's Republic of China, as well as on other matters of interest to both sides. In addition, Secretary of State William Rogers and Foreign Minister Chi Pengfei held talks in the same spirit . . .

The leaders of the People's Republic of China and the United States of America found it beneficial to have this opportunity, after so many years without contact, to present candidly to one another their views on a variety of issues. They reviewed the international situation in which important changes and great upheavals are taking place and expounded their respective positions and attitudes.

The U.S. side stated: Peace in Asia and peace in the world requires efforts both to reduce immediate tensions and to eliminate the basic causes of conflict. The United States will work for a just and secure peace: just, because it fulfills the aspirations of peoples and nations for freedom and progress; secure, because it removes the danger of foreign aggression. The United States supports individual freedom and social progress for all the peoples of the world, free of outside pressure or intervention. The United States believes that the effort to reduce tensions is served by improving communication between countries that have different ideologies so as to lessen the risks of confrontation through accident, miscalculation or misunderstanding. Countries should treat each other with mutual respect and be willing to compete peacefully, letting performance be the ultimate judge. No country should claim infallibility and each country should be prepared to re-examine its own attitudes for the common good. The United States stressed that the peoples of Indochina should be allowed to determine their destiny without outside intervention; its constant primary objective has been a negotiated solution; the eight-point proposal put forward by the Republic of Vietnam and the United States on Jan. 27, 1972, represents a basis for the attainment of that objective; in the absence of a negotiated settlement the United States envisages the ultimate withdrawal of all U.S. forces from the region consistent with the aim of self-determination for each country of Indochina. The United States will maintain its close ties with and support for the Republic of Korea; the United States will support efforts of the Republic of Korea to seek a relaxation of tension and increased communication in the Korean peninsula. The United States places the highest value on its friendly relations with Japan; it will continue to develop the existing close bonds. Consistent with the United Nations Security Council Resolution of Dec. 21, 1971, the United States favors the continuation of the ceasefire between India and Pakistan and the withdrawal of all military forces to within their own territories and to their own sides of the ceasefire line in Jammu and Kashmir; the United States supports the right of the peoples of South Asia to shape their own future in peace, free of military threat, and without having the area become the subject of great power rivalry.

The Chinese side stated: Wherever there is oppression, there is resistance. Countries want independence, nations want liberation and the people want revolution—this has become the irresistible trend of history. All nations, big or small, should be equal; big nations should not bully the small and strong nations should not bully the weak. China will never be a superpower and it opposes hegemony and power politics of any kind. The Chinese side stated that it firmly supports the struggles of all the oppressed people and nations for freedom and liberation and that the people of all countries have the right to choose their social systems according to their own wishes and the right to safeguard the independence, sovereignty and territorial integrity of their own countries and oppose foreign aggression, interference, control and subversion. All foreign troops should be withdrawn to their own countries.

The Chinese side expressed its firm support to the peoples of Vietnam, Laos and Cambodia in their efforts for the attainment of their goal and its firm support to the seven-point proposal of the Provisional Revolutionary Government of the Republic of South Vietnam and the elaboration of February this year on the two key problems in the proposal, and to the Joint Declaration of the Summit Conference of the Indochinese Peoples. It firmly supports the eight-point program for the peaceful unification of Korea put forward by the Government of the Democratic People's Republic of Korea on April 12, 1971, and the stand for the abolition of the "U.N. Commission for the Unification and Rehabilitation of Korea." It firmly opposes the revival and outward expansion of Japanese militarism and firmly supports the Japanese people's desire to build an independent, democratic, peaceful and neutral Japan. It firmly maintains that India and Pakistan should, in accordance with the United Nations resolutions on the India-Pakistan question, immediately withdraw all their forces to their respective territories and to their own sides of the ceasefire line in Jammu and Kashmir and firmly supports the Pakistan Government and people in their struggle to preserve their independence and sovereignty and the people of Jammu and Kashmir in their struggle for the right of self-determination.

There are essential differences between China and the United States in their social systems and foreign policies. However, the two sides agreed that countries, regardless of their social systems, should conduct their relations on the principles of respect for the sovereignty and territorial integrity of all states, nonaggression against other states, noninterference in the internal affairs of other states, equality and mutual benefit, and peaceful coexistence. International disputes should be settled on this basis, without resorting to the use or threat of force. The United States and the People's Republic of China are prepared to apply these principles to their mutual relations.

With these principles of international relations in mind the two sides stated that:

—progress toward the normalization of relations between China and the United States is in the interests of all countries;

—both wish to reduce the danger of international military conflict;

—neither should seek hegemony in the Asia-Pacific region and each is opposed to efforts by any other country or group of countries to establish such hegemony; and

—neither is prepared to negotiate on behalf of any third party or to enter into agreements or understandings with the other directed at other states.

Both sides are of the view that it would be against the interests of the peoples of the world for any major country to collude with another against other countries, or for major countries to divide up the world into spheres of interest.

The two sides reviewed the long-standing serious disputes between China and the United States. The Chinese side reaffirmed its position: The Taiwan question is the crucial question obstructing the normalization of relations between China and the United States; the Government of the People's Republic of China is the sole legal government of China; Taiwan is a province of China which has long been returned to the motherland; the liberation of Taiwan is China's internal affair in which no other country has the right to interfere; and all U.S. forces and military installations must be withdrawn from Taiwan. The Chinese Government firmly opposes any activities which aim at the creation of "one China, one Taiwan," "one China, two governments," "two Chinas," and "independent Taiwan" or advocate that "the status of Taiwan remains to be determined."

The U.S. side declared: The United States acknowledges that all Chinese on either side of the Taiwan Strait maintain there is but one China and that Taiwan is a part of China. The United States Government does not challenge that position. It reaffirms its interest in a peaceful settlement of the Taiwan question by the Chinese themselves. With this prospect in mind, it affirms the ultimate objective of the withdrawal of all U.S. forces and military installations from Taiwan. In the meantime, it will progressively reduce its forces and military installations on Taiwan as the tension in the area diminishes.

The two sides agreed that it is desirable to broaden the understanding between the two peoples. To this end, they discussed specific areas in such fields as science, technology, culture, sports and journalism, in which people-to-people contacts and exchanges would be mutually beneficial. Each side undertakes to facilitate the further development of such contacts and exchanges.

Both sides view bilateral trade as another area from which mutual benefit can be derived, and agreed that economic relations based on equality and mutual benefit are in the interest of the peoples of the two countries. They agree to facilitate the progressive development of trade between their two countries.

The two sides agreed that they will stay in contact through various channels, including the sending of a senior U.S. representative to Beijing from time to time for concrete consultations to further the normalization of relations between the two countries and continue to exchange views on issues of common interest.

The two sides expressed the hope that the gains achieved during this visit would open up new prospects for the relations between the two countries. They believe that the normalization of relations between the two countries is not only in the interest of the Chinese and American peoples but also contributes to the relaxation of tension in Asia and the world.

The Soviets watched with palpable discomfort as Nixon and Mao embraced and saluted each other's flags, and they quickly raised the premium on improving relations with Washington. Efforts to this end had been frustrated by a series of crises: a buildup of Soviet jets in Egypt and Jordan, the discovery of a Soviet submarine base under construction in Cuba in 1970, and Nixon's escalations of the war in Southeast Asia. Substantial moves toward East–West détente had already been made in Europe, however. Following de Gaulle's lead, the West German foreign minister, Willy Brandt, a Socialist and former mayor of West Berlin, had made overtures toward Moscow. After becoming chancellor in 1969 he pursued a thorough *Ostpolitik* ("eastern policy") that culminated in treaties with the U.S.S.R. (August 1970), renouncing the use of force in their relations, and with Poland (December 1970), recognizing Germany's 1945 losses east of the Oder–Neisse Line. Brandt also recognized the East German government (December 1972) and expanded commercial relations with other eastern European regimes. Both German states were admitted to the UN in 1973. Support for *Ostpolitik* among West Germans reflected the growing belief that German reunification would more likely be achieved through détente, rather than confrontation, with the Soviet bloc.

The United States, Britain, and France seconded Brandt's efforts by concluding a new Four Power Accord with the U.S.S.R. on Berlin in September 1971. The Soviets made what they considered a major concession by agreeing to retain their responsibility under the Potsdam Accords for access to West Berlin and achieved in return Western recognition of the status quo in eastern Europe and access to West German technology and credits.

ARMS-LIMITATION NEGOTIATIONS

The centrepiece of a bilateral U.S.–Soviet détente, however, had to be the Strategic Arms Limitation Talks (SALT), which began in 1969. After a decade of determined research and deployment the Soviet Union had pulled ahead of the United States in long-range missiles and was catching up in submarine-launched missiles and in long-range bombers. Indeed, it had been American policy since the mid-1960s to permit the Soviets to achieve parity in order to stabilize the regime of mutual deterrence. Stability was threatened, however, from the technological quarter with the development of multiple independently targeted reentry vehicles (MIRVs), by which several warheads, each aimed at a different target, could be carried on one missile, and antiballistic missiles (ABMs), which might allow one side to strike first while shielding itself from retaliation. In the arcane province of strategic theory, therefore, offense (long-range missiles) became defense, and defense (ABM) offense. Johnson had favoured a thin ABM system to protect the United States from a Chinese attack, and in 1969 Nixon won Senate approval of ABM deployment by a single vote. He intended, however, to use the program as a bargaining chip. The Soviets had actually deployed a rudimentary ABM system but were anxious to halt the U.S. program before superior American technology left theirs behind. The public SALT talks stalled, but back-channel negotiations between Kissinger and Ambassador Anatoly Dobrynin produced agreement in principle in May 1971 to limit long-range missiles and ABM deployment. The American opening to China made the Soviets increasingly eager for a prompt agreement and summit meeting, while the Americans hoped that Moscow would encourage North Vietnam to be forthcoming in the peace talks.

Since 1968 North Vietnamese negotiators had demanded satisfaction of Premier Pham Van Dong's "four points" of 1965, including cessation of all U.S. military activity in Indochina, termination of foreign military alliances with Saigon, a coalition government in the South that included the NLF, and reunification of Vietnam. The United States demanded withdrawal of all foreign troops from the South, including the PAVN. This deadlock, plus Hanoi's anxiety over the possible effects of détente, prompted another North Vietnamese bid for victory on the battlefield. In March 1972 they committed 10 of their 13 divisions to a massive offensive. Nixon responded by ordering the resumption of bombing of the North for the first time since 1969 and the mining of the harbour at Haiphong, North Vietnam's major port. The offensive stalled.

Nixon's retaliation against North Vietnam prompted speculation that the U.S.S.R. would cancel the planned summit meeting, but Soviet desire for détente prevailed. Kissinger visited Moscow in April 1972 to work out details on SALT and draft a charter for détente. Nixon instructed him "to emphasize the need for a single standard; we could not accept the proposition that the Soviet Union had the right to support liberation movements throughout the world while insisting on the Brezhnev Doctrine inside the satellite orbit." The Soviets, however, refused to make explicit concessions and defined détente as a means of preventing the inevitable struggle between "progressive" and "reactionary" forces from escalating into war. The result was a vague statement of 12 "basic principles of mutual relations" committing the two parties to peaceful coexistence and normal relations based on "sovereignty, equality, non-interference in internal affairs, and mutual advantage." Nixon then proceeded to Moscow in May 1972 and signed 10 documents providing for cooperation in economics, science and technology, outer space, medicine, health, and the environment. Most important were the SALT accords: an Interim Agreement limiting ballistic-missile deployment for five years and the ABM Treaty limiting each side to two ABM

In Focus: Strategic Arms Limitation Talks (SALT)

Negotiations between the United States and the Soviet Union aimed at curtailing the manufacture of strategic missiles capable of carrying nuclear weapons were known as the Strategic Arms Limitation Talks (SALT). The first agreements, known as SALT I and SALT II, were signed by the United States and the Union of Soviet Socialist Republics in 1972 and 1979, respectively, and were intended to restrain the arms race in strategic (long-range or intercontinental) ballistic missiles armed with nuclear weapons. First suggested by U.S. Pres. Lyndon B. Johnson in 1967, strategic arms limitation talks were agreed on by the two superpowers in the summer of 1968, and full-scale negotiations began in November 1969.

Of the resulting complex of agreements (SALT I), the most important were the Treaty on Anti-Ballistic Missile (ABM) Systems and the Interim Agreement and Protocol on Limitation of Strategic Offensive Weapons. Both were signed by Pres. Richard M. Nixon for the United States and Leonid Brezhnev, general secretary of the Soviet Communist Party, for the U.S.S.R. on May 26, 1972, at a summit meeting in Moscow.

The ABM treaty regulated antiballistic missiles that could theoretically be used to destroy incoming intercontinental ballistic missiles (ICBMs) launched by the other superpower. The treaty limited each side to only one ABM deployment area (i.e., missile-launching site) and 100 interceptor missiles. These limitations prevented either party from defending more than a small fraction of its entire territory, and thus kept both sides subject to the deterrent effect of the other's strategic forces. The ABM treaty was ratified by the U.S. Senate on Aug. 3, 1972. The Interim Agreement froze each side's number of ICBMs and submarine-launched ballistic missiles (SLBMs) at current levels for five years, pending negotiation of a more detailed SALT II. As an executive agreement, it did not require U.S. Senate ratification, but it was approved by Congress in a joint resolution.

The SALT II negotiations opened late in 1972 and continued for seven years. A basic problem in these negotiations was the asymmetry between the strategic forces of the two countries, the U.S.S.R. having concentrated on missiles with large warheads while the United States had developed smaller missiles of greater accuracy. Questions also arose as to new technologies under development, matters of definition, and methods of verification.

As finally negotiated, the SALT II treaty set limits on the number of strategic launchers (i.e., missiles that can be equipped with multiple independently targetable reentry vehicles [MIRVs]), with the object of deferring the time when both sides' land-based ICBM systems would become vulnerable to attack from such missiles. Limits were put on the number of MIRVed ICBMs, MIRVed SLBMs, heavy (i.e., long-range) bombers, and the total number of strategic launchers. The treaty set an overall limit of about 2,400 of all such weapons systems for each side. The SALT II treaty was signed by Pres. Jimmy Carter and Brezhnev in Vienna on June 18, 1979, and was submitted to the U.S. Senate for ratification shortly thereafter. But renewed tensions between the superpowers prompted Carter to remove the treaty from Senate consideration in January 1980, after the Soviet Union's invasion of Afghanistan. The United States and the Soviet Union voluntarily observed the arms limits agreed upon in SALT II in subsequent years, however. Meanwhile, the renewed negotiations that opened between the two superpowers in Geneva in 1982 took the name of Strategic Arms Reduction Talks, or START.

sites, one protecting the national capital, the other a long-range missile site. The treaty also enjoined the signatories not to interfere with each other's "national technical means of verification," a de facto recognition of each side's space-based reconnaissance satellites.

The preliminary SALT agreement appeared to be a significant achievement, but there was in some ways less to it than met the eye. The treaty mandated controlled increases, not decreases, in the Soviet arsenal, while failing to ban development of cruise missiles, space-based weapons, or the MIRVing of existing launchers by the United States or the U.S.S.R. Thus the superpowers sacrificed the right to defend their attack missiles with ABMs while failing to ensure the stability of mutual deterrence. In sum, the limitation of one sort of nuclear launcher (long-range missiles) did not preclude a continuing arms race in other sorts of launchers or in technological upgrades. To be sure, the mere fact of a U.S.–Soviet agreement seemed of psychological value, but only if both sides were genuinely seeking to reduce arsenals and not simply to maneuver diplomatically for a future advantage. Hence the practical value, or danger, of SALT would be revealed only by superpower behaviour in years to come.

END OF THE VIETNAM WAR

The American achievement of détente with both Moscow and Beijing and the failure of North Vietnam's spring 1972 offensive moved both protagonists in that conflict to bargain as well. In October the secret talks in Paris between Kissinger and Le Duc Tho finally produced an agreement on a cease-fire, the release of prisoners of war, evacuation of remaining U.S. forces within 60 days, and political negotiations among all Vietnamese parties. South Vietnam's president, Nguyen Van Thieu, then balked: The plan might indeed allow the Americans to claim "peace with honour" and go home, but it would leave Thieu to deal with the Communists while 100,000 PAVN troops remained in his country. When North Vietnam sought to prevent any last-minute changes by releasing in public the Paris terms, Kissinger was obliged to announce on October 26 that "peace is at hand." After his landslide reelection a week later—a victory aided by the prospect of peace—Nixon determined to force compliance with the terms on both Vietnamese states. Nixon ordered 11 days of intensive bombing over Hanoi itself (December 18–28) while sending Thieu an ultimatum threatening a separate peace and cessation of U.S. aid if Saigon did not accept the peace terms. The United States was castigated worldwide for the "Christmas bombing," but, when talks resumed in January, Hanoi and Saigon quickly came to terms. A Vietnam cease-fire went into effect on Jan. 27, 1973, and the last American soldiers departed on March 29.

Vietnam had been America's longest and most divisive war, and public and congressional opinion flatly opposed any resumption of the agony. The 1973 accords, therefore, were a fig leaf hiding the fact that the United States had just lost its first war despite an estimated expenditure of $155,000,000,000, 7,800,000 tons of bombs (more than all countries dropped in all of World War II), and some 58,000 American lives. Estimates of Vietnamese dead (North and South) totaled more than 2,000,000 soldiers and civilians. In its proportional impact on Vietnamese society, the Vietnam War, 1955–75, was the fourth most severe in the world since 1816.

The end of U.S. involvement in Southeast Asia also brought to a close 15 years of astounding change in world politics that featured the arrival of the space and missile age, the climax of decolonization, the assertions of Maoist China and Gaullist France, the shattering of the myth (fostered by Washington and Moscow alike) of a monolithic Communist world, and the relative decline of American power. In 1969, the very moment when astronauts were setting foot on the Moon to fulfill Kennedy's pledge to prove American superiority, Nixon and Kissinger were struggling to adjust to the new realities and manage a limited American retreat. They succeeded brilliantly in establishing a triangular relationship with Moscow and Beijing and appeared to have replaced Cold War with détente. Likewise, they appeared to have escaped from Vietnam and implemented the Nixon Doctrine. New crises and reversals were in the offing, however, that would prove that the American decline had not yet been arrested. Given these reversals, détente might be judged as much an exercise in American presumption as the Vietnam War. The U.S.S.R. could not be expected to cease its quest for real values in world competition just because the United States was prepared to acknowledge it as a military equal. Rather, with the United States less able to cope, that very equality opened up new opportunities for Soviet expansion. Khrushchev's boast about the new correlation of forces in the world may have brought the Soviets a series of embarrassments from 1957 to 1962, but a decade later it seemed perversely justified.

THE VIETNAM WAR IN PERSPECTIVE

The human costs of the long conflict were harsh for all involved. Not until 1995 did Vietnam release its official estimate of war dead: as many as 2 million civilians on both sides and some 1.1 million North Vietnamese and Viet Cong fighters. The U.S. military has estimated that between 200,000 and 250,000 South Vietnamese soldiers died in the war. In 1982 the Vietnam Veterans Memorial was dedicated in Washington, D.C., inscribed with the names of 57,939 members of U.S. armed forces who had died or were missing as a result of the war. Over the following years, additions to the list have brought the total past 58,200. (At least 100 names on the memorial are those of servicemen who were actually Canadian citizens.) Among other countries that fought for South Vietnam on a smaller

Vietnam veterans look for the names of their fellow soldiers on the 20th anniversary of the opening of Vietnam Veterans Memorial Wall in Washington, D.C., 2002. *Tim Sloan/AFP/Getty Images*

scale, South Korea suffered more than 4,000 dead, Thailand about 350, Australia more than 500, and New Zealand some three dozen. In its proportional impact on Vietnamese society, the Vietnam War, 1955–75, was the fourth most severe in the world since 1816.

Vietnam emerged from the war as a potent military power within Southeast Asia, but its agriculture, business, and industry were disrupted, large parts of its countryside were scarred by bombs and defoliation and laced with land mines, and its cities and towns were heavily damaged. A mass exodus in 1975 of people loyal to the South Vietnamese cause was followed by another wave in 1978 of "boat people," refugees fleeing the economic restructuring imposed by the communist regime. Meanwhile, the United States, its military demoralized and its civilian electorate deeply divided, began a process of coming to terms with defeat in its longest and most controversial war—a process that has not yet ended, despite the reestablishment of formal diplomatic relations between the countries in 1995.

Glossary

adversary An enemy or foe.
amphibious landing In tactical military terms, an attack by troops landed by naval ships.
anathema Something that is detested.
antebellum Before, or existing before, the start of a war.
arcane Known by very few people.
atrophy To deteriorate.
attrition A wearing down or weakening of resistance or an enemy force.
auspices Patronage; support.
autocratic A ruler having unlimited power.
autonomy Independence.
barrage A heavy onslaught of military fire to stop the advance of enemy troops.
blockade The closing off of a certain area by troops to prevent the enemy from entering or exiting.
bulwark Something that serves as a defense.
cadre The key group of officers necessary to establish a new military unit.
callous Insensitive.
cessation A temporary or complete stop.
clandestine Characterized by secrecy.
communique An official report.
constabulary The body of officers of the peace on a military base.
counterinsurgency Political or military action taken to defeat insurgency, usually in guerrilla warfare.
defoliant An agent to cause widespread loss of leaves; in wartime, used to deprive enemy troops of concealment.
demarcation The separation by distinct boundaries.
dictatorship A form of government in which absolute control is held by one leader.
expediency Adherence to self-interest.
expeditionary Sent on or designed for military operations abroad.
guerrilla A warfare tactic involving harassing the enemy with surprise attacks.
hegemony The dominance of one group over another.
hubris Arrogance.
imperial Relating to an empire's rule over its dependencies.
impetus An impulse.
incursion A hostile invasion.
ineluctable Inescapable.
intractable Not easily controlled; unmanageable.
linchpin A central source of stability.
magistrate A civil officer who is responsible for administration of the law.
omnipotence Having unlimited power and authority.
picketer A person protesting outside of a building.
pragmatic Related to a practical point of view.
premeditated Planned in advance.

promulgate To declare; to set forth publicly.

prophetic Pertaining to the foretelling of events.

protectorate A weaker state that is partially controlled and protected by a stronger state.

protocol Customs and regulations.

pylon A finlike device used to attach objects to an aircraft wing.

ratify To confirm by giving formal approval.

repatriate To send a person, particularly a prisoner of war or refugee, back to their country of origin.

scapegoat A person that is made to bear the blame of someone else.

stalemate A position of deadlock.

unanimity An undivided opinion.

unilateral Involving only one side.

vehement Strongly emotional.

viaduct A bridge that conveys a road or railroad across a valley or river.

vociferously Crying out noisily.

Bibliography

The Korean War

Monographs

Histories of the Korean War written for a popular audience should be used with care. The best are Michael Hickey, *The Korean War: The West Confronts Communism, 1950–1953* (1999); Jon Halliday *and* Bruce Cumings, *Korea: The Unknown War* (1988); Callum A. MacDonald, *Korea: The War Before Vietnam* (1986); Kim Chum-kon (Chŏm-gon Kim), *The Korean War, 1950–53* (1980); and David Rees, *Korea: The Limited War* (1964, reissued 1970).

For students who want more detail on ground operations, the best lines of departure are Roy E. Appleman, *Disaster in Korea: The Chinese Confront MacArthur* (1989), and *Ridgway Duels for Korea* (1990); Clay Blair, *The Forgotten War: America in Korea, 1950–1953* (1987); and Max Hastings, *The Korean War* (1987, reissued 2000).

Russian and Chinese sources, though still limited in availability, have allowed the publication of books written from the perspective of the Soviets, North Koreans, and communist Chinese. They include Shu Guang Zhang, *Mao's Military Romanticism: China and the Korean War, 1950–1953* (1995); Chen Jian (*Jian Chen*), *China's Road to the Korean War: The Making of the Sino-American Confrontation* (1994); Sergei N. Goncharov, John W. Lewis, *and* Xue Litai (Litai Xue), *Uncertain Partners: Stalin, Mao, and the Korean War* (1993); and Dae-Sook Suh, *Kim Il Sung: The North Korean Leader* (1988, reissued 1995).

Video Documentaries

Documentary films outside Russia, China, and North Korea almost always focus on the U.S. military experience in Korea. The following documentaries, though hardly "balanced," at least provide interpretations that compete with the American view: *The Korean War* (1992), produced by the Korean Broadcasting System (Hanguk Pangsong Kongsa); *Korea: The Unknown War* (1988), produced by Phillip Whitehead for Thames Television; and *Korea: War at the 38th Parallel* (1989), produced by the BBC (British Broadcasting Corporation).

Reference Sources

The most useful references for specific information are Spencer C. Tucker (ed.), *Encyclopedia of the Korean War: A Political, Social, and Military History*, 3 vol. (2000); James Hoare and Susan Pares, *Conflict in Korea: An Encyclopedia* (1999); James I. Matray (ed.), *Historical Dictionary of the Korean War* (1991); and Lester H. Brune (ed.), *The Korean War: Handbook of the Literature and Research* (1996).

North Korean History
Politics and history are addressed in Robert A. Scalapino and Chong-sik Lee, *Communism in Korea*, 2 vol. (1972); Chong-sik Lee, *The Korean Workers' Party: A Short History* (1978); Dae-sook Suh, *The Korean Communist Movement, 1918–1948* (1967), *Kim Il Sung: The North Korean Leader* (1988), a well-written and the most objective biography to date; Koon Woo Nam, *The North Korean Communist Leadership, 1945–1965* (1974); Chin O. Chung (Chin-wi Chŏng), *P'yongyang Between Peking and Moscow: North Korea's Involvement in the Sino-Soviet Dispute, 1958–1975* (1978); Robert Scalapino and Jun-yop Kim (Chun-yŏp Kim) (eds.), *North Korea Today: Strategic and Domestic Issues* (1983); Tai Sung An, *North Korea in Transition: From Dictatorship to Dynasty* (1983); and Chong-sik Lee and Se-hee Yoo (eds.), *North Korea in Transition* (1991). Thomas H. Henriksen and Jongryn Mo (eds.), *North Korea After Kim Il Sung: Continuity or Change?* (1997); and Dae-Sook Suh and Chae-Jin Lee (eds.), *North Korea After Kim Il Sung* (1998), cover political and economic developments and external relations, especially U.S.–North Korean relations and nuclear issues of North Korea. Tae Hwan Ok and Gerrit W. Gong (eds.), *Change and Challenge on the Korean Peninsula: Past, Present, and Future* (1996), surveys the various political relationships on the peninsula in detail. Chong Bong-uk (ed.), *North Korea: Uneasy, Shaky Kim Jong-il Regime* (1997), introduces the political and socioeconomic situation of the country under the younger Kim. Helen-Louise Hunter, *Kim Il-Song's North Korea* (1999), describes Kim's life and the social situation in detail in North Korea. Jae Kyu Park (ed.), *North Korea in Transition and Policy Choices* (1999), provides a range of papers that give a general description of the country's political, economic, and social structure. Don Oberdorfer, *The Two Koreas: A Contemporary History*, new ed. (2001), is a news correspondent's firsthand account of inter-Korean relations from the 1970s through the early 21st century.

South Korean History
Studies of South Korea's history include John Kie-chiang Oh, *Korea: Democracy on Trial* (1968), beginning with Syngman Rhee's administration; Sŭng-ju Han, *The Failure of Democracy in South Korea* (1974), a study of the causes of the collapse of Chang Myŏn's liberal democratic government in May 1961; Donald N. Clark (ed.), *The Kwanju Uprising: Shadows Over the Regime in South Korea* (1988); Harold C. Hinton, *Korea Under New Leadership: The Fifth Republic* (1983); Frank Gibney, *Korea's Quiet Revolution: From Garrison State to Democracy* (1992); Jasper Kim, *Crisis and Change: South Korea in a Post-1997 New Era* (2005); and Ju Kim, *The Development of Modern South Korea: Civilisation, State, Capitalism, and Nationalism* (2006).

The Vietnam War

General Overviews in Print and Video

William S. Turley, *The Second Indochina War: A Short Political and Military History, 1954–1975* (1986), is the best short introduction to political and military developments in Vietnam. The best general account of the Vietnam War from the American perspective is George C. Herring, *America's Longest War: The United States and Vietnam, 1950–1975*, 4th ed. (2002). The North Vietnamese perspective is found in *The Military History Institute of Vietnam, Victory in Vietnam: The Official History of the People's Army of Vietnam, 1954–1975*, trans. by Merle L. Prebbenow (2002).

The following exhaustive television documentaries, based on hours of film footage and personal interviews, are available on video: *Vietnam—A Television History* (1983), produced by WGBH Boston for the Public Broadcasting Service; and *Vietnam: The Ten Thousand Day War* (1980), written by American war correspondent Peter Arnett.

Vietnamese History

Keith Weller Taylor, *The Birth of Vietnam* (1983), is the definitive treatment of early history to the 10th century. Joseph Buttinger, *The Smaller Dragon: A Political History of Vietnam* (1958, reprinted 1966), is the standard history from the rise of the Vietnamese state to the colonial era. Alexander Barton Woodside, *Vietnam and the Chinese Model* (1971, reprinted 1988), compares the governments of these two countries in the first half of the 19th century. Milton E. Osborne, *The French Presence in Cochinchina and Cambodia: Rule and Response (1859–1905)* (1969), analyzes French policies during the first stages of colonial rule. Hue-Tam Ho Tai, *Radicalism and the Origins of the Vietnamese Revolution* (1992, reissued 1996), plumbs the sources of anticolonial thought. David G. Marr, *Vietnamese Anticolonialism, 1885–1925* (1971), is a sensitive account, *Vietnamese Tradition on Trial, 1920–1945* (1981, reissued 1984), explores the social and intellectual changes taking place under colonial rule, and *Vietnam 1945: The Quest for Power* (1995, reprinted 1997), explains the August Revolution. Ellen J. Hammer, *The Struggle for Indochina* (1954, reissued 1969), dramatically treats the final stages of French rule. Huynh Kim Khánh, *Vietnamese Communism, 1925–1945* (1982, reissued 1986), is the definitive account of the rise of the Vietnamese communist movement. Alexander B. Woodside, *Community and Revolution in Modern Vietnam* (1976), argues that the search for community is a key factor in the Vietnamese revolution. Thomas Hodgkin, *Vietnam* (1981), recounts in detail the background of the Vietnamese revolutionary struggle. Bernard B. Fall, *The Two Viet-Nams*, 2nd rev. ed. (1967, reprinted 1984), dated but still useful, examines the period after the division of the country. William J. Duiker, *Sacred War: Nationalism and Revolution in a*

Divided Vietnam (1995), focuses on Vietnamese communist perspectives and strategy, and his *Ho Chi Minh* (2000) is the most comprehensive account of the communist leader's life. David W.P. Elliott, *The Vietnamese War: Revolution and Social Change in the Mekong Delta* (2003), is a detailed analysis of communist techniques and popular responses; while Truong Nhu Tang, David Chanoff, and Doan Van Toai, *A Vietcong Memoir* (1985; also published as *Journal of a Vietcong*, 1986), is a firsthand account of the organization. Ken Post, *Revolution, Socialism, and Nationalism in Vietnam*, 5 vol. (1989–94), is a Marxist interpretation of the Vietnamese revolution. Jeffrey Race, *War Comes to Long An* (1972), is the classic study of factors behind the communist success in one province of South Vietnam. William S. Turley and Mark Selden (eds.), *Reinventing Vietnamese Socialism: Doi Moi in Comparative Perspective* (1993); and Börje Ljunggren (ed.), *The Challenge of Reform in Indochina* (1993), assess social, political, and economic developments since the war's end. Adam Fforde and Stefan de Vylder, *From Plan to Market* (1996), analyzes the causes and dynamics of the transition to a market economy. Sophie Quinn-Judge and Odd Arne Westad (eds.), *The Third Indochina War: Conflict Between China, Vietnam, and Cambodia, 1972–1979* (2006), is a collection of essays based on more recently available archives that shed new light on Vietnam's wars with China and Cambodia.

Index

A

B

C

D

E

F

G

H

I

J

K

L

M

N

S

T

U

V

W

X

Y

Z